50

UNCONVENTIONAL CLINICAL CAREERS FOR PHYSICIANS

Unique ways to use your medical degree without leaving patient care

SYLVIE STACY, MD, MPH

AAPL books are available at special quantity discounts to use as premiums and sales promotions, or for use in corporate training programs. For more information, please write to Special Sales at journal@physicianleaders.org

This publication is designed to provide general information and is sold with the understanding that neither the author nor the publisher is engaged in rendering legal, accounting, ethical, or clinical advice. If legal or other expert advice is required, the services of a competent professional person should be sought.

13   8 7 6 5 4 3 2 1

Copyedited, typeset, indexed, and printed in the United States of America

PUBLISHER
Nancy Collins

PRODUCTION MANAGER
Jennifer Weiss

COPYEDITOR
Pat George

DESIGN & LAYOUT
Carter Publishing Studio

*"Let each day's work absorb your entire energies,
and satisfy your wildest ambition."*
—WILLIAM OSLER

Table of Contents

About the Author

Sylvie Stacy, MD, MPH, received her medical degree from the University of Massachusetts Medical School and completed a residency at Johns Hopkins. She holds board certifications in preventive medicine and addiction medicine. She is also the author of *50 Nonclinical Careers for Physicians: Fulfilling, Meaningful, and Lucrative Alternatives to Direct Patient Care* (2020). She lives in Alabama with her husband, Scott.

Preface

After the release of *50 Nonclinical Careers for Physicians: Fulfilling, Meaningful, and Lucrative Alternatives to Direct Patient Care*, I was interviewed for the American Association for Physician Leadership's podcast, SoundPractice. I talked about self-reflection questions for doctors contemplating a nonclinical career pathway. One of them was "Do you truly dislike patient care?"

I suggested that doctors contemplating a nonclinical job may simply dislike the patient care style they are engaged in or the setting in which they are doing it. In these cases, a nonclinical job may not be the solution. Perhaps a transition to a different type of clinical job is a better approach.

"I could write an entire other book on the unconventional types of clinical careers," I added as an afterthought.

Two years later, Nancy Collins, the organization's senior vice president of content development, reminded me that I had made this statement and suggested it was time discuss it.

She's right, it is time to discuss it. Physician burnout remains pervasive, and many talented, capable doctors express a desire to quit medicine. Few, however, are fully aware of the options available to them.

The concept of an unconventional clinical career is near and dear to me.

In my final year of residency, I was exploring my next steps. I liked many aspects of preventive medicine but wasn't sure which direction to head. My broad search led me to a job listing for a corporate medical director position with a national provider of healthcare services in correctional facilities.

I had never envisioned having a job in which my patients were incarcerated. Nor had I ever pictured myself passing through a sallyport on my way to work. However, the job's responsibilities appeared to be ones I would enjoy: Providing clinical oversight. Implementing strategies to improve care quality. Making clinical utilization management decisions. Ensuring compliance with healthcare regulations. Liaising between information technology and clinical staff for electronic health record (EHR) enhancements.

It all sounded appealing. As a bonus, the face-to-face patient care would be limited.

So I applied for the job, interviewed, and got a solid job offer. I cogitated. I was hesitant about the idea of working in correctional medicine. *Was I adequately prepared? What about the high lawsuit rate? Would I pigeonhole my career?*

I could not get past my concerns, so I declined the job offer. I immediately felt a sense of regret.

Two weeks later, the regret still lingered. I wanted that job. I asked the hiring manager if he could re-extend the offer. Fortuitously, the job was still available and he did.

I have worked in correctional medicine for more than nine years now — nine satisfying years with good work–life balance and compensation that reflects the value of my work. Along the way, a handful of unconventional clinical side gigs have expanded my skill set.

My hope is that you, too, find fulfillment in your work and have a career that is deeply satisfying — however unconventional it may be.

SYLVIE STACY
November 2023

Introduction

The Oxford dictionary defines conventional as "established by general agreement." This suggests that convention is arbitrarily or artificially determined. What is conventional is not what is inherently right. It is not necessarily better than alternative methods. Perhaps most importantly, it is not optimal for every individual.

This insight — that what is deemed conventional is not automatically the most effective or beneficial approach — has major implications for the work we do as doctors and the satisfaction we derive from our work. It challenges us to critically evaluate the standard practices and to consider other approaches that might better serve our individual needs and preferences.

WHAT MAKES A PHYSICIAN'S CAREER UNCONVENTIONAL?

For doctors, conventional jobs entail being in private practice or employed by a hospital or healthcare system and delivering customary patient care within a specialty: A family doctor providing primary care at a local clinic, for example. A surgeon performing scheduled and emergent procedures in a hospital operating room. A dermatologist diagnosing and treating a range of skin conditions in a group specialty practice. These and other standard roles incorporate the archetypal doctor–patient interactions within the most established and visible parts of the U.S. healthcare infrastructure.

Physicians' conventional jobs are the result of a long transformation in medical practice. Historically, doctors primarily had broad-based solo practices. They had few treatment options and relied more on opinion than science. Today, organization-based roles, specialization in medical disciplines, and adherence to established care standards care are the norm.

Advances in medical science, medical education, and societal needs have driven this evolution. Demographic shifts, patient expectations, new technologies, regulatory changes, financial incentives, and corporate interests have all been influential, as well. Changes to physician roles and the healthcare system over time have not only reshaped the "typical" job for a doctor, but also created new, less conventional possibilities.

There are many ways to deviate from conventional work in medicine. Jobs can involve practice settings beyond the hospital or outpatient medical office. They can concentrate on a discrete patient population brought together by a shared medical condition, location, interest, or other characteristic. They can have a unique clinical focus or set themselves apart by adopting cutting-edge medical technologies and treatments. Another source of deviation can be the way the physician works, such as employment type, schedule, or approach to patient care.

The terms *job* and *career* are used interchangeably, but they are distinct. A career encompasses the entirety of a person's employment-related experiences, including various positions, roles, and professional activities over time. You can hold both conventional and unconventional jobs throughout your career or build a career entirely from unconventional jobs. Each chapter in this book delves into a career area; most describe multiple possible job opportunities within those areas.

Labeling unconventional careers

The word *unconventional* offers a perspective that other labels don't capture as well. The careers described in the following sections are not necessarily *alternative* careers. They are not alternatives to medicine; they are an integral part of it. Further, alternative implies a sense of last resort. For some, pursuing an unconventional path does feel like a last resort as they fight frustration and burnout from conventional medicine. Ideally, though, all physicians should consider unconventional jobs at all career stages.

The careers covered are not *nontraditional* either. This term does not acknowledge medicine's changing nature and how what is typical today may not align with tradition.

Most unconventional careers are not *unusual*. Unusual conveys rarity, but many jobs explored in this book are both available and attainable to many physicians, with a minority being truly rare.

Career transitions among doctors are sometimes equated with a switch to *nonclinical* work. Nonclinical careers like working for the pharmaceutical industry, a consulting firm, or a health insurer are an amazing option if your interests align with them. Yet, most students enter medicine with a primary aspiration to care for patients. Moreover, medical school and residency focus on equipping us with the skills and knowledge needed to do just that. The idea of transitioning to a nonclinical job is daunting for many physicians. Some fear they will miss seeing patients; others believe they will underutilize their medical degree.

In this context, an unconventional clinical career is a compelling choice.

Patient care and clinical work

Unconventional clinical careers enable you to continue doing what you set out to do in medical school while still making a transition of sorts. They offer a compromise for anyone hesitant to fully depart from clinical practice.

Clinical work encompasses a wider range of activities than most people realize. It is not only the time spent with a patient in a hospital room, exam room, or operating room. It includes reviewing medical documentation and test results, consulting with other clinicians, responding to emergencies, supervising other healthcare professionals, communicating with families, and making many types of medical decisions.

Some clinical work lends itself to unconventional jobs. Tightly regulated healthcare domains often require licensed physicians to perform or oversee certain duties. Medical and technological advances provide opportunities for pioneering new approaches and subfields in medicine. Jobs caring for vulnerable populations necessitate unconventional roles to address the specific needs of these groups. Many physical settings outside of hospitals and outpatient offices in which individuals require healthcare services offer unconventional positions, too.

Though they remain fundamentally oriented toward patient care, many clinical jobs also involve nonclinical responsibilities. These can be administrative duties, quality assurance activities, and teaching, as a few examples.

Most clinical roles — even unconventional ones — require a medical license, often accompanied by board certification and completion of a post-graduate training program. You usually need professional liability insurance because nearly every type of clinical work carries the risk of a malpractice accusation. These requirements may seem like hurdles; however, they are evidence of the expertise, qualifications, and specialized knowledge physicians have. We are indispensable assets in healthcare delivery, even when our clinical roles are out of the ordinary.

RATIONALE FOR AN UNCONVENTIONAL CAREER IN MEDICINE

Why consider an unconventional career? Ultimately, it is about finding happiness and fulfillment. There is a strong correlation between a sense of career success and overall life satisfaction, as well as mental wellbeing. There are numerous reasons that an unconventional career could help you accomplish this.

First, an unconventional job can help prevent or address burnout. A 2020 survey found that 58% of physicians have feelings of burnout, up from 40% just two years prior.[1] Overwhelming workloads and bureaucratic complexities are prevailing reasons for burnout. The subsequent chapters cover many roles somewhat removed from these major sources of burnout, allowing more leeway to practice on your own terms.

Even for doctors who do not feel burned out, a general feeling of apathy is common. A mere 10% of physicians are actively engaged in their work.[2] This can be detrimental to our careers and to patient care. Unconventional work can be a remedy. Many less conventional jobs offer novelty and excitement. They can transform listlessness into an opportunity for personal and professional growth.

Practical matters come into play as well. Some physicians gravitate toward unconventional careers for their flexibility and convenience. A range of healthcare industry entities offer positions with schedules that accommodate personal obligations and can help optimize work–life balance. In many cases, unconventional jobs require less time spent at work. This is significant, as more hours worked by physicians correlates with lower satisfaction.[3]

Other logistical reasons have to do with job availability and financial details. The economy, location, and individual qualifications can make standard jobs unappealing or difficult to land. An unconventional job can be a way to earn a great living in a saturated market. For medical fields with high demand, unconventional positions can sometimes offer better pay and benefits, especially when the schedule and total hours worked are factored in.

The rationale for pursuing an unconventional career does not need to stem from negativity or frustration. Ideally, we should be proactive in contemplating unconventional opportunities alongside conventional ones. Having broader and more varied options can help in finding roles that align with our passions, skills, and goals.

UNCONVENTIONAL CAREERS NEED MORE ATTENTION

Discontent with their careers leads many physicians to think about leaving medicine. But quitting medicine is rarely the best solution. Healthcare remains the largest U.S. economy segment. There is a wealth of opportunities to explore within it. Simply changing your career trajectory to something less conventional is a great alternative to leaving the profession altogether.

Many doctors have limited knowledge of career options beyond their medical school and residency exposure, which revolves around large academic medical centers. Even among physicians who are aware of some less conventional paths, misconceptions are standing in the way. Some believe unconventional jobs are exclusive to particular specialties, to those holding business degrees or other special certifications, or to those facing licensure or credentialing issues. These preconceived notions are often untrue.

Apprehension also stems from the perception that transitioning into an unconventional clinical practice requires more effort than securing a "regular" job. This can be true; however, the long-term benefits far outweigh the effort required on the front end.

Physicians with unconventional careers may be told that they are a sell-out, that they are wasting their medical degree, or that they will never earn the salary that they deserve. These myths persist due to a dearth of knowledge about varying practice settings, reimbursement structures, and the legal issues surrounding medical practice.

In light of these challenges and misconceptions, it is clear that there is a great need for the information covered in the 50 chapters that follow. Physicians and medical students need encouragement to entertain the full spectrum of career options. And they need to be armed with high-quality, balanced insights and guidance about these options.

WHAT TO EXPECT FROM THIS BOOK

The main portion of this book is organized into 10 sections, each describing a different category of unconventional careers. Within each section is a selection of chapters focused on specific career areas or concepts. While some groupings may seem arbitrary, they serve the purpose of organizing a wide array of career options for easier and more deliberate exploration. You can read this book cover to cover or choose chapters that pique your interest.

Many chapters cover multiple job opportunities within their respective topics. For example, the chapter on treating athletes discusses working as a team physician, conducting pre-participation sports exams, and running an athletic performance medicine practice. These are all distinct roles in different physical work settings and with different responsibilities. You could incorporate just one of these jobs into your career, or potentially all of them.

Some chapter titles might strike you as fairly conventional. Rest assured each one delves into unconventional employment or practice options within that field or setting. For instance, there is a chapter on careers focused on managing chronic pain. Nearly all physicians treat chronic pain in some way, and pain medicine is a well-recognized medical sub-specialty. However, this chapter explores ways to have a career concentrating on pain management in less conventional ways, such as without completing a pain medicine fellowship or by dedicating your practice to a specific type of chronic pain, such as headaches.

Overlap between chapters is inevitable, as many topics are highly inter-connected. Some, like telemedicine, make an appearance in multiple chapters due to their relevance in various contexts.

The current state of the medical profession influences the content of some chapters. Well-established specialties and subspecialties result in clearly defined career areas, while emerging fields tend to have less distinct boundaries. One aim of this book is to shed light on medical fields that lack formal recognition, but that still present great career opportunities.

The book is a guide. It offers practical advice and information to help you make informed decisions about your career path. It won't tell you which career is best for you. It won't explain precisely where or how to find your dream job. It won't rejuvenate your love of medicine unless you act on the knowledge you glean from reading it.

CAREERS WITH UNCONVENTIONAL PATIENT POPULATIONS

In most contexts, *population* simply refers to the total number of people living in a certain region. But in medicine, it is so much more. A patient population is a specific group sharing common characteristics or attributes that may affect their health, how and where they obtain medical care, or the treatment they receive.

Physicians can offer specialized services targeting particular populations. We can work in organizations that tailor their approach to meet the specific care needs and financial opportunities presented by distinct population segments.

Most doctors encounter members of the populations described in the upcoming chapters from time to time, regardless of specialty or practice setting. However, few put in the effort to become experts on treating these specific groups. Becoming skilled in treating a population can lead to better care, improved health outcomes, and patients who feel heard and understood.

This section delves into populations that can form the focal point of one job or your entire career. Perhaps one of these resonates with you. If not, use this information as inspiration to identify your own niche patient population. Immigrants and refugees, those with intellectual and developmental disabilities, and even foster youth could all be the cornerstones of an unconventional career, and there are many others to explore.

Adolescents and students

Reflecting on your teens and early 20s, your dominant memories might be wild weekends partying, long nights studying, or anything in between. Despite our vastly different experiences, we all agree these were formative years. We encountered new relationships, heightened responsibility, and self-discovery.

Adolescence is also a phase of distinctive health needs driven by physical, cognitive, and psychosocial development. These needs are often met by embedding medical services in educational environments or offering specialized programs targeting this age group, creating several attractive, lesser-known career options for physicians.

STUDENT HEALTH PRACTICE SETTINGS

The two primary settings for physicians to treat a student patient population are university health centers and school-based health centers.

College and university health centers

The majority of the nation's more than 4,400 college campuses offer student health services, together providing care to nearly 20 million undergrads.[4] On a typical day, a university health center physician treats a combination of acute issues, chronic diseases, and mental health conditions, and provides preventive services, referrals, and administrative oversight of the clinic's services.

Many patient encounters mimic those seen in a typical primary care practice. Some are more specific to the university setting, such as infections resulting from communal living or issues related to students' new independence like mental health fluctuations and unhealthy behaviors.

Besides individual patient care, doctors take an active role in resource management and quality improvement activities. They may serve on university committees and work with university leadership in response to health-related issues and events on campus, such as an infectious disease outbreak. They may collaborate with collegiate sports programs on processes relating to student athlete health. In larger clinics, physicians may supervise one or more advanced practice providers (APPs).

Medical care at college health centers is financed by a combination of student health fees, university-administered health insurance and, to a lesser extent, third-party insurance billing. Physicians are less burdened with insurance billing than in a typical outpatient practice. Yet, since many students remain insured under their parents' health plans, they can still be referred to outside specialists when their medical needs are complex or exceed the college health center's capabilities.

Working in a university health center is more relaxed than conventional outpatient primary care practice. Both part-time and full-time positions for physicians are available. The position includes the benefits of being a university employee — library access, fitness center access, a lighter schedule during summer and winter breaks — without the traditional obligations of being a faculty member.

School-based health centers

About 2,300 grade schools run a school-based health center. This is more than double the number that existed two decades ago.[5] The concept of school-based health centers, which was initially promoted by the American Academy of Pediatrics, is based on the premise that students can't reach their full potential at school unless they are physically and mentally healthy. These programs lead to reduced school absences[6] and address health disparities.[7]

School-based health centers resemble college health centers in many ways, providing care in a convenient location (in the main school building or adjacent to it) at an accessible time (while students are at school). Most programs offer management of minor acute medical needs and certain chronic care needs. More so than college health centers, school-based health centers focus on conditions likely to affect attendance, academic performance, and participation in school activities. They are equal parts health promotion and medical care.

School districts run most school-based health centers with funding through a combination of government grants, private sector grants, and reimbursement through Medicaid and private insurance. They use various models for care delivery. Many employ a full-time APP complemented by a part-time physician, as well as nurses and medical assistants. Some programs have mental health providers, health educators, counselors, dental hygienists, and nutritionists. Affiliations with nearby hospital systems and medical groups are common.

Physicians working in school-based health centers can expect to manage asthma exacerbations, food allergies, hypoglycemic episodes, and playground injuries, as a few examples. They provide or oversee general health assessments, anticipatory guidance, immunizations, and screenings, such as for vision and hearing. They are involved in individual and school-wide responses to bullying, drug abuse, and violence. In this setting, doctors must keep in touch with the school culture, environment, and trends like risky activities fueled by social media.

Despite their expansion, fewer than 2% of schools have a school-based health center. This shortfall represents an opportunity for physicians to initiate a school-based health center in their community.

OTHER UNCONVENTIONAL CAREER OPTIONS

Medical needs during the transition from pediatric to adult care has been an area of interest, with several national bodies concurring that "all youth need education, guidance, and planning to prepare to assume appropriate responsibility for their health and well-being in adulthood."[8] Traditional adolescent primary care practices address many of this population's routine needs, although there are targeted programs giving rise to a few less conventional career options, some of which are described here.

Eating disorder treatment centers hire physicians for patient care and administration. Most are residential treatment facilities, although some centers offer intensive outpatient programs, virtual treatment, and other formats. They provide medical management, nutritional guidance, education, and therapy for a full scope of eating disorders. Several programs, such as Alsana, Eating Recovery Center, and The Emily Program, have a large national or regional presence.

There are 1,323 residential facilities housing justice-involved juveniles operated by the state and local governments throughout the United States.[9] Many of the adolescents and young adults housed in them have medical needs. Most of these facilities provide primary care and mental health services within their walls.

Job Corps is a residential job training and education program for at-risk adolescents. Participants receive housing, activities, and living necessities, including basic medical care. Although funded through the U.S. Department of Labor, the programs fulfill most day-to-day operations through contracts with private organizations that hire their own staff. Physician positions are part-time and can include direct patient care and oversight of other clinicians.

GETTING INTO STUDENT HEALTH AND ADOLESCENT MEDICINE

Pediatrics, family medicine, and internal medicine are the most relevant specialties within careers treating students and adolescents. Although not required for all jobs, fellowship training in adolescent medicine is available. It is a recognized subspecialty with board certification offered collaboratively by the American Board of Pediatrics, the American Board of Internal Medicine, and the American Board of Family Medicine. Fellowships are two or three years in length. A combined internal medicine and pediatrics residency program is another option.

Psychiatry training followed by a fellowship in child and adolescent psychiatry is a path for those with an interest in mental health.

For educational resources and networking, look into the Society for Adolescent Health and Medicine, the American College Health Association, and the American School Health Association.

COMPENSATION

In 2021, adolescent medicine subspecialists earned an average of $211,688 per year.[10] Public job listings for full-time physicians in university health centers at the time of this writing indicate salary ranges between $200,000 and $265,000 annually.

Physicians in part-time roles at school-based health centers earn an hourly rate or negotiate billing arrangements based on services rendered, either invoicing the program directly or billing patient insurance.

Athletes

Americans love sports. We love participating and spectating. More than three-quarters of us partake in sports and fitness activities.[11] An estimated 160 million Americans tuned in to the most recent Olympics.[12] The NFL generates an impressive $12 billion per year.[13] Few other pastimes approach these levels of enthusiasm.

But sports carry significant injury risk for players and, to perform at their best, athletes need to be in excellent health. Physicians contribute to maintaining athletes' health and performance.

MORE THAN ORTHOPEDIC SURGERY

Many medical students dismiss orthopedic surgery as a specialty choice because competition is high for residency positions and the day-to-day work is grueling. But, even if you have ruled out orthopedic surgery or have already completed residency in another field, don't dismiss the idea of a career concentrating on athletes.

The medical care of athletes goes far beyond surgically treating bone, muscle, and joint injuries. It includes medical risk assessment, medical issue management on and off the field, rehabilitation, and performance optimization. It is feasible for nearly any physician who wishes to focus a portion of their career on this population to do so.

PRACTICE OPTIONS

Work settings for physicians treating athletes are not limited to medical offices and hospitals; they include schools, universities, gyms, and professional sports facilities.

Team physician
Team physicians provide medical care and expertise to sports teams, including during games and practices, and outside of training sessions.

Most professional sporting leagues require teams to have a team physician.

For this position, you must have knowledge of sports medicine, orthopedics, and general medicine. During games, team physicians provide urgent evaluation of injured and ill players. They are responsible for making return-to-play clearance decisions for injured players. Off the field, they monitor health and provide ongoing medical care, working closely with the team's coaches, athletic trainers, physical therapists, nutritionists, and other sports and healthcare professionals. Administrative duties can include developing injury prevention strategies, establishing a chain of command for addressing player medical issues, and educating athletes, coaches, and trainers on medical issues.

At the high school and college levels, team physicians may be part-time positions that are less involved.

Sideline physicians provide coverage at games or sporting events without being affiliated with a particular team. Ringside physicians in combat sports serve a similar role.

Athletic performance medicine

Athletic performance medicine is a growing field geared toward optimizing capability and functioning in a sport while reducing injury risk. Unlike sports medicine, which focuses on sports-related injury treatment and prevention, it is concerned with helping athletes achieve their full potential.

Most athletic performance medicine practices take a comprehensive approach, offering traditional medical services along with some combination of athletic training, strength and conditioning coaching, physical therapy, nutrition planning, biomechanical analysis, and sports psychological counseling. Many patients pay out-of-pocket for this type of service, which makes it more feasible for practices to offer emerging technologies and treatments to improve athletic performance, such as sports ultrasound and platelet-rich plasma (PRP) injections.

Patient panels in this type of practice are not restricted to competitive athletes. Many practices attract recreational athletes seeking to improve their performance, achieve personal fitness goals, or regain their abilities after an injury.

Pre-participation sports exams

The most straightforward option for most physicians to get started in a career treating athletes is by conducting pre-participation sports exams. These consist of a medical history and physical exam, and may also include an electrocardiogram (EKG), labs, and other diagnostic testing, if indicated. Their purpose is to identify any underlying health conditions putting athletes at risk for injury, illness, or sudden death during sports. Assessing risk of sudden cardiac death is a major component, especially for high school athletes.

With nearly 8 million high school athletes participating in sanctioned sports every year,[14] there is a need for physicians to dedicate a portion of their practice to conducting pre-participation exams. Multiple professional medical organizations have published guidance on sports exams, although state law and school district policy determine whether these exams are required.

PATHS TO A CAREER TREATING ATHLETES

Most team physicians are subspecialists in sports medicine. Physicians with primary board certification in emergency medicine, family medicine, internal medicine, pediatrics, and physical medicine and rehabilitation (PM&R) are eligible for one-year fellowships in nonsurgical sports medicine. Separate fellowships in orthopedic sports medicine are available to orthopedic surgeons. Although not accredited by the Accreditation Council for Graduate Medical Education (ACGME), sports cardiology fellowships are available at several large universities.

The American Academy of Orthopaedic Surgeons published a consensus statement describing the qualifications for team physicians, although it is not universally followed. Many team physicians supplement their medical training by becoming certified strength and conditioning specialists. Advanced life support certification may be required. Familiarity with drug testing policies and procedures of professional sports leagues and organizations is important.

Team physicians may also need to complete media training, given the significant media attention professional and collegiate sports teams receive, as well as special training on the medicolegal and ethical issues that may arise when treating athletes.

Any primary care physician with a basic understanding of sports medicine and the medical issues affecting athletes can conduct pre-participation sports exams in most areas; a few states and organizations require formal training in sports medicine.

The American Medical Society for Sports Medicine, the American College of Sports Medicine, the American Orthopaedic Society for Sports Medicine, and the Association of Ringside Physicians are resources for more information.

COMPENSATION

The median salary for family physicians with subspecialization in sports medicine was $311,439 in 2021.[10]

Compensation for sports team physicians depends heavily on the physician's specialty, the sport, and level. At the high school level, physicians may be employed by the school district or may even volunteer their time to cover local games. Teams and universities hire professional and collegiate team physicians, respectively, as employees or contractors. Public information on how much professional team physicians are paid is limited. In addition to a sizeable base salary, they may receive signing bonuses, bonuses based on the team's performance, and a per-diem allowance when traveling with the team.

Executives, celebrities, and other VIPs

Any individual who holds influence, prominence, or importance within their respective field or within society might qualify as a very important person, or VIP. VIPs can be celebrity entertainers, sports figures, business moguls, corporate executives, cultural icons, politicians, foreign dignitaries, and others who are wealthy, well-known, or well-connected.

VIPs share two commonalities that affect their medical care. First, to maintain their status, they need to function at their peak. Second, they have the means to curate the services and support needed to reach that peak. These are the basis of what makes VIPs an unconventional patient population.

EXECUTIVE HEALTH PROGRAMS

Working in an executive health program is an attainable way to incorporate this population into your career. These programs aim to optimize the health of busy professionals. Despite the name, patients include directors, senior management, entrepreneurs, and other business professionals, in addition to executives.

There are many programs of this type across the country and they have proven successful in most medium- to large-size cities. Most physicians who oversee executive health programs come from primary care backgrounds. Being well-connected or well-known in your area is not necessary.

Patients can enroll on their own, although many companies now offer membership to an executive health program as an benefit for certain employees.[15] Employers hope this will improve recruitment and retention, lower long-term business risk, decrease health insurance costs, and increase productivity.

The cornerstone of most executive health programs is a baseline comprehensive health assessment, sometimes called the executive physical. This extends far beyond a routine check-up, with numerous appointments condensed into one or two dedicated days. Much of the assessment focuses on prevention and early detection.

Patients see a primary care doctor and sometimes specialists, depending on the program's scope and the patient's pre-evaluation screening. Baseline testing can include lab panels, imaging studies, EKGs, pulmonary function tests, and screenings for hearing and vision, skin cancer, mental health conditions, and more. There is often an element of fitness assessment, such as with maximal oxygen consumption testing or body composition testing. Patients may meet with a dietitian, fitness professional, wellness coach, and even a genetic counselor.

Results from the initial evaluation serve as a foundation for a personalized plan addressing medical concerns, risks, and other factors that affect overall health and work performance. Programs vary in their scope and extent of follow-up care, with some offering a less intensive health assessment on an annual basis.

Executive health programs are designed to optimize the patient's time. Clinic spaces can resemble a combination of doctor's office, health club, and upscale business suite, offering amenities for added comfort and for patients to get work done between appointments. A healthcare navigator or medical liaison schedules appointments, relays test results, and coordinates follow-up care. They may even book travel and accommodations for out-of-town patients.

Some executive health programs are hosted by large medical centers, including Mayo Clinic, Cleveland Clinic, and Emory, to name a few. Some are operated by corporations, such as EHE Health. Countless smaller, physician-owned practices focus on executive health as well.

The cost of an executive physical ranges from less than $1,000 to well above $5,000.[16] In many cases, the patient's employer is billed directly. Private health insurance may be billed for certain covered services.

NICHE VIP PRACTICES

Relatively few people are rich and famous, but their impact within the healthcare industry is substantial. They have significant discretionary income and have high expectations for healthcare services. For many, medical care is not just a necessity; it is a service that should indulge their specific needs and lifestyles. Even individuals with lower-level notoriety or more modest wealth increasingly expect — and are willing to pay for — exclusive and tailored care.

Private practices that attract VIPs

Solo and group practices of many types can cater to VIPs. One way to attract this population is by offering medical services they use more than the general public, such as cosmetic surgery. However, the success of a VIP practice more commonly hinges on factors like organization, strategic positioning, and amenities rather than the core medical services offered. This is accomplished by offering a personalized experience prioritizing privacy and comfort.

VIP practices need to see patients when and where it is convenient for the patient. Waiting areas may need to accommodate patients' personal staff and assistants. Amenities include spa-like atmospheres, valet parking, escorts, business centers, and prescription delivery service. Owners of conventional medical practices often dismiss these features because they are cost prohibitive for a practice that is dependent on insurance reimbursement and they do not make sense if your goal is to keep costs low for patients.

Many VIP practices use a concierge model; pricing reflects the fact that wealthy individuals will pay more for their care. News outlets have reported annual membership fees between $25,000 and $80,000.[17-19]

Healthcare systems that treat VIPs

Working within healthcare systems or hospitals renowned for accommodating VIP patients is another option. Cedars-Sinai Medical Center in Hollywood is well-known among celebrities, offering a range of amenities and options like deluxe maternity suites. Similarly, the entire Mayo system has developed a strong reputation among the VIP crowd. The Suites at Saint Mary's are Mayo's luxury accommodations for high-profile patients. A wing at New York-Presbyterian Medical Center known as Greenberg 14 South features large, private rooms that are nicer than most hotel rooms and come with extra security, a butler, and a concierge.

Working as a personal physician

Hiring a personal physician is a common practice among those with significant wealth and influence. Oprah Winfrey, Warren Buffett, Bill Gates, and Tom Hanks are only a few of the most notable individuals who have openly acknowledged having a personal doctor. The U.S. president, too, has a personal physician who also directs the White House Medical Unit. A job as a personal physician is among the most exclusive in the medical field. Although there are relatively few opportunities, it is an option particularly for physicians with strong connections and reputations.

PATHS TO A CAREER TREATING VIPS

Broad specialties like internal and family medicine set a good foundation for working in an executive health program and in many private practices geared toward VIPs. Due to high demand in the entertainment industry, specialties that incorporate cosmetic procedures, such as plastic surgery and dermatology, are excellent choices for physicians aiming to treat celebrities. With the right planning and effort, though, nearly all specialties can tailor a practice to this population.

Word of mouth and personal referrals are some of the best marketing for VIP practices. It takes some effort to network and build connections within the entertainment, business, and high-profile communities.

Depending on your goals, geographic location can be important. Certain areas have a high density of wealthy and famous people. Being in southern California, New York City, Miami, and other celebrity hotspots greatly increases your chances of finding a job centering around this population.

VIPs wield power and are regarded with special attention. Overtreatment and confidentiality breaches are risks when a patient's fame or status influences clinician judgment. There have been celebrity deaths attributed to misguided treatment approaches driven, in part, by so-called "VIP syndrome." Maintain your ethical bounds and remember that VIP status does not exempt us from our responsibilities as physicians.

COMPENSATION

Compensation for physicians who treat this patient population mirrors the extremely wide range of wealth among VIPs themselves. Employed physicians in executive health programs earn salaries on par with internists. Private practice physicians have the potential to earn significantly more, limited only by their ability to attract and retain VIP clientele. As one example, primary care physicians at the VIP concierge practice Private Medical earn an annual salary between $500,000 and $700,000.[19]

Indigenous peoples

For most of us, the United States became home after our families emigrated from other countries. But for some, this is their ancestral land. There are more than five million indigenous people in the United States, belonging to 565 tribes. Interestingly, the indigenous population is growing faster than the general population.[20] Providing healthcare to this group is distinct in many ways, creating some less conventional career options for physicians.

THE POPULATION

Indigenous peoples are descended from the original inhabitants of a particular region or territory, identified by their cultural practices, languages, and traditional knowledge, as well as their social, economic, and political structures. In the United States, they include Native Americans, Alaska Natives, and Native Hawaiians. Examples from around the world are the First Nations people of Canada, Māori people of New Zealand, Adivasi people of India, and Inuit people of the arctic regions.

Indigenous groups have faced challenges related to colonization, forced displacement, discrimination, and marginalization. Many continue to struggle to protect their rights, cultures, and ancestral environments.

Health and medical needs of indigenous communities

Indigenous peoples in the United States face a range of health challenges and disparities. Compared to the general population, they have a significantly shorter life expectancy.[21] Many tribes are disproportionality affected by chronic diseases, including diabetes, heart disease, respiratory disease, obesity, and certain cancers. They experience higher rates of mental health issues, including depression, anxiety, substance use disorders, and post-traumatic stress disorder (PTSD).

Settler colonialism likely contributed to these disparities through introduction of foreign infectious diseases, contamination of natural resources, and other means. The disparities are exacerbated by broader social determinants, including poverty and insufficient access to education and social services.

For many doctors who treat indigenous peoples, the geographic location they practice in is unconventional. Communities may be remote or rural with limited access to hospitals and medical facilities. Economic challenges can mean that doctors need to work amid limited technology, infrastructure, and equipment.

Cultural differences can play a significant role in care, particularly for physicians who are not part of these communities themselves. Many indigenous groups have a long history of experiencing trauma and discrimination. Physicians need to be knowledgeable about patients' cultures and beliefs, advocate for them, and do what they can to address systemic issues. Understanding a tribe's traditional healing practices can also be helpful, as these practices often can be used in conjunction with contemporary, evidence-based medical treatments.

CAREER PATHS

There is a healthcare provider shortage in many indigenous communities, with fewer physicians available per capita for American Indians and Alaska Natives compared to the general population.

Indian Health Service

The most common way for physicians to work with these populations is through the Indian Health Service (IHS). IHS is a division within the U.S. Department of Health and Human Services responsible for providing medical and public health services to federally recognized tribes. They operate healthcare facilities in most states.

IHS offers jobs in several settings ranging from remote clinics to urban hospitals. There are roles for general practitioners and all types of specialists in different capacities. Alongside patient care, physicians may work as program directors or consultants in various capacities, such as for disease prevention initiatives.

One way to work for IHS is to become a federal civil servant employed directly by IHS. Another is to join the U.S. Public Health Service

(USPHS) Commissioned Corps, a uniformed service comprised of physicians, nurses, scientists, and others. Officers have considerable autonomy in selecting their work assignments, which can include IHS facilities and other tribal healthcare programs.

Physicians can also seek employment by a tribal health program that has a contract with the IHS through what is known as the Tribal 638 program. Under the Indian Self-Determination and Education Assistance Act, tribes can contract with the federal government to manage and operate healthcare programs for their own people.

Other practice settings

Other career options are well-suited for those who wish to treat indigenous peoples as a just portion of their work.

Nonprofit organizations like the National Council of Urban Indian Health and the Alaska Native Tribal Health Consortium provide healthcare services and support to urban and rural indigenous populations, respectively.

There are strategies to make private solo or group practice appealing to indigenous patients and help to retain them. You can build credibility and rapport by engaging with an indigenous community and learning about its culture and health needs. This could include attending community events, collaborating with leaders, and seeking input and feedback from patients about the care provided in the practice.

PATHS TO A CAREER TREATING INDIGENOUS PEOPLES

The minimum qualifications to work for IHS are completion of residency and a current medical license from any state. Because IHS employees and USPHS commissioned corps officers are federal employees, they are authorized to practice across state lines in an assigned area. Opportunities exist for all specialties, although there Is a particular need for primary care.

The most common way to get a job with the IHS is to apply for a direct hire position through a public job listing. Another option is to work as a contractor or locum tenens physician through various staffing agencies that partner with IHS. Tribal Health is a leading staffing agency in this field.

Training in providing culturally sensitive care can be useful. Many continuing medical education (CME) providers have started offering courses on this topic. Depending on the specific indigenous community you are working with, proficiency in the local language may be beneficial or necessary to provide effective care.

Sources of additional information include the National Indian Health Board, the National Council of Urban Indian Health, and the Alaska Native Tribal Health Consortium.

COMPENSATION AND FINANCIAL CONSIDERATIONS

IHS physician salaries are similar to those of other federal government agencies. Working in rural or remote areas often comes with special pay which increases overall compensation.

The National Health Service Corps offers a scholarship program for medical students who commit to working in underserved communities after completing their training. It also has several loan repayment programs for those who work in qualifying centers.

Physicians who belong to an indigenous group themselves may have financial support for training programs and scholarships geared toward indigenous medical workforce development. The IHS Scholarship Program provides full tuition, fees, and a stipend for students majoring in health professions who agree to work in Indian health programs after graduation. Other examples are the Association of American Indian Physicians scholarship programs, the Indians Into Medicine program, and the Tribal Health Profession Opportunity Grants program.

Performing artists

You've heard the phrase "art in medicine" as it relates to using expressive and creative arts therapies in healthcare. Less familiar is the concept of "medicine in the arts." The unusual needs of performing artists present several unconventional career options for physicians who have a dual passion for medicine and art.

PERFORMERS AND THEIR MEDICAL NEEDS

Performing artists are dancers, singers, musicians, actors, and other performers who present their art to an audience. They are professionals, amateurs, and students of diverse backgrounds. Many use precise and repetitive motions with isolated and sometimes odd physical demands. Perfecting their performance necessitates long hours and there is no off-season for recovery. They endure high stress levels that are both the root of complaints and a consequence of underlying medical issues.

All the performing arts combine artistic and physical components. It is the artistic component that attracts audiences; however, physicians who work with performers need to be equally focused on both.

Musicians and singers

Musicians have been referred to as "small-muscle athletes," reflecting how they hone specific muscle groups to play their instruments. Each instrument has its own physiological demands that can cause or contribute to symptoms.

Musculoskeletal complaints are common and characterized by pain and loss of function. They can be related to practice habits, playing intensity and duration, and technique. Issues are cumulative due to the recurring and rhythmic movements required to play an instrument. Some conditions, like tendinitis, may be straightforward to recognize and treat; others are complex. Neurological issues are common, especially nerve entrapment and focal motor dystonia.

Singers face unique issues resulting from using their voice as their instrument. Laryngopharyngeal reflux, muscle tension dysphonia, poor posture, and vocal cord pathologies can all affect singing ability.

Dancers

Each dance genre — ballet, jazz, tap, modern, hip hop — puts different demands on a dancer's body. The majority of medical issues stem from the interaction between the dancer's technique, their repertoire, and their physical attributes.

Musculoskeletal conditions, especially involving the feet and ankles, are prevalent. Injuries are caused by a single event or by repetitive use. Reinjury after treatment is common. Joint hypermobility in dancers can cause susceptibility to joint instability and overuse injuries. Young dancers face additional risks, such as growth plate fractures and eating disorders.

Theater and circus performers

Theatrical genres include drama, musicals, comedy, and the circus arts. A common thread among these is that the performers embody characters on stage. They move in dynamic patterns and through extreme ranges of motion. Movements are quick and repetitive. Performers sing and dance simultaneously, exposing them to issues related to both vocal exertion and musculoskeletal injury. Heavy costumes, poorly fitting footwear, bright lights, and stage props are added risks.

PERFORMERS AS PATIENTS

Few physicians see enough performing artists to fully understand their medical needs. Physicians who are not well versed in performing arts medicine may resort to a generic diagnosis like overuse injury and a generic treatment recommendation such as to practice and perform less. Failing to account for a patient's complaints in the context of their art can lead to suboptimal management, delays in care, and frustrated patients.

The daily workflow for most physicians who treat performers is like other outpatient specialty clinics, but there are distinctive aspects. Patient evaluation needs to go beyond a traditional clinical encounter to include both a medical history and performing arts history. The patient's recent practice habits and performance schedules are relevant.

The physical exam may focus on aspects of flexibility, strength, and posture that are relevant to the demands of each art form. You may need to watch a musician play their instrument or observe a dancer doing specific moves to assess their technique and positioning.

Even with an appropriate understanding and contextualization of symptoms, there might not be a clear pathological diagnosis to explain a patient's presentation. Some complaints might even seem trivial compared to those we assess in a broader patient population. But they still require strategic evaluation and treatment to avoid long-term impairment for performers.

Effective treatment includes measures related to the art itself. For example, you might treat chronic pain caused by an instrument's weight by having the patient use an instrument stand. The patient's choreographer, director, or conductor may be involved in the treatment plan as well.

Physicians in this field are frequently asked for guidance on whether the patient should continue rehearsing or performing. This decision is a weighty one since, for many performers, their art is their livelihood. Suggesting performance modifications or conducting specialized return-to-play assessments can be helpful.

PRACTICE OPTIONS

Although careers focusing on performers are unconventional, they are not as scarce as you might think. There are more than 2.5 million artists in the U.S. workforce[22] and even more amateur and student performers. Most musicians and dancers have at least one injury or other medical issue related to their art at some point in their career.[23,24]

The primary practice setting is an outpatient clinic, but there are instances where doctors may find themselves working in the field, such as in a performance venue or rehearsal space.

Performing arts medicine centers

Most performing arts medicine centers are affiliated with academic medical centers. A few large universities with both medical schools and arts schools have developed performance medicine programs through a collaboration between the two. A few examples are the Harkness Center for Dance Injuries at the New York University Langone Orthopedic Hospital, the Center for the Performing Artist at Weill Cornell Medicine, and Eastman Performing Arts Medicine at the University of Rochester. Smaller programs operate within healthcare systems' sports medicine or orthopedics departments.

Many physicians in this field dedicate a portion of their time to performance medicine while also seeing other patients or engaging in teaching or research. This way, programs can offer specialty care by physicians with very niche expertise. The Houston Methodist Hospital Center for Performing Arts Medicine, for instance, is staffed by more than 100 physicians with various specializations.

Working and consulting in the performing arts industry

Another career possibility is working in the arts and entertainment industry. Troupes, conservatories, and other performing arts groups hire physicians as consultants. Prominent groups such as the New York City Ballet have a physician on staff. The Cirque du Soleil Entertainment Group has an entire performance medicine department, employing physicians, physical therapists, athletic trainers, and other clinicians. Many professional orchestras have a physician who travels on tour.

GETTING INTO PERFORMING ARTS MEDICINE

Performing arts medicine lacks a widely recognized or standardized training pathway or credentials. You need to be proactive in tracking down opportunities and creative in carving out your niche. You also need to be where performers are. This could mean a geographic area with a high density of performers or an institution that trains or employs artists.

A variety of medical specialties are fitting. Internal medicine and other primary care specialties have broad training covering many medical issues faced by performers. Sports medicine, orthopedic surgery, PM&R, and neurology are options for those interested in treating performance-related musculoskeletal and neuromuscular conditions. Otolaryngology is the best choice for a practice catering to singers. Even psychiatry is an option for physicians with a particular interest in artists' mental health and the psychological aspects of performance.

The ACGME does not recognize performance medicine fellowships. The Texas College of Osteopathic Medicine offers a one-year, unaccredited performing arts medicine fellowship. With some legwork, residents and fellows in any training program may be able to arrange an elective to gain some experience in the field.

Other educational offerings are not specific to medical doctors, but may still be fitting, depending on your experience. Shenandoah University has a part-time performing arts medicine certificate program. The Performing Arts Medicine Association and certain schools with physical therapy programs have online and in-person courses on performing arts health.

Most physicians in this field are musicians or performers themselves. You need to have at least a baseline knowledge of the art or performance type practiced by your patients, since musicians describe symptoms in musical terms and dancers refer to specific dance moves that cause symptoms. Observing performers can be simultaneously entertaining and educational, so attend performances, concerts, shows, and arts festivals whenever possible.

Finding opportunities

Few job openings in performing arts medicine are publicly posted on job boards. Networking with other physicians in the field is one of the best ways to find opportunities. Start building connections through involvement with the Performing Arts Medicine Association or the Physicians for Musicians network of the Musician Treatment Foundation.

To grow the performing arts medicine component of your practice, reach out to performance groups in your local community. Introduce yourself to dance studios, theater companies, musical ensembles, or cultural organizations to let them know about your services.

COMPENSATION

Salaries for physicians in performing arts medicine are not reported separately. For many, salary is comparable to the average salary for their specialty.

Focusing on vocal conditions in singers may command higher compensation than other niches within performing arts medicine. Otolaryngologists earn an average of $485,000 per year.[25]

Medical consultants for conservatories, orchestras, troupes, and other performing arts groups can negotiate their compensation. This could be an hourly rate, a monthly retainer, or flat fee per patient seen.

PHYSICIAN PROFILE

Kelli Naylor, MD

College Health Physician, University of Rhode Island Student Health Services

Practice setting

University of Rhode Island Student Health Services is an outpatient clinic that provides a broad spectrum of medical care for 18,000 enrolled undergraduate and graduate students. These services include primary care, acute care (for injuries, illnesses, and mental health crises), sexual and reproductive health, mental health, and nutrition counseling.

Within the acute care branch of the clinic, we can manage a wide variety of acute medical and traumatic conditions seen in a typical emergency department. We have a holding unit for delivery of intravenous (IV) fluids and medications, a full lab, an x-ray department, and an in-house pharmacy.

Employment type and schedule

I work three days a week, including one evening until 8:00 p.m. I am a per-diem employee and receive an hourly pay.

I also have a second part-time job as a wound care specialist in nursing homes.

Patient population and clinical work

The majority of my patients are between the ages of 17 and 30, although there are occasionally older graduate students. Many are generally healthy; however, a significant percentage of the student population has at least one chronic medical condition. Some examples include asthma, cystic fibrosis, sickle cell anemia, inflammatory bowel disease, depression, anxiety and other mental health conditions, and a variety of autoimmune and rheumatologic conditions.

I spend approximately 75% to 80% of my time in direct patient care. The remainder is spent on charting and attending weekly staff meetings.

Student health clinics vary dramatically depending on the size of the college or university. Medium to large universities provide a vastly greater variety of services in their clinics compared to smaller schools.

A typical day at work

A typical day includes seeing patients with a variety of complaints, such as simple upper respiratory illnesses, dermatologic conditions, urinary or sexually transmitted illnesses, or more complex issues like allergic reactions, appendicitis, pneumonia, abscesses requiring drainage, and acute mental health crises. Common traumatic presentations include lacerations, burns, concussions, and orthopedic injuries, to name a few. We schedule patients every 15 minutes, with more time allocated for complex cases. Between appointments, I follow patients in our holding unit for up to several hours.

Unconventional aspects

My work serves a relatively small patient demographic, and my schedule is structured around the university's academic calendar. I do not work over winter or summer breaks. This was particularly appealing to me while I was raising three children. Once my children went off to college, I chose to add my second part-time job in wound care. Having two part-time jobs allows greater flexibility for my schedule (as opposed to one full-time position). It also supplements my income and broadens my scope of practice.

Best parts of the job

I started my career as an emergency physician. After nearly a decade of rotating through morning, evening, and overnight shifts, as well as covering every other weekend and holidays, I felt I needed a change. The transition to college health allowed me to be a more present mother while providing medical care to a dynamic and fascinating patient population. I find college students to be well-informed, engaging, and appreciative patients, who are taking charge of their healthcare for the first time in their lives. It is very rewarding work.

I will often continue to follow a patient who I initially met in an acute presentation for the remainder of their time at the university. The ability to provide emergency care followed by ongoing primary care for my patients has been another welcomed change from my former career in the emergency department.

Challenges faced

There are some challenges in student health. The greatest current challenge is access to mental health specialists. We do have a counseling center with part-time psychiatrists and a mental health nurse practitioner (NP) on staff. However, the need far exceeds their availability. I believe this is a nationwide issue currently, which worsened significantly during and after the COVID-19 pandemic.

Another important consideration is the economic limitations for many students. The University of Rhode Island has students from dozens of countries and a wide socioeconomic spectrum. Not all students enroll in the medical coverage provided by the university. As a result, some are not able to afford all options for evaluating and managing their particular complaint. We make a concerted effort to provide the best care within these constraints.

Qualifications and skills needed for this career

College healthcare providers can range from those with backgrounds in primary care to emergency medicine. You should be comfortable with a variety of diagnostic skills and be adept at minor procedures like suturing, abscess drainage, gynecologic exams, and orthopedic splinting.

Advice for students and physicians

As an aspiring physician, it had never occurred to me how my choice of discipline may impact my personal life. As much as I thrived professionally as an emergency physician, I was unable to dedicate the time I wanted and needed to my children's upbringing. I would ask yourself prior to committing to a career path, "Where do I see myself in five or 10 years?" and "What do I want my average work week to look like as a spouse or a parent?" Having said that, in medicine there are so many fulfilling career options, it is relatively easy to change course as the needs of your personal and family life evolve.

CAREERS WITH UNCONVENTIONAL CLINICAL CONCENTRATIONS

The concept of specialization in medicine has evolved. Medical specialties recognized by the ACGME are becoming increasingly compartmentalized. There are several reasons for this, including that medicine is growing in complexity. As medical science advances, so does the depth of understanding required to practice as a doctor. There is also a growing demand among patients for specialized and tailored care.

Some clinical concentrations covered in this section correspond to recognized subspecialties. Addiction medicine, for example, is a newer ACGME-recognized subspecialty. However, having an area of clinical concentration frequently does not require board certification. As you will read in the upcoming chapters, there are ample job opportunities for doctors who have developed expertise through experience, coursework, and self-directed learning.

Some less conventional clinical concentrations are not regarded as discrete subfields of medicine. They may not have relevant national associations, fellowships, or certification programs. But there is often sufficient patient demand for entire practices or employment positions to focus on them. There are doctors whose daily work centers around a condition as narrow as chronic fatigue syndrome, eating disorders, hair loss, or late-life depression.

By focusing your efforts and expertise on a specific clinical concentration, you can gain recognition, earn patient trust, operate efficiently, and more easily stay at the forefront of the latest research and practice guidelines in your area.

Addictions and toxicology

Addictions are taking a toll on the United States. Nearly 17% of the population has a substance use disorder,[26] but the majority are not receiving treatment. Many are uninsured, misinformed about treatment options, or face other obstacles to getting treatment. One barrier is an insufficient physician workforce offering treatment. This shortage is exacerbated by lingering stigma about addictions and strict regulatory requirements.

Opioid overdose deaths have surpassed 100,000 per year in recent years.[27] This further highlights the need for addiction treatment, but also for expertise in the field of toxicology. Amid an increasing prevalence of poisonings and overdoses from various substances, there are only about 500 medical toxicologists in the United States.[28]

ADDICTION MEDICINE PRACTICE SETTINGS

Addiction medicine centers around the management of alcohol, nicotine, opioid, stimulant, and other substance use disorders. It also includes behavioral addictions such as gambling disorder. There are medications approved by the U.S. Food and Drug Administration (FDA) for alcohol, opioid, and nicotine use disorders; off-label medications are commonly used to treat other addictions. Physicians work closely with therapists, social workers, and recovery support groups for the psychosocial aspects of treatment.

The regulatory landscape of opioid use disorder treatment is especially cumbersome. Some doctors avoid treating opioid addiction, viewing it as an unnecessary risk to their professional license; however, the regulation is partially to thank for the unconventional nature of careers in this field.

Certified opioid treatment programs

Methadone is one of the most effective medications for opioid use disorder but must be dispensed in an opioid treatment program (OTP) that is registered with the Drug Enforcement Administration (DEA), the Substance Abuse and Mental Health Services Administration, and the state's opioid treatment authority. The program must adhere to federal guidelines as well as state-specific regulations, some of which are stricter than the federal guidelines in terms of staffing ratios, lab testing requirements, and other aspects.

There are roughly 2000 OTPs in the United States.[29] Each clinic is required to have a medical director who is responsible for administering the program's medical services and ensuring compliance with applicable laws. Federal guidelines require the medical director be present at the facility for a "sufficient number of hours" to perform these duties. Some states specify the minimum number of hours necessary. Completion of a residency, an active state medical license, and at least one year of experience in addiction medicine is required.[30]

National corporations own most private, for-profit OTPs and contract with independent physicians for medical director services. A few of the largest corporations are BAART Programs, BayMark Health Services, Behavioral Health Group, and New Season. For some physicians, a draw to working at an OTP is flexible, early-morning hours conducive to moonlighting.

Residential addiction treatment and detox programs

Medical detoxification and residential treatment programs differ in the range and intensity of services they offer and therefore in their need for medical professionals. They may employ physicians on a full-time or part-time basis, depending on the size and scope of the program.

Detox programs need a physician to evaluate substance withdrawal risk, order medications for withdrawal, and manage complicated withdrawal. Ongoing care after the withdrawal period can include prescribing long-term treatment for addiction and managing co-morbid mental health conditions. Acadia Healthcare, Caron, and Hazelden Betty Ford Foundation are a few of the larger corporations with residential treatment programs in multiple states.

Physician-owned private practice

Many patients with addictions can be appropriately managed in the outpatient primary care setting. Treatment for opioid use disorder tends

to follow a structured protocol, incorporating medication management, counseling, drug testing, and follow-up visits. This structure can
streamline the practice's processes, thereby reducing overhead costs and
ensuring consistent billing.

Physician health programs

Most states have a physician health program that provides confidential
treatment to physicians (and sometimes other healthcare professionals)
with addictions and other conditions that cause impairment at work.
Evaluation and treatment by an impartial doctor is part of the process.
Working as a consultant physician for this type of program is a way to
practice addiction medicine while also helping your peers and upholding
the integrity of our profession.

TOXICOLOGY PRACTICE

Medical toxicology concentrates on the diagnosis, treatment, and prevention of poisoning and adverse effects of drugs and other substances on the
human body. Common exposures include medication overdoses, toxic
ingestion of illicit drugs, poisoning by household chemicals or carbon
monoxide, and exposure to industrial chemicals. Treatment includes
antidotes to specific substances, when available, and supportive care
such as ventilation or dialysis.

Many medical toxicologists work in academic practice, splitting their
time between hospital consult services and outpatient visits.

A part-time job option is working in one of 55 poison control centers
that provide telephone guidance for nearly three million calls about
human poison exposures each year. These centers are staffed by spe-
cially trained pharmacists, physicians, and nurses. A medical director
provides guidance and support to staff and is consulted to give input and
guidance on patient care in complex and severe cases. Because poison
centers operate around the clock, medical directors may cover a variety
of shifts and work remotely.

While most medical toxicologists practice clinically, many have a component of nonclinical work within their careers. This might include forensic
toxicology, in which they provide expert opinions and testimony for law

firms, or consulting for insurance companies and other organizations needing guidance on toxicology-related issues.

GETTING INTO ADDICTION MEDICINE AND TOXICOLOGY

The American Board of Medical Specialties (ABMS) and the American Osteopathic Association (AOA) recognize addiction medicine as a subspecialty. It is one of the few subspecialties for which doctors of any primary specialty are eligible. Fellowship lasts one year. Psychiatrists have an additional option of subspecializing in addiction psychiatry.

Board certification in medical toxicology requires a two-year fellowship. About 90% of toxicologists have an emergency medicine background,[31] but physicians of other specialties can pursue it as well. Many programs accept residency graduates coming from internal medicine, pediatrics, and occupational medicine; fewer accept family medicine and other specialties. Most fellowship programs are housed within emergency medicine departments and, due to program structure and funding, some depend on their fellows to cover general shifts in the emergency department.

You do not necessarily need board certification in addiction medicine or medical toxicology to practice in the settings described above. Physicians with an interest in these fields can acquire the necessary knowledge through experience and CME. Getting a master's degree in toxicology science is also an option.

The Providers Clinical Support System, which is federally funded, is a great free resource on addiction treatment. Look into membership with the American Society of Addiction Medicine, the American Academy of Addiction Psychiatry, and the American College of Medical Toxicology for educational and networking opportunities.

COMPENSATION

In 2023, the average annual income for addiction medicine specialists was $292,100.[32] Recent national physician salary surveys have not reported on the average salary for medical toxicologists. Toxicologists with primary certification in emergency medicine often continue to practice in emergency departments, aligning their annual income with the average $385,554 for emergency medicine physicians.[33]

Chronic pain

More than 20% of adults live with chronic pain;[34] it is among the most common reasons for seeking medical care.[35] Chronic pain takes a toll on society as well as on individuals, costing the United States $635 billion annually.[36] Its impact is great enough that the Institute of Medicine called for chronic pain to be addressed as a public health issue.[37] Despite this, many careers focusing on pain management are anything but ordinary.

UNCONVENTIONAL ASPECTS OF PAIN MEDICINE

What sets a career in chronic pain management apart? Nuances, misunderstandings, and a few unexpected pathways make for more varied career options than most physicians realize.

Historical influences

The history of pain medicine as a subspecialty has shaped and limited its scope. The field's foundation was laid by an anesthesiologist who felt the cornerstone of chronic pain treatment was anesthetic interventions.[38] Since then, pain medicine has largely been viewed as a branch of anesthesiology. Interventional procedures are the bread and butter of pain medicine fellowships and pain management specialty practices; however, our understanding of chronic pain and how to treat it has progressed considerably. We know high-quality pain management requires a multifaceted approach.

The complicated relationships between doctors and opioid prescribing also leads to misunderstandings about chronic pain management. Our profession unintentionally got involved in the War on Drugs. Licensing and regulatory bodies became aggressive, states began demanding mandatory education on opioid prescribing, and standards for prescribing and reporting grew complicated. As a result, many physicians are reluctant to prescribe opioids or even to oversee chronic pain management cases.

Difficulties of treating chronic pain

The two approaches to chronic pain treatment described above — interventional procedures and opioids — receive the most attention, but actually can lead to the under-treatment. This is worsened by the subjective nature of pain, making it difficult to assess. There also are high rates of misinformation and negative attitudes about pain among healthcare professionals.[39]

At least 40% of patients with chronic pain receive inadequate treatment,[40] and its treatment is only growing more complicated. Treatment techniques are advancing. Practice guidelines now incorporate medical, behavioral, integrative, and rehabilitative approaches, but many physicians don't follow them in practice.[41] So, putting in the time and effort to become adept at treating chronic pain can really set you apart.

COMPREHENSIVE PAIN MANAGEMENT CENTERS

One way to concentrate your career on chronic pain management in a less conventional way is by working with a comprehensive pain management center. Some centers are part of large medical institutions, such as the pain centers at Mayo, Johns Hopkins, and Cleveland Clinic. Others are smaller, private practices. These are a great career option for physicians who have entered pain medicine through a nontraditional path, including primary care physicians who take on a "pain generalist" role.

What distinguishes these from most specialty pain practices is the focus on offering and balancing multiple modalities for pain treatment, including medication management, procedures, and nonpharmacologic treatments. Some offer onsite physical therapy, gyms, mental health counseling, mindfulness-based programs, and other services.

HEADACHE MEDICINE

One distinct type of chronic pain carved out as its own medical subfield is headaches. Despite how common headaches are, there are high rates of misdiagnosis and misclassification by primary care providers.[42] Effective treatment depends on having a strong understanding of headache subtypes and their treatments, many of which are not used for other pain conditions.

The therapeutic options for headaches are also expanding, making it more difficult for primary care providers to treat them. In fact, some insurance plans even restrict primary care providers from prescribing monoclonal antibodies for headaches.

Although there is a clear need for doctors with expertise in headaches, we lack adequately trained specialists. There are currently fewer than 600 certified headache specialists — less than five times the estimated need.[43]

Headache specialists can find positions in academic practice, private neurology practices, and headache specialty practices; however, there are less conventional job options, too. Headache infusion centers, as one example, address the problem of poor headache management in emergency rooms, where patients tend to receive unnecessary imaging and inappropriate medications. They provide IV treatment on an urgent basis, primarily for established patients who have not responded well to standard treatments.

Comprehensive headache centers are another possibility. These facilities treat patients with refractory and severe headaches, offering Botox injections, neuromodulation, and other interventions. The Veterans Health Administration operates a Headache Centers of Excellence Program with more than a dozen clinics throughout the country.

PATHS TO A LESS CONVENTIONAL CAREER IN CHRONIC PAIN MANAGEMENT

You do not need to be an anesthesiologist to pursue training and certification in pain medicine. The ABMS recognizes pain medicine as a subspecialty of PM&R, emergency medicine, neurology, psychiatry, family medicine, and radiology. The AOA takes a similar approach. Many fellowship programs limit which primary specialties they accept, so applicants who have not trained in anesthesiology may need to put more effort into justifying their interest in pain medicine subspecialization. Most fellowships are one year in length.

The American Board of Pain Medicine offers an alternative pathway to certification in pain medicine for those who have not completed an accredited fellowship. There are also nonaccredited pain medicine fellowships, many of which are embedded within private pain practices.

A career focused on chronic pain is also possible without fellowship training. The most straightforward way to go this route is by developing expertise in the most common chronic pain presentations seen in your specialty. For instance, an oncologist might carve out a niche in managing cancer-related pain and a neurologist may focus their practice on neuropathic pain management.

Headache medicine is not an ABMS-recognized subspecialty. Fellowship programs and board certification are overseen by the United Council of Neurologic Subspecialties. Most programs are one year long. Some accept only neurologists, while others are open to applicants from other primary specialties. The council also offers alternative pathways for headache medicine certification, such as through practice experience. Other ways to gain competency and credentials in treating headaches include a Certificate of Added Qualification through the National Headache Foundation and courses offered by the American Headache Society.

COMPENSATION

Insurance companies pay more for procedures than for history-taking, counseling, or medication management, which affects physician compensation for different types of pain treatment. In 2021, the median salary for specialists in non-anesthesia pain management was $497,101; for anesthesiologists subspecializing in pain medicine, it was $538,718.[10]

End-of-life care

In his bestseller *Being Mortal*, Atul Gawande wrote, "People with serious illness have priorities besides simply prolonging their lives."[44] They may want to minimize distressing symptoms or nurture relationships with loved ones, for example. These priorities are, to a large extent, what makes end-of-life care an unconventional clinical concentration for physicians.

Most of what is practiced in modern medicine focuses on curing diseases and achieving quantifiable health outcomes. But approaches used at the end of life, such as hospice care and palliative treatment, don't align with this focus. Consequently, physicians may be reluctant to recommend these end-of-life approaches.

End-of-life care merges two common reasons for entering medicine: a love of the science and a compassionate drive to alleviate suffering.

MEDICAL CARE AT THE END OF LIFE

Approximately three million people die in the United States each year.[45] Disease precedes most deaths, but end-of-life planning and palliative measures often are not provided or not offered early enough in the disease process.

There is a growing body of evidence demonstrating that dedicated end-of-life care services can control costs, improve quality, and increase patient and family satisfaction in the setting of serious and life-threatening illnesses.

Differences in the approaches used in end-of-life care can be important when it comes to care coordination, patient education, and insurance billing. *Palliative care* aims to optimize quality of life and relieve discomfort in patients with serious medical problems. It is not limited to individuals near the end of life and can be provided alongside treatment with curative intent, such as through aggressive symptom management and psychosocial support.

Hospice care is both a support philosophy and a structured insurance benefit. It incorporates palliative measures, but a key differentiator from palliative care is its focus on patients with a terminal prognosis of six months or less.

Most physician jobs in end-of-life care include several desirable features. Many positions are part-time and have flexible hours, and administrative tasks can often be performed remotely. Jobs are not difficult to find. The need for end-of-life care is growing as the population ages. There have been more hospice and palliative care health insurance claims in the past five years than in any other specialty areas.[46]

JOBS WITH HOSPICE AGENCIES

Hospice care is a booming business, with more than 4,700 hospice agencies in the United States alone.[47] There has been a trend toward private, national corporations in the hospice market, with two-thirds run by for-profit entities.[48] A large program can have several hundred patients at once. Hospices run by nonprofits, government, and hospitals tend to have smaller censuses. Most programs provide in-home services, while some use hospitals or free-standing hospice facilities.

To be eligible for Medicare's hospice benefit, a patient's life expectancy must be six months or less. There is no limit on the duration of care, as long as the patient is reassessed regularly and continues to meet criteria for ongoing coverage. Commercial insurance hospice coverage policies largely mirror those of Medicare.

Medicare defines four service levels to capture different intensities of care needed over the course of terminal disease. These are (1) routine home care, (2) continuous home care, (3) general inpatient care, and (4) inpatient respite care. The hospice agency is reimbursed a flat daily rate for each patient, which varies by level of care.

The hospice care team includes physicians, nurses, health aids, case managers, social workers, counselors, and chaplains. At one time, hospices were nurse-driven programs, but Medicare standards have evolved to require more physician involvement at several levels.

For example, each hospice must have a medical director who leads and ultimately bears responsibility for the program's medical components. This physician provides certification and recertification of a patient's terminal illness and life expectancy. The role involves both direct patient interaction and oversight tasks, and usually requires visiting patients' homes, nursing facilities, or hospitals to conduct face-to-face visits. Small programs have a part-time medical director; the largest agencies need a full-time medical director plus one or more assistant or associate medical directors.

Medicare also defines the role of a hospice team physician who is responsible for providing medical care to patients on a day-to-day basis. Although this role is not required, many agencies have one or more team physicians on staff, depending on the agency's size and needs. Team physicians can be delegated certain responsibilities by the medical director.

Hospice programs must provide around-the-clock access to care. Because many aspects of care require physician orders, the on-call burden for hospice medical directors and team physicians can be high.

Medical directors and team physicians are either employed by or contracted with the hospice and are compensated directly by the agency. The two other physician roles outlined in Medicare's rules — attending physicians and consulting physicians — may also be involved in hospice patients' care but are independent from the hospice agency.

JOBS WITH PALLIATIVE CARE PROGRAMS

Unlike hospice, palliative care does not adhere to stringent Medicare eligibility criteria and there are no restrictions related to life expectancy, meaning more flexibility in program design and delivery. Programs include inpatient consult services, dedicated inpatient palliative care units, outpatient palliative care clinics, community-based services, and even telemedicine-based practices.

Hospital-based roles are a traditional avenue for palliative care careers; however, hospitals have been expanding their palliative care capabilities, potentially offering a career option for physicians of more varied backgrounds and interests. More than 80% of hospitals with 50 or more beds now incorporate palliative care teams, up from a mere 25% in 2000.[49]

Corporations are increasingly getting into the palliative care business. Major players like VITAS Healthcare and Optum offer comprehensive palliative care programs geared toward individuals who do not qualify for hospice care, but who can benefit from similar services. As with hospice, these programs depend on medical directors and staff physicians for oversight, patient assessments, and medical orders.

MEDICAL AID IN DYING

Medical aid in dying is a concept and process in which a terminally ill patient with limited life expectancy obtains prescription medication that they self-administer to end their life. In 1997, Oregon became the first state to legalize medical aid in dying. Since then, nine more states have passed similar legislation,[50] each with their own regulations and safeguards. Cumulatively, 6,378 individuals have ended their lives in this manner.[51]

As you might expect, medical aid in dying has very strict legal oversight. An attending physician must establish that a patient has decision-making capacity, the ability to take and respond to medications, and an expected six months or less to live, as well as submit required documentation to the state.

Many physicians choose not to get involved in medical aid in dying due to lack of the requisite knowledge, for moral reasons, or because they work for health systems that prohibit this practice. In Oregon and Washington, for example, fewer than 1% of licensed physicians write prescriptions to aid in dying.[52] Thus, there is a need for doctors who are willing to develop specialized expertise and incorporate this niche clinical area into their careers. Demand will likely increase as more states enact legislation to legalize this process.

GETTING INTO END-OF LIFE CARE

Hospice and palliative medicine is one of the newest and fastest growing ABMS-recognized medical subspecialties. Physicians from a wide range of primary specialties are eligible to pursue it, including anesthesiology, emergency medicine, family medicine, internal medicine, neurology, OB/GYN, pediatrics, PM&R, psychiatry, radiation oncology, and surgery.

Some training programs, however, only allow applicants from certain specialties. Internal medicine and family medicine are by far the most common specialties from which to enter the field.

Fellowships are one year long. Several fellowship programs offer a specific concentration such as pediatric or geriatric palliative care. Integrated programs combining residency with palliative care fellowship training are available as well.

Part-time fellowships geared toward mid-career physicians are a newer option for training in hospice and palliative medicine. The ACGME approved this type of "time-variable competency-based" fellowship in response to a specialist shortage in this field, providing a path to board eligibility without leaving your existing job.

Not all careers in end-of-life care require board certification in hospice and palliative care. Medicare mandates that hospice medical directors hold an MD or DO, although most other qualifications are set by the hospice agency. Some agencies require subspecialization or a minimum amount of hospice experience. Some require or prefer certification as a hospice medical director, which is offered by the Hospice Medical Director Certification Board and focuses on the administrative, regulatory, and legal competencies needed to oversee hospice care.

A few organizations offering education and other professional resources are the American Academy of Hospice and Palliative Medicine, the Society of Palliative Care Physicians, and the National Hospice and Palliative Care Organization.

For physicians with an interest in medical aid in dying, the American Clinicians Academy on Medical Aid in Dying is a resource. The advocacy organization Compassion & Choices offers a confidential consultation line called Doc2Doc, which allows doctors to speak to a fellow physician experienced in end-of-life care.

COMPENSATION

The median salary for hospice and palliative care specialists was $262,164 in 2022.[53]

Hospice medical director roles at large hospice agencies are often full-time, salaried positions. Part-time medical directors may get paid hourly or with a stipend. There may be additional hourly or daily pay for on-call responsibilities. Sometimes the hospice medical director role is a component of full-time employment with a healthcare system that operates a hospice; whether there is extra pay for the medical directorship can vary

Forensics and law enforcement

The public is fascinated by crime and forensics. The popular media's portrayals of crime and investigation produce unrealistic expectations of what forensic evidence can accomplish. This so-called *CSI-effect* can have real consequences, such as increased demand for forensic evidence in criminal trials and misunderstandings among jurors about the significance of evidence.

This surge of interest in forensics presents opportunities for physicians. Many criminal cases and legal disputes require medical evidence and expert medical opinion. You can have a career applying medical knowledge and skills within a legal context, with the shared goals of helping patients, keeping society safe, and ensuring justice is served.

UNCONVENTIONAL ASPECTS OF CLINICAL FORENSIC MEDICINE

Forensic medicine is a misunderstood field; some clinicians believe it is primarily concerned with medical malpractice, misconduct, or fraud, and others equate it with forensic pathology and misunderstand it as a scientific laboratory discipline.

Clinical forensic medicine involves individuals who are involved in legal proceedings or who have suffered harm resulting from criminal activity. It includes examining assault and abuse victims, providing medical evidence for courts, and evaluating the physical and mental health of individuals involved in legal proceedings.

Forensic medicine lacks the extensive standards of care and evidence-based practice guidelines used by other fields of medicine. Practitioners often rely on individual experience and customary practices to formulate their expert opinions.

The individuals evaluated and treated are patients, but also victims and potential crime suspects. Doctors are accustomed to ensuring privacy and confidentiality for our patients; however, some findings and opinions in forensic medicine need to be public. Age of consent, competency, and the physician's role in emergencies are other ethical issues that can differ from most medical fields.

Complete and accurate documentation is important for all physicians, but in forensic medicine, it is essential. Physicians' written reports are critical in determining the outcome of a trial and the guilt or innocence of a suspect. Reports are the principal means of communication between the physician and the legal team.

Aside from clinical work, physicians in forensics frequently take on various nonclinical roles in legal cases, including expert witness, factual witness, and law firm consultant.

CLINICAL FORENSIC EXAMS

A forensic exam evaluates the physical state of an individual claiming to be a victim of assault or other offense. Evaluations may be related to physical assaults, self-harm, child abuse, or sexual offenses. Occasionally, the alleged offender is also examined, such as for their fitness to be detained. Exams can take place in healthcare facilities such as emergency departments, or other settings like law enforcement agencies.

Exam requirements vary by jurisdiction. Forensic exams involve a medical history, physical exam, mental health evaluation, and collection of samples for forensic testing. They may be conducted in combination with limited medical treatment, such as prophylaxis for infections and pregnancy prevention in the case of sexual assault.

Results are documented in a report that details the patient's injuries and any evidence collected during the exam, such as DNA samples. The report is sent to law enforcement and any other relevant groups, such as the prosecutor's office or child protection agency, and is used as evidence. In some cases, the physician may provide testimony in court.

CAREER OPTIONS IN LAW ENFORCEMENT

Criminal investigation is the responsibility of law enforcement officials, but the information they need to investigate a case effectively comes from a variety of sources, including physicians.

The Federal Bureau of Investigation (FBI) investigates a range of criminal activity, including terrorism, organized crime, cybercrime, public corruption, and civil rights violations. One role for physicians within the FBI is supporting the Operational Medicine Program (OpMed). OpMed physicians are involved in training and drills, and may deliver medical care to FBI personnel, conduct fitness-for-duty exams, provide medical support during FBI operations, and implement medical protocols. Other possible FBI roles for physicians include intelligence analyst and forensic examiner.

Less commonly, physicians work in federal law enforcement with other agencies, such as the DEA.

Local and state law enforcement agencies may contract with physicians for their expertise in criminal investigations. Some use the title police surgeon, although most doctors in this role are not surgeons.

GETTING INTO FORENSICS AND LAW ENFORCEMENT

Emergency medicine is a fitting specialty for clinical forensic medicine, as injuries and health concerns that arise during criminal activities are often evaluated in emergency departments. Similarly, OB/GYNs encounter cases of sexual assault in their patient populations, pediatricians assess child abuse cases, and psychiatrists conduct forensic mental health evaluations.

Forensic exams draw from principles of pathology, pharmacology, toxicology, and other adjunct disciplines. So, while physicians of various specialties conduct these exams, the necessary skill set extends beyond the usual scope of each specialty. It can also be necessary to apply principles of disciplines outside of medicine. Injury cases, for instance, may rely on knowledge of applied physics and biomechanics.

Pediatricians can complete a three-year fellowship in child abuse pediatrics, which may be required for certain positions such as medical director for a child advocacy center. Psychiatrists can subspecialize in forensic psychiatry by completing a one-year fellowship. Otherwise, most residency and fellowship programs do not include much training in clinical forensic medicine, so you may need to find self-directed learning content.

The National Protocol for Sexual Assault Medical Forensic Examinations outlines best practices for conducting sexual assault forensic exams. The American Academy of Forensic Sciences is another source of information.

Basic requirements for employment with the FBI include U.S. citizenship, between 23 and 37 years of age, excellent physical fitness, and the ability to pass a rigorous background investigation. OpMed Medical Officer positions require a medical license and clinical experience.

Emergency medicine is the most well-suited specialty for the FBI, though others may be accepted. Once hired, OpMed physicians must complete the FBI's training program for special agents, which includes training in firearms, defensive tactics, law enforcement procedures, disaster response, crisis negotiation, and more.

COMPENSATION

Clinical forensic exams are typically paid for by state governments through a combination of federal funding, state-funded programs, and grants. Patients' health insurance can cover certain exam components, as well. As a result, physician compensation comes from a variety of sources, depending on the location, setting, and circumstances. Some states impose a reimbursement maximum for forensic exams, which tends to be low for the amount of work required.

Subspecialists with board certification in child abuse pediatrics or forensic psychiatry may command higher salaries than generalists in their respective fields for jobs in clinical forensic medicine, though this depends on demand for services and other factors.

Physicians working for the FBI and other federal government agencies are paid in accordance with the federal employee pay scale and may have more limited earning potential compared to those who work in private practice.

Taking on contract work as an expert witness or subject matter expert for legal cases can substantially increase overall compensation. Expert witnesses negotiate a fee structure with their client that can include hourly rates, retainers, and contingency fees. Hourly rates for this work range from a few hundred dollars to more than $1,000 per hour.

Obesity and weight loss

In 2013, the American Medical Association classified obesity as a disease requiring medical treatment and interventions. Yet, medical training and practice have not kept pace with the science supporting obesity treatment. Issues other than obesity take priority when patients see their doctors. As a result, high-quality obesity treatment is underutilized; consequently, there is significant opportunity for physicians to dedicate their attention to this field.

THE NEED FOR PHYSICIANS IN OBESITY MANAGEMENT

Obesity rates among adults in the United States have increased sharply over the past several decades, from 15% in 1980 to 42% in 2022.[54] Weight-related complications caused or exacerbated by obesity include diabetes, cardiovascular disease, fatty liver disease, infertility, obstructive sleep apnea, osteoarthritis, and many others. The effects go beyond morbidity and mortality, with obesity imposing an economic burden on healthcare systems and society.

Obesity is a multifactorial disease with genetic, biologic, environment, behavior, and psychosocial determinants, making treatment challenging for clinicians and patients. Sustained weight loss often requires a multi-modal approach. The challenges of obesity treatment are compounded by a $150 billion weight loss industry[55] that is largely driven by trends and gimmicks. We need doctors invested in obesity treatment to provide balanced, evidence-based care.

Expanding treatment options

Uptake of FDA-approved medications for obesity treatment was relatively low until a few years ago. Some of the older options like lipase inhibitors, sympathomimetics, and antidepressants are associated with significant side effects and were withdrawn from the market due to safety concerns.

Glucagon-like peptide-1 receptor agonists, including liraglutide and semaglutide, were approved for weight loss beginning in 2021. They showed remarkable efficacy and quickly became the first-line choice for many patients. The spotlight on this drug class intensified with media coverage and celebrity endorsements, increasing public awareness and demand.

We can anticipate new drug approvals, more targeted indications, and refined treatment protocols moving forward. As a result, clinicians will find it increasingly challenging to offer obesity treatment without specialized knowledge and ongoing education in this field.

The weight loss market and specialization

Despite how much we hear about weight loss programs, clinics, products, and memberships, the market is far from saturated — especially when it comes to physician-led weight loss services. Fewer than half of obese patients have been advised by a healthcare professional to lose weight,[56] yet patients want their doctors to be involved in their weight loss[57] and they are willing to pursue and pay for physician-directed weight management services.

Although some primary care doctors treat obesity, it has become a specialist-driven issue. Most primary care visits are too short to adequately address weight; when weight is addressed, patients are often told to lose weight but not given a specific treatment plan. Moreover, obesity does not receive much attention in internal and family medicine training programs, leaving many primary care doctors ill-equipped to treat it.

PRACTICE AND EMPLOYMENT OPTIONS

The commercial weight loss marketplace offers services ranging from meal delivery to personalized coaching. These businesses occasionally hire physicians to serve as consultants and medical advisors; however, far more opportunities are available in medical and surgical weight loss.

Medical weight loss clinics

Medically supervised weight loss programs center around the use of medication to treat obesity. This differentiates them from nonmedical programs, such as Weight Watchers and LA Weight Loss Centers.

Many physicians find success with independent solo or group medical weight loss practices. Most aim to programmatize their services while still offering individualized care. This is particularly effective for a weight loss practice, since many individuals seek a structured program for weight loss and it aligns with the common perception that weight loss should be regimented. A structured weight loss program also facilitates time-limited plans — such as a 12- to 16-week commitment — making it easier for clinic staff to manage the patient panel and for patients to follow recommendations.

To incorporate other revenue sources into a medical weight loss clinic, you can hire dietitians, exercise physiologists, and psychologists to offer tailored education, assessments, or behavioral counseling. Specialized diets accompanied by discounted supplements and weight loss products offer value for some patients. Hormonal therapy, vitamin B shots, IV nutrition therapy, food sensitivity testing, and body composition analysis are potential revenue-generators.

Because the weight loss industry is so commercialized, if you start an independent weight loss clinic, strong marketing and branding are important. You also need to be aware of any state-specific regulations governing obesity treatment, many of which were implemented decades ago in response to overuse of amphetamine derivatives for weight loss.

Working for a national or regional corporate medical weight loss chain is another option. Some corporations hire physicians directly; others work with medical providers through franchising, licensing, and other turn-key models. Some of the largest companies are Center for Medical Weight Loss, Let's Lose, Lindora Clinics, and Medi-Weightloss.

Surgical and procedural weight loss practices

Surgery is recommended for many patients who do not meet weight loss goals with diet, exercise, and drug therapy. Surgeons naturally have career options in this area; however, nonsurgical obesity medicine specialists can provide pre- and peri-surgical care to bariatric patients. These jobs are found in comprehensive weight management centers associated with academic medical centers or larger healthcare systems.

The scope of minimally invasive procedural interventions for weight loss is broadening, creating additional career opportunities. Many procedures are performed endoscopically, including gastric balloons, endoscopic sleeve gastroplasty, and the Pose procedure.

GETTING INTO OBESITY MEDICINE AND MEDICAL WEIGHT LOSS

A range of medical specialties provide a good foundation for obesity medicine and medical weight loss. An internal medicine subspecialty certification in endocrinology, diabetes, and metabolism requires a two-year fellowship. Given the increase in endoscopic bariatric procedures, we will likely see more gastroenterologists focusing their practices on obesity management.

There is a growing need for pediatricians to practice obesity medicine, as childhood obesity rates are rising and new guidelines from the American Academy of Pediatrics stress the need for early and intensive treatment.[58]

Although not ACGME-accredited, a growing number of clinical obesity medicine fellowships are available. The American Board of Obesity Medicine offers certification through either a CME or fellowship pathway. Applicants must be board-certified by an ABMS member board to be eligible.

Most surgeons who perform bariatric surgery are general surgeons. The American Board of Surgery offers a Focused Practice Designation in metabolic and bariatric surgery, and there are some surgical fellowships focused on bariatric surgery.

Medical school curriculums tend to lack in-depth training on nutrition, so taking a course or two on this topic can be helpful. Motivational interviewing and counseling skills are also valuable.

National professional organizations that are reputable sources of additional information are the Obesity Medicine Association, The Obesity Society, and the American Society of Metabolic & Bariatric Surgery.

COMPENSATION AND FINANCIAL CONSIDERATIONS

Physicians employed in a medical weight loss center can expect to earn a salary on par with most primary care physicians. The average annual income for nonsurgical obesity medicine specialists was $291,972 in 2021.[10] The earning potential for nonsurgical practice owners is far higher. The average revenue of a medical weight loss clinic has been reported as $543,000 per year, with a profit margin of 36%.[59]

Not surprisingly, surgeons treating obesity are compensated more than nonsurgical physicians, with bariatric surgeons earning an average annual salary of $576,461 in 2021.[10]

William Andrew "Andy" Lemons Jr, MD

OB/GYN and Addiction Medicine Specialist

Practice setting

I work for two large corporate entities that provide treatment for addictions in outpatient clinics. We mainly provide medication-assisted treatment, but also counseling and referrals for other medical, mental health, and social needs.

I also work as a physician advisor for a large health insurance agency.

Employment type and schedule

I serve each of my three positions as an independent contractor. All are part-time positions, but collectively amount to a full-time schedule.

I have one day each week divided between clinic in the morning and insurance reviews in the afternoon. The other days are divided between the two clinics, sometimes spending the morning at one clinic and the afternoon at the other.

I spend over 90% of my time on direct patient care, either face-to-face with patients or in consultation with other clinicians. My physician advisor position is computer-based and accounts for no more than 10% of my time.

On-call responsibilities are limited to two weekends monthly and are strictly responding to nurse calls regarding patient needs and medication dosing. There is no overnight call and no need to go in on the weekends. One of the clinics does have patient appointments one to two Saturdays each month, but those are staffed by other providers at this time.

Patient population and clinical work

I focus on patients with opioid addiction, though many have poly-substance use disorder. Many are quite stable and are in maintenance treatment, while others are in the peak of the grips and illness associated with their addictions, its poor decision-making tendency, and the consequences of those. Addictions have no societal or economic barriers, and I find my patients have extensively varied backgrounds, variability in their work status, family support, and level of commitment to their own recovery.

A typical day at work

One of the clinics opens at 5:00 a.m., so my days begin very early. I do intake assessments on new patients and follow-ups with existing patients. I review labs, urine drug screens, and confirmation testing. I conduct team visits with patients, their counselor, a clinical supervisor, and the program director when specific needs arise. There is also a weekly staff meeting in which we discuss complex cases.

Unconventional aspects

The most unconventional aspect for me is the early hours. Five o'clock comes early. I definitely had to adjust my social, family, and sleep-wake patterns to accommodate this.

The patients themselves have unique traits. Most are truly interested in stability, recovery, and improving their lives. A few work the system, divert medication and drug screens, and continue illicit use. A lot of patient education is needed. I try to function as a life coach who also has the credentials to assist with medication.

Treatment in a certified opioid treatment program is very team-oriented. I have to balance what I would recommend or implement as the licensed and responsible prescribing provider with input from counselors, regional directors, and supervisors.

Corporate ownership of the clinics comes with a few unconventional elements. It is different than privately owned practice. The corporation determines technology and equipment choices (such as the EHR), how staff are utilized and retained, and how compliance is ensured.

Best parts of the job

I enjoy working with patients who are turning their lives around. There are patients who overcome an inability to repair their car, keep a job, or manage their family because they were spending all their time, money, energy, and resources on pursuing drug use and trying to prevent withdrawal. Witnessing them conquer these hurdles is quite rewarding.

I do miss the surgical and obstetric career I had prior to focusing on addiction medicine. However, my current work is fulfilling in its own way. I work directly with pregnant patients in both clinics, which allows me to combine my prior specialty with my newer field.

Challenges faced

The biggest challenge is the assortment of social, economic, family, and mental health struggles of patients. These contribute to and underly their addictions. Many have limited resources, limited access to insurance benefits, limited support systems, and limited education. Many have fallen prey to self-limiting belief patterns, old labels, and a sense of learned helplessness. Assisting them in overcoming these obstacles can be frustratingly challenging.

Qualifications and skills needed for this career

A strong understanding and expertise in the field coupled with communication skills is needed. Patients need to see you as an authority, but also an advocate. Learning the harm-reduction role is important. Accountability and grace can co-exist while avoiding the enabling behaviors often seen in this group. The ability to explain induction protocols, the medications used to treat addictions, and the time frames needed to establish stability while also establishing expectations is also helpful. Gaining trust, establishing boundaries, balancing advocacy with compliance expectations are all among the needed tools.

It's also important to be able to separate your interest in patients' success from your own professional fulfillment. Despite your efforts, a subset of patients with addiction may continue to make poor choices and will have little improvement in treatment.

Advice for students and physicians

You can treat addictions without being board-certified in addiction medicine. But attaining board certification provides a level of excellence and expertise to help you to best serve this underserved — and often stigmatized — group of patients.

CAREERS IN UNCONVENTIONAL PRACTICE SETTINGS AND SURROUNDINGS

A career in medicine is not confined to a hospital or clinic. Doctors are needed for patient care in varied and unexpected settings ranging from prisons to retrofitted vans to remote mountainsides. The number of physicians working in nontraditional settings will grow in coming years due, in part, to expanding healthcare needs of diverse and aging populations, technological advances, and an emphasis on preventive care.

Each setting has its own culture, operational dynamics, patient flows, and other distinctions that might address a source of discontent or frustration you have faced in hospitals and office-based practices. Or, these settings can be a means to focus within a niche or on treating a specific patient type.

It is difficult to point to any clear evidence in support of improved career satisfaction through working in an unconventional practice setting. But it stands to reason that if you find yourself dreading your next walk down the hospital corridor, you may feel more at home elsewhere.

Blood and transfusion centers

Blood transfusions are the most frequently performed procedure during hospitalization.[60] Since transfusion relies on individual donors, blood procurement procedures are common as well. Nearly 7 million people in the United States donate blood each year.[61] Given this statistic, you might think healthcare practitioners would be well-acquainted with blood procurement and transfusion; however, most of us lack knowledge on these subjects.[62] Physicians with an interest (whether they are pathologists or not) have career opportunities across various stages of the blood supply chain.

BLOOD PROCUREMENT

Blood donation centers ensure a reliable supply of blood products for transfusion. Most are nonprofit organizations that rely on volunteer donors. Together, the American Red Cross and America's Blood Centers manage most of the blood supply. Other key organizations with national or regional presence include Blood Centers of America, ImpactLife, Vitalant, LifeSouth, and New York Blood Center.

Many centers primarily procure whole blood, although specialized facilities focusing on plasma donation are common. Plasma donation has advanced as an industry in itself due to high demand and profitability. Private, for-profit organizations run most plasma centers. Major players include BioLife Plasma Services, CSL Plasma, Grifols, Octapharma Plasma, and Plasma Centers of America.

Donation center physician oversight

Blood donation is a heavily governed series of processes, which significantly impacts the role of physicians.

FDA's authority extends beyond food and drugs to include blood products. Requirements address donor eligibility criteria, screening and testing procedures for infectious diseases, proper collection and storage practices, documentation and record-keeping protocols, and adverse event reporting. Some states have additional requirements.

FDA uses the term *responsible physician* to refer to the physician who assumes overall responsibility for the medical aspects of the donation center's operations. The physician does not always need to be present onsite, as some tasks can be conducted by phone. Certain duties can be delegated to a physician substitute working under the responsible physician's supervision.

The Association for the Advancement of Blood & Biotherapies (AABB) accredits blood banks. Their standards similarly require that a center's medical director have responsibility for all medical and technical policies and processes. Donation centers must also comply with the Clinical Laboratories Improvement Act to ensure accurate and reliable blood sample testing. This requires each center to have a qualified lab director.

These regulations and standards largely define the scope and nature of physician roles in blood donation centers. In many centers, a single physician is the responsible physician, lab director, and medical director.

Oversight tasks include reviewing policies and procedures, conducting chart reviews, and providing staff training. Physicians may be involved in donor evaluation, physical exams, and counseling in plasma centers. Since many responsibilities are delegated to phlebotomists, nurses, and medical lab technologists, centers often limit physician involvement as much as possible in order to control expenses.

The time commitment for a donation center physician may be as little as an hour or two per week. A few states impose certain requirements regarding the physician's hours. Connecticut, for example, requires a doctor to be present at the center during at least half of its normal working hours.

BLOOD TRANSFUSION

Transfusion centers receive blood products from donation centers for storage and distribution. Many doctors never step foot in their hospital's transfusion center; however, physicians are there, overseeing the entire transfusion process from patient evaluation to post-transfusion care.

A physician's work in a transfusion center involves a combination of administrative duties, lab oversight, and patient care. Most tasks revolve around ensuring the appropriate and safe blood product use, such as through blood compatibility testing. They supervise specialized procedures like therapeutic apheresis, evaluate and manage transfusion reactions, and consult with other physicians on issues related to transfusions.

Blood banking and transfusion medicine intertwines medical knowledge, laboratory expertise, supply chain management, and quality assurance. It is one of the few pathology subfields that involves direct patient interaction and treatment.

PATHWAYS TO PRACTICING IN A BLOOD OR TRANSFUSION CENTER

Most blood banking and transfusion medicine subspecialists are pathologists; however, you do not need to be a pathologist to seek fellowship training and board certification in this field. The rationale for this is that many concepts and practices of transfusion medicine have relevance across multiple medical disciplines, including hematology/oncology, surgery, emergency medicine, and critical care. Board eligibility requires a 12-month fellowship. Not all fellowship programs accept applicants who are not trained in pathology.

One job in many blood and transfusion center jobs is lab director. Qualifications are based on the complexity level of procedures performed. Depending on your credentials, this may require a 20-hour, online CME course.

Although not required, it is fairly common for physicians in blood banking and transfusion medicine to hold a PhD. This is an option if you want more in-depth knowledge or research experience in molecular pathology, cytopathology, hematopathology, or another area of lab medicine.

Donation center physician qualifications

The FDA requires the responsible physician for a blood donation center to be licensed in the state in which the center is located and to be "adequately trained and qualified" to carry out their responsibilities.[63] It does not stipulate what "adequately trained and qualified" means. Similarly, AABB requires the donation center medical director to be "qualified by training, experience, and facility-defined relevant continuing education" but does not specifically state what training or experience is acceptable.

Some states have strict rules about the qualifications for a donation center medical director. California, for instance, requires at least six months experience in blood banking methods, transfusion principles, and transfusion practices. In Connecticut, medical directors must have at least one year of training or experience in blood banking or be board-certified in pathology.

Donation centers or the corporations running them may set additional requirements for their medical directors. Some require physicians to be board-certified in blood banking and transfusion medicine, while others do not.

COMPENSATION

Pathologists earned an average salary of $357,384 in 2022.[33] Even the most in-depth physician salary surveys fail to provide a breakdown of compensation for blood banking and transfusion medicine subspecialists.

Hourly rates for contracted medical directors at blood product donation centers range from about $100 to $300 per hour. Experience, prevailing market rates, scope of responsibilities, and other factors influence this figure.

Convenient care centers

Convenient care centers have a lot to offer patients. With nearly 10,000 centers across the United States[64] and an average wait time under 15 minutes,[65] they are, as the name suggests, convenient. They are affordable, too, with an average urgent care visit costing $168, compared to $2,200 for an emergency department visit.[66] Convenient care centers serve nearly 160 million patients per year.[65]

But the benefits are not limited to patients. Convenient care is a great career option for physicians seeking something a bit out of the ordinary.

THE CONVENIENT CARE INDUSTRY

Convenient care refers to a limited scope of medical services provided by clinics offering an alternative to primary care office visits and certain types of emergency department visits. Although their scope of services varies significantly, nearly all provide unscheduled care (some also allow for scheduled appointments) and offer access to care outside of traditional office hours.

Types of convenient care

Medical providers staff urgent care centers, providing workup and treatment for a range of common medical problems, such as minor infections, common acute illnesses, and sprains and strains. In a typical clinic, patients are triaged upon arrival and are assessed, diagnosed, and treated by a provider. The provider may order tests and medications, as well as arrange for follow-up care. Notable urgent care chains include CareNow, FastMed, and MedExpress.

Retail clinics provide less advanced services and procedures. They can treat minor illnesses such as upper respiratory infections and rashes, and offer vaccinations, physicals, and screenings. Many are located in busy retail outlets and co-located with drugstores or supermarkets. CVS, Walgreens, and Walmart are major players in the retail clinic sector.

Other terms used in the field of convenient care include immediate care, minor emergency center, walk-in clinic, minute clinic, quick care clinic, express care, after-hours care, and same-day care. These terms vary regionally and by healthcare organization, but they refer to the same concept of providing quick, affordable on-demand care.

Convenient care ownership and outlook

Increasing numbers of hospital systems own and operate urgent care clinics. Although there are still a sizeable number of independently owned facilities, fewer than a third of urgent care centers are physician-owned.

Regardless of ownership, convenient care can provide substantial cost savings for the healthcare industry, primarily by preventing unnecessary emergency department visits. Many urgent care centers also accept insurance and charge copays similar to those of primary care physician visits. This can be a major advantage for patients who need immediate care but cannot afford the higher copays and deductibles of emergency room visits. As opposed to emergency departments, which are bound by legal obligations to treat all patients who come through their doors, urgent care centers in most states can choose patients by payer type.

The demand for convenient care is expected to increase. Urgent care centers are increasingly being integrated into larger healthcare networks, allowing for coordination across levels and types of care. Telehealth urgent care is gaining popularity, as patients can receive medical attention from the comfort of their homes.

PRACTICING IN A CONVENIENT CARE CENTER

Approximately 20,000 physicians practice urgent care medicine.[67] The patient population includes patients of all ages, backgrounds, and medical histories. Physicians need to be comfortable handling a high patient volume and a broad range of minor and acute illnesses and injuries.

Urgent care staffing models vary depending on the size and needs of the facility. Most centers are physician-led; the majority employ at least one physician, although some hire multiple part-time physicians. More than half also employ APPs.[68] In retail clinics, non-physician providers conduct the majority of care, while physicians are mainly responsible for clinical oversight and administrative work.

Another unconventional aspect is the work schedule. Urgent care clinics are open evenings, weekends, and holidays, leading to nontraditional work hours compared to other outpatient practices. A typical shift is eight to 12 hours, with many clinics offering flexible scheduling or part-time work options.

GETTING INTO CONVENIENT CARE

Due to increased awareness and improved standards, urgent care medicine has increasingly become a deliberate career choice for physicians, rather than a fallback option.

Urgent care is not a recognized specialty of the ABMS or the AOA, although several medical specialties lend themselves to a career in these settings. Family medicine is the most common specialty of doctors staffing urgent care centers, followed by emergency medicine and internal medicine.[69] Pediatrics is another option, as the number of pediatric urgent care clinics is increasing.

Although their skills are well-suited for urgent care, emergency physicians will find the compensation does not compete with what they can earn by working in an emergency department. Hiring emergency medicine specialists can actually be cost-prohibitive for convenient care clinics, so many clinics target their searches toward primary care physicians.

Several healthcare organizations offer urgent care fellowship and certification programs. Whether these are helpful for gaining relevant skills or landing jobs in convenient care will depend on your background. The Urgent Care Association is a resource for networking and continuing education.

COMPENSATION

In 2022, the median salary for a physician practicing full-time urgent care was $289,464.[53] Compensation in convenient care can be salaried or hourly, depending on the work arrangement and schedule. Use of value-based compensation models is growing.

Clinics hiring full-time physicians typically offer benefits packages and malpractice insurance. Physician-owned convenient care clinics may offer ownership and partnership opportunities.

Correctional facilities

The U.S. Constitution creates an unconventional career path for physicians. In the 1976 landmark case *Estelle* v *Gamble*, the Supreme Court ruled that deliberate indifference to an inmate's serious medical needs amounted to a violation of the Eighth Amendment, which prohibits "cruel and unusual punishments." This set the precedent that prison and jail authorities provide medical treatment.

Providing treatment is not easy. Transporting inmates to a doctor's office or hospital for every medical need poses security risks, logistical challenges, and substantial costs. The viable alternative for large jails and prisons is to establish clinics within their walls and bring in clinicians and equipment to deliver medical care onsite, thus creating this under-recognized practice setting.

INCARCERATION IN THE UNITED STATES

There are almost 2 million individuals behind bars in the United States.[70] Despite the fact that this number has gradually decreased since 2009, the United States still has among the highest incarceration rates in the world.[71]

The U.S. criminal justice system uses multiple institution types. Prisons are long-term facilities operated by state or federal authorities, housing those convicted of serious offenses and serving longer sentences. There are 1,161 prisons,[72] ranging from minimum to maximum security. The Federal Bureau of Prisons houses federal offenders; state correctional systems are responsible for those convicted of state-level crimes. State prison populations range from 1,300 inmates in Vermont to over 133,000 in Texas.[73]

Jails are shorter-term facilities operating at the county or city level. They hold individuals awaiting trial or serving shorter sentences. Most house fewer than 100 inmates; only 4% are large jails with 1,000 or more inmates, although these house over a third of all inmates.[74] This range of size and population creates wide variation in the operational dynamics of jails.

The correctional system also includes detention centers designed for specific purposes such as housing immigration detainees, juvenile detention centers for underage offenders, specialized medical facilities, and pre-release centers focused on preparing individuals for transition back into society.

Health and healthcare in correctional facilities

Inmates are housed in close quarters and exposed to potentially unhealthy conditions. Rates of asthma, hepatitis B, hepatitis C, human immuno-deficiency virus (HIV), and certain other medical conditions, including many mental health conditions, are higher in correctional facilities compared to the general population. Suicide, homicide, and overdose are leading causes of death.[75]

Harsher sentencing policies, longer incarceration periods, overcrowding, and the aging of the prison population have compounded the prevalence of medical and mental health problems. Despite a decreasing incarceration rate, the average acuity level has increased, resulting in more demand for medical and behavioral health services.

Concerns about the quality of medical care in jails and prisons are long-standing. Legal interventions have continued since *Estelle v Gamble*, addressing such issues as lack of resources to meet the population's needs, mental healthcare provision, and excessive use of force by prison staff.

Healthcare operations in jails and prisons utilize a few different structures. A self-operated system, where the facility manages and delivers healthcare services internally, is one approach. Privatized healthcare services, involving contracts with private correctional healthcare vendors, is another model. Some use a combination of these, relying on contracts for specific aspects such as staffing, lab services, radiology, or dental care. Some jurisdictions have established partnerships with large healthcare systems or academic medical institutions to provide medical care.

JOBS FOR PHYSICIANS IN PRISONS AND JAILS

The size and specific needs of a jail or prison influence the nature of employment. Many physicians at larger facilities are in full-time roles. Part-time positions at smaller jails may require just a few hours per week and offer significant flexibility in scheduling.

Staff physician

The work of a staff physician falls in line with primary care, although it overlaps with emergency and hospital medicine. They conduct chronic care clinics, treat acute medical needs, and round in infirmaries or medical units. Physicians in large facilities with multiple medical staff may have a specific area or service they focus on.

A dedicated medical unit is used for most routine care, but there are urgent and emergent medical situations to respond to throughout the facility. Doctors may also round on patients who are housed in isolation, suicide watch cells, or other special housing that complicates patient movement and transport. When not providing direct patient care, they may coordinate with offsite specialists, review hospital records, and follow-up on lab and imaging results. Correctional facilities rely heavily on APPs, so many physicians take on a supervision role, as well.

Medical director

A site medical director has clinical authority over one facility and may oversee staff physicians and other providers. Regional or state-wide medical directors have broader oversight, managing the clinical aspects of an entire state prison system or facilities within a geographic area. When not traveling to the facilities within their region, most work from a corporate office or from home.

These leadership positions involve a balance of nonclinical and clinical responsibilities. Medical directors participate in quality improvement initiatives, infection control measures, accreditation surveys, policy development, and other administrative tasks.

Psychiatrist

Mental healthcare is a huge component of correctional medicine. Staff psychiatrists manage medications and oversee treatment plans.

They work with a team of mental health professionals, including social workers, therapists, counselors, and psychologists. There are mental health leadership positions analogous to those of medical staff, such as psychiatric director.

Specialist consultant

Some correctional facilities opt to bring in medical specialists to provide dedicated clinics for specific medical needs, avoiding the need to send patients offsite for specialty services. This is particularly common for OB/GYN in facilities housing women and nephrology in prisons with onsite dialysis units. Many specialists serving as consultants do so at more than one facility, and most keep up a practice outside of the correctional setting.

Increasingly, jails and prisons are using telemedicine, particularly for specialty services. This expands the opportunities for doctors who cannot easily get to a facility or who do not wish to physically work in one.

UNCONVENTIONAL ASPECTS OF CORRECTIONAL MEDICINE

Physicians encounter a range of clinical, ethical, and legal challenges when working in correctional facilities. Overall facility operations center around security. Doctors are occasionally asked to participate in custody activities, such as performing body cavity searches or obtaining lab specimens for forensic purposes. Patient privacy is limited; security staff are present during patient visits, and you may need to examine patients who are restrained.

You may face legal mandates from lawyers representing inmates. Facilities might need to operate under consent decrees or other legal agreements that influence healthcare services.

Some facilities have limited resources and budgets. The field is burdened by understaffing, which can exacerbate resource constraints.

Despite these challenges, practicing in the correctional setting has several advantages. There is far less involvement with insurance companies, billing, and coding than in traditional practice settings. Because patients are housed and receive medical care in the same place, closer monitoring and more frequent follow-up than in the outpatient setting is possible. Many doctors appreciate the heterogeneous patient population, steady patient volumes, and contribution to reduced recidivism rates.

GETTING INTO CORRECTIONAL MEDICINE

Staff physicians and medical directors come from a range of backgrounds and specialties, including internal medicine, family medicine, emergency medicine, preventive medicine, and even OB/GYN and general surgery. Psychiatrists are in high demand. Juvenile detention centers hire pediatricians. Part-time contract work is available in other specialties and subspecialties.

Most employers require physicians to be board-certified in their specialty; however, some accept licensed general practitioners. Prior experience working in a jail or prison is desirable, but rarely required.

The ACGME is developing a designation for correctional medicine fellowships, which will lead to significantly more training opportunities within jails and prisons. National organizations offering education and other resources on correctional medicine include the National Commission on Correctional Health Care and the American College of Correctional Physicians.

COMPENSATION

Some doctors are surprised to hear that correctional medicine pays well. Most physicians earn a salary comparable to what they would earn in traditional healthcare settings. The California Correctional Health Care Services, which serves one of the largest state prison systems, offers an annual salary up to $317,556 for internal medicine physicians and $343,596 for psychiatrists in 40-hours-per-week positions. These figures increase to $372,588 and $389,328 for leadership roles, respectively.[76]

In 2023, postings on USAJOBS listed base salaries of up to $243,000 for medical doctors and $282,000 for psychiatrists working for the Bureau of Prisons.

Unlike government-operated facilities, private vendors are for-profit companies, so there may be more opportunity for salary negotiation.

Given that positions can be difficult to fill, employers may be willing to offer sign-on bonuses, retention bonuses, relocation packages, and other incentives.

House calls

The image of a doctor delivering care to a sick patient at home is a deeply ingrained symbol of compassion, dedication, and expertise. Today, treating patients in their homes is sometimes viewed as outdated and impractical, yet home visits are a potential setting for an unconventional career.

HOUSE CALLS ARE MAKING A COMEBACK

More than one in three patient visits were house calls in the 1930s.[77] By 1980, they accounted for fewer than 1% of patient encounters.[78] This decline resulted, in part, from advances in diagnostic technologies making it more feasible for patients to visit a medical facility. There was also a trend toward physician specialization and an increasing emphasis on productivity, which pushed physicians to treat patients in clinics.

Beginning in the late 1980s, home visits picked up some steam. Although it never returned to its previous level of use, home care was the most rapidly growing segment of Medicare's budget for a full decade.[79] Interestingly, physicians in England make house calls at a rate of 10 times that of U.S. physicians today,[80] suggesting the capacity to further revive house calls.

Benefits of house calls

Patients, their families or caregivers, and physicians can all benefit from house calls.

Patients may find it easier to receive care in their own homes, especially when they have limited transportation or mobility. But convenience is a relatively minor advantage when you consider that house calls can lead to improved care. Studies involving older adults have shown that house calls reduce hospitalizations, days spent in the hospital, emergency department visits, and admissions to long-term care.[81] House calls also promote improved collaboration with home health agencies and give clinicians a deeper understanding of environmental factors affecting their patients' health.

Physicians report a great deal of satisfaction from providing house calls.[82] Appointment volume is lower and the pace is slower than what we're used to in a regular medical office. The average home visit provider sees about 10 patients per day.[83] In many cases, doctors can take more time with patients and have a break between encounters during driving time.

Without many of the overhead costs stemming from office-based practice, profit margins can be higher. For physicians who already have a physical office, adding home visits is a way to grow their practice without adding more space. It can also give practice owners better access to their target patient population.

The range of house call services

Patients who have mobility restrictions, conditions that could be exacerbated by going to an office, or complex medical issues with functional or cognitive limitations make up the bulk of house call visits. However, they can be suitable for addressing a wide scope of medical needs for a broad range of patients — even those who are ambulatory and relatively healthy.

House calls should be differentiated from home care, in which nurses or aids provide personal assistance or services to patients at home due to illness or injury. You may also come across the term *home-based primary care*, which is a model incorporating house calls, telemedicine, monitoring devices, and other services to offer comprehensive primary care within the home.

HOUSE CALLS CAREER OPTIONS

House calls programs range in size from small office-based practices that reserve a few appointment slots for home visits to large, multistate groups with or without brick-and-mortar locations.

The career option with the lowest barriers to entry is employment with a healthcare system that has a formalized house call program. MedStar Health and Ascension Health, through its Ascension at Home program, are two examples. Many larger hospitals and networks have realized that robust house call programs can improve their bottom line, mainly through decreases in unnecessary hospital readmissions and emergency department visits. Some now hire physicians who are dedicated full-time to house calls, rather than requiring them to juggle office visits with home visits.

Numerous private healthcare companies have launched house call services. Some offer primary care services: for example, One Medical Seniors specializes in primary care for older adults and Landmark Health focuses on complex care needs. Specialty in-home care practices have emerged as well. Evergreen Nephrology, for instance, provides home visits to patients on dialysis, and NayaCare offers perinatal care. Depending on their business model, these companies hire doctors for full-time or part-time roles, often through a physician-run professional corporation or other medical group entity.

Private practice is a career option through two main avenues: adding house call services to an existing practice or running a practice exclusively conducting house calls. The former may be more doable in a group practice, so there is in-office coverage when one provider is out of the office making house calls. New programs can initially allocate one to two sessions weekly for home visits, expanding as the house call component grows and becomes self-sufficient.

CAREER ENTRY AND PRACTICE PLANNING

Most house calls physicians are in primary care, with many fellowship-trained in geriatrics or palliative medicine. Surgery, OB/GYN, nephrology, and other specialties are also relevant, given the increase in organizations offering more specialized home visit services.

In addition to clinical skills and solid bedside manner, you need sufficient business acumen to manage the operations of a house calls practice. Without a physical clinic, you need to carefully select equipment and supplies to carry with you. The modern-day doctor's bag is more of a rolling suitcase, given the availability of hand-held technologies and point-of-care testing.

Scheduling requires extra effort to cluster visits within a particular geographic area on a given day and to minimize travel time. Larger programs may hire a driver so physicians can use travel time to catch up on charting and other tasks.

House call medicine requires attention to your safety. Have a plan for responding to urgent situations, visiting higher crime areas, inclement weather, car accidents, and traveling to remote areas without satellite service. Be prepared to respond to unexpected clinical scenarios without the resources of a fully staffed medical office. There may be pets, pests, sanitation issues, or extra family members to contend with in patients' homes.

There have been relatively few litigations relating to house calls, but there are pertinent legal issues. You need adequate protection for motor vehicle accidents and injuries occurring on a patient's property. Patient abandonment may be a concern if a physician refuses to make a house call and the patient cannot otherwise access necessary care. There are state regulations applicable to some practices relating to medication storage and provision of certain services outside of a medical setting.

The American Academy of Home Care Physicians, the Home Centered Care Institute, and the National Home-Based Primary Care Learning Network offer guidelines, training programs, and peer connections.

COMPENSATION AND REIMBURSEMENT

For primary care doctors employed by a health system, compensation is comparable to office-based primary care physicians.

Profit and compensation for private practice doctors depend on volume, scope of services, specialty, billing procedures, and other factors. House call physicians primarily bill Medicare, as most patients are older. In an effort to encourage the use of house calls, Medicare increased physician payments for home visits in 2000; however, many still believe reimbursement is inadequate.

Being a house call doctor is conducive to certain supplementary income sources, such as working as a medical director for hospice programs or home health agencies.

Long-term care and rehab facilities

Acute care hospitals and outpatient medical offices do not meet all the healthcare needs of many chronically ill, elderly, and impaired individuals. The full care continuum necessitates medical services in post-acute and long-term care settings, which are mainly comprised of skilled nursing homes and rehabilitation centers.

MEDICAL NEEDS IN LONG-TERM CARE FACILITIES

A skilled nursing facility offers care to residents around the clock. More than 15,500 skilled nursing facilities house 1.3 million individuals across the United States,[84] with an average of 109 beds per facility.[85] Nearly 90% of patients are long-term residents,[86] though many centers also house temporary residents for post-acute care or rehab following hospitalization.

Nursing homes are predominantly for-profit; more than half are part of regional or national chains.[87] Many geographic areas have a competitive long-term care market.

Nursing home residents are debilitated, with multiple chronic conditions requiring treatment. Psychosocial issues are common. Although most residents are older, practicing in this setting is not synonymous with geriatric care. About 15% of patients are young with complex medical and social needs. They may have developmental disabilities, hemiplegia and quadriplegia, chronic neurological disorders, or perioperative needs.

The term *skilled nursing* stresses the role of nurses, but doctors are the ones who evaluate residents and give orders for treatments, medications, diets, and other medical care that nursing staff implement. Nursing home residents have gotten more medically complex over time, increasing the need for physicians in this setting.

Nursing home regulations

Long-term care is a highly regulated industry. Nursing homes must comply with Medicare rules and regulations, unless they accept only private pay patients (which is rare). Regulations cover staffing ratios, qualifications for healthcare providers, and other operational issues. There are specific guidelines about patient admissions, discharges, and transfers. They require that physicians provide timely patient assessments, after-hours coverage, and proper documentation. Many states have regulations further delineating care standards.

Assisted living and other long-term care settings

Similar settings in which physicians can practice include assisted living facilities, independent living communities, and intermediate care facilities. These do not face the same federal government regulatory oversight of skilled nursing facilities; however, many offer clinical services and staffing, which can include part-time physicians.

PHYSICIAN ROLES AT NURSING FACILITIES

The goal in any post-acute or long-term care setting is for patients to reach their highest expected level of functioning in the least restrictive environment.

Residents newly admitted to a facility need to be assessed by a physician for stability, functional and cognitive status, and appropriateness for the nursing home level of care. This assessment helps the staff formulate an initial treatment plan. Subsequent encounters focus on monitoring and updating the care plan and addressing any acute needs. This often requires coordinating with specialists, nursing staff, and family members.

Medical director

Skilled nursing facilities must designate a physician as the medical director. Federal regulations broadly define the medical director's responsibilities, which include implementing resident care policies and coordinating medical care within the facility. Serving as a nursing home medical director is not a passive way to earn a monthly stipend by signing off on a few forms. Medicare's intent is for the medical director to take an active role in helping facilities deliver effective medical care.

Most medical directors provide general oversight and guidance to facility staff, attend routine meetings to discuss care issues, review reports, and contribute to policy and procedure development. The responsibilities are extensive enough that some facilities hire an assistant or associate medical director.

Treating physician

While the medical director provides general service to the nursing home, Medicare's rules refer to treating physicians as those who take primary responsibility for the medical care of individual residents. They can be employed by the facility either part-time or full-time or maintain a private practice and see nursing home residents via a contractual agreement.

The medical director is responsible for monitoring and improving the care delivered by treating physicians, but rarely provides direct supervision of them. Many medical directors also work as a treating physician. Many facilities also employ APPs, although Medicare imposes restrictions on the tasks that can be delegated to them.

Practice structure

Most long-term care centers are too small to require a full-time doctor. Physicians often have significant flexibility in the days and times they work and in scheduling patient visits. Depending on their contract, they may be on-call during off hours for all patients, for only their own patients, or not at all.

It is common for physicians to maintain a community practice and work in a nursing home on an as-needed or part-time basis. However, a growing cadre of physicians have a dedicated skilled nursing facility practice, which appears to improve clinical outcomes and quality of care.[88] Some doctors split their time across two or more facilities.

GETTING INTO POST-ACUTE AND LONG-TERM CARE

Nursing home medicine has been proposed as a medical specialty,[89] but is not currently recognized as such. Nearly all physicians who practice in skilled nursing facilities are family medicine or internal medicine specialists.[90] About one-quarter of nursing home physicians have training in geriatric medicine.[90] Geriatric fellowships are one year in length and are required to provide fellows with direct experience in nursing home care as part of their curriculum.

Psychiatry with subspecialization in geriatric psychiatry is another possible route for practicing in a long-term care setting, given the high prevalence of mental health conditions among long-term care residents.

To be a skilled nursing facility medical director, Medicare mandates licensure in the state where the facility is located, but otherwise does not have specific qualifications.

The American Board of Post-Acute and Long-Term Care Medicine offers a Certified Medical Director designation to physicians with demonstrated commitment to practicing in the long-term care setting. Eligibility requires completion of a residency and spending a minimum of eight hours each month working at a nursing facility. Certification is usually optional, although some facilities and jurisdictions (like California) require it for their medical directors.

The American Medical Directors Association, the American Geriatrics Society, and the Society for Post-Acute and Long-Term Care Medicine are resources for more information.

COMPENSATION AND FINANCIAL CONSIDERATIONS

Employment and compensation arrangements for nursing home medical directors vary. They can receive a flat hourly or monthly fee as a contractor, with the expectation that they spend the necessary time needed to fulfill the duties of the role. Anecdotally, rates fall between $3,000 to $4,000 per month or $250 to $350 per hour. A flat fee per resident is used less often.

Some nursing homes opt to hire treating physicians as salaried employees or contractors paid by the hour, although most rely on insurance reimbursements. Daily rates paid by Medicare or other insurance plans to nursing homes do not include payments for medical services. Payment for medical services is made directly to the healthcare provider.

Therefore, treating physicians can see patients and bill the insurance as they would in a traditional outpatient practice. Physicians and nursing homes can have agreements in place to split the revenue; for example, the physician earns 70% while the facility earns 30%.

Physicians acting in a dual role of medical director and treating physician may have an arrangement combining the above approaches.

Of note, Medicare does not reimburse physicians for time spent on activities outside of direct medical encounters. This includes talking with nursing staff or family members on the phone, coordinating interdisciplinary care, or traveling to the nursing facility.

Some nursing homes contract with specialized medical practices for certain services. Vohra Wound Physicians, as one example, hires physicians to provide wound care services in their contracted nursing homes. Working for a third-party company of this type can simplify coordination and scheduling for physicians wishing to provide care at multiple facilities.

Mobile medical clinics

Vehicles are not solely for transportation anymore. Food trucks, pop-up retail stores, and marketing event vehicles have increased in popularity. It is no surprise that the healthcare industry has also recognized the benefits of mobility. Mobile medical units have become a realistic way for healthcare practitioners to bring their services directly to patients. They also offer unconventional practice options for physicians.

THE MOBILE CLINIC MARKET

Services offered by mobile clinics include primary care, dental care, mental health, women's health, pediatric care, and more. They operate with the same quality and professionalism as a traditional medical office, but with the added flexibility of being able to change locations.

The history of mobile health clinics dates to the 1920s when they were used to address the tuberculosis epidemic. It was not until the 1960s that mobile clinics began expanding to include general medical care. A more significant rise in recent years can be attributed to healthcare provider shortages and a need for innovative ways to deliver care to hard-to-reach communities. Natural disasters and public health emergencies have also highlighted the need for — and demonstrated the utility of — mobile health clinics to provide emergency medical care and support services.

The U.S. mobile clinics market is valued at an impressive $1.7 billion.[91] There are more than 1,200 mobile medical units operating across the United States.[92] Most are affiliated with universities and healthcare systems; some are independent. On average, a single mobile clinic conducts nearly 3,500 visits per year.[93]

Mobile clinics tailor their care to meet the needs of the communities they serve, although certain services have more readily available funding and are more manageable to deliver in a mobile setting. More than 40% provide primary care services.[94]

Benefits to patients who receive care from mobile units include greater accessibility, convenience, and cost savings. Mobile clinics can eliminate the need for patients to travel long distances or take time off work for medical appointments. They prevent emergency department visits and yield better clinical outcomes for certain chronic conditions, such as hypertension and asthma.[95,96]

GETTING INTO MOBILE MEDICINE

Primary care lends itself to mobile clinics, but specialists should not be dissuaded from a mobile practice. Market research and some creativity can identify specialty services that will make for a successful mobile practice. As a brief illustration, the surge of interest in remaining child-free following the overturning of *Roe* v *Wade* in 2022 prompted mobile vasectomy clinics to hit the streets.

An independent mobile clinic can operate as an adjunct to a brick-and-mortar medical practice or as an entirely mobile practice. Physicians can also own and operate a mobile health clinic that offers services primarily delivered by non-physician clinicians, such as mobile diagnostic imaging, IV hydration therapy, counseling, and occupational health services. In many cases, you can supervise van-based clinicians or technicians without being on the road yourself.

Equipment is one of the biggest differences between a traditional medical office and a mobile clinic, starting with the mobile unit itself. Planning patient flow patterns and dealing with space constraints requires thought. You can purchase medical vehicles of various types and sizes, new or used, or modify a nonmedical vehicle. Many companies offer van retrofitting packages, with some specializing in medical modifications. Medical equipment must be selected carefully to ensure fit and function in a van.

Determining where to park a mobile unit while seeing patients is another major decision. Leasing private parking or using a public lot are options. Community centers and churches may offer their parking lots. You can also partner with local establishments or corporations. This was the tactic mobile health provider DocGo used when it affiliated with Dollar General to provide medical services in their store parking lots.[97]

Another career option is employment with an organization that owns a mobile medical fleet. Some of the most well-known names in healthcare — CVS Health, MedExpress, Kaiser Permanente, and Mercy Health — as well as many smaller systems have mobile medical programs. Most physicians employed by these organizations do not spend all their time in mobile units themselves; rather, they are involved in mobile medical program planning and oversight. They may also supervise APPs who staff mobile clinics.

Mobile Health Map, which is a network of mobile clinics, offers resources and best practice guidelines for mobile medicine.

Mobile medical clinic regulation

New regulations in healthcare often restrict medical practice; however, recent regulatory changes and funding initiatives have had a positive impact on the ability to practice out of a mobile unit. In 2021, the DEA released new rules allowing certified Opioid Treatment Programs to operate mobile vans without obtaining a separate registration for each unit. The MOBILE Health Care Act, passed in 2022, expands the ability of federally qualified health centers to establish mobile clinics in rural areas and underserved communities by allowing them to utilize federal funds to do so.

During the COVID-19 pandemic, the FDA and Centers for Disease Control and Prevention (CDC) authorized healthcare providers to administer vaccines in mobile units. These examples pertain to specific healthcare services, but they indicate a general trend toward the acceptance of mobile units as a legitimate way to practice medicine.

Some states have laws relevant to practicing out of a mobile unit. These may be related to vehicle inspections, business licensing and registration, and mobile unit size and safety features.

FINANCIAL CONSIDERATIONS

Mobile clinics are not a cheap way to practice medicine. The average cost to launch a mobile health clinic is $300,000.[98] Vehicle fuel and maintenance costs can also be pricey.

Medical coding, billing, and reimbursement for services rendered out of a mobile van follow the same general principles as traditional healthcare settings, with the exception of mobile units having a unique place of service identifier.

It is common for mobile clinics to receive philanthropic or federal financial support when they provide services in underserved areas or to underserved populations. This support can help offset costs associated with operating a not-for-profit mobile clinic.

Public health departments

The United States is committed to safeguarding and promoting the population's health. Every one of our 50 states has a public health department that functions alongside a network of nearly 3,500 local health departments across the country[99] assisted by nine federal agencies comprising the U.S. Public Health Services. More than 1,000 physicians are employed by state health departments and an even higher number by local health departments.[100]

Public health is not glamourous, however. It operates behind the scenes (until something goes wrong) and as a result, few physicians view health departments as career destinations. But these settings offer huge potential for professional satisfaction.

PUBLIC HEALTH INFRASTRUCTURE AND WORKFORCE

Public health encompasses a range of efforts, strategies, and interventions aimed at preventing diseases, promoting healthy behaviors, and addressing the social, economic, and environmental factors influencing health outcomes. The scope and services provided by a health department depend on the needs and priorities of their specific jurisdictions, as well as their statutorily defined authority. Likewise, a department's workforce varies in size and structure, but generally is comprised of epidemiologists, environmental health specialists, public health nurses and physicians, health educators, nutritionists, lab scientists, and policy analysts.

Funding comes from multiple sources, including federal, state, and local governments, as well as grants and fees for services.

Health department activities include monitoring the population's health, developing policies, and enabling equitable access to health, among others. Medical care is not actually deemed an essential public health service, and whether clinical services should be provided has been debated. Despite the debate, almost all local health departments offer certain clinical services, particularly child immunizations and testing and treatment for certain communicable disease. Many have prenatal care, primary care, dental care, or other expanded clinical programs. Some departments offer more specialized services like smoking cessation programs or treatment for victims of domestic violence.

The widespread inclusion of clinical services means physicians are needed in both administrative capacities and in roles involving direct patient care.

JOBS IN STATE AND LOCAL HEALTH DEPARTMENTS

Physicians serve as department administrators, program directors, clinicians, and consultants. Positions range from full-time to very limited part-time.

State health agencies have an average of 15 physicians on staff.[101] The largest local health departments have an entire team of full-time doctors; small departments may function with the part-time help of one physician who practices elsewhere in the community.

Health officer

The health commissioner or health officer in a state or local health department is at the highest leadership level, akin to the chief executive officer of the department. This is a primarily nonclinical job involving overall strategic direction, policy development, and administration of public health initiatives. In many departments, the health commissioner position requires medical licensure.

Medical director

Health department medical directors oversee specific bureaus, programs, or divisions within the department. These areas can include environmental health, epidemiology, maternal and child health, tuberculosis testing and management, and community field services. Responsibilities are contingent on the director's assigned area and medical specialty but tend to focus on program management and administrative functions.

In departments offering clinical services, medical directors overseeing clinical programs may spend a portion of their time involved in patient care or supervising other clinicians who are providing that care. They may work closely with a nursing director or other clinical leadership staff.

Attending physician

Health departments with more robust clinical programs have a need for physicians beyond the medical director who oversees the program. This is particularly true for large departments that offer safety net services to indigent patients. Attending physicians provide care in outpatient clinics operated by the department. Most are in primary care, although infectious disease specialists, OB/GYNs, and other specialists are needed. Local physicians in private practice or with other employment may be hired on a part-time basis for these roles.

Consultant services

Health departments engage physicians as consultants for expertise that does not require a full-time specialist. This can be for ongoing needs or specific, time-limited projects. Consulting physicians may provide guidance on clinical protocols, review and analyze medical data, contribute to program development, conduct trainings, participate on a task force, or engage in policy formulation, as a few examples. Depending on the nature of the project or program, consultants with clinical expertise may advise on individual patient management — for example, offering treatment recommendations for tuberculosis cases.

PUBLIC HEALTH CAREERS AT THE FEDERAL LEVEL

Public health is driven at the state and local levels, but it is supported on a national level. Several federal agencies, including CDC, FDA, and National Institutes of Health (NIH), heavily invest in public health initiatives. These agencies have positions for doctors; most are primarily focused on the population level, engaging in research, program management, policy development, or public health surveillance.

A unique option for those wanting to work in federal public health is joining the USPHS Commissioned Corps. Officers serve in numerous federal agencies and departments, with the ability to transition between agencies and geographic areas as needs and preferences change. This avenue increases the likelihood of incorporating clinical work into a public health career, as Commissioned Corps officers are called on to provide direct assistance and support in public health threats and emergencies, such as disease outbreaks and natural disasters. They may be deployed to affected areas to coordinate emergency response efforts, provide medical care, or conduct epidemiological investigations.

PREPARING FOR A CAREER AT A HEALTH DEPARTMENT

Working in a health department as a physician requires a solid foundation in both medicine and public health.

Medical training

Most health department jobs requiring an MD or DO also require a medical license and board certification. Aside from specialist medical director positions, there is flexibility in terms of specialty.

Preventive medicine is highly compatible with many physician-level jobs in public health. It combines clinical medicine with a population health perspective and public health training. Residencies after internship are two years long, with most including all the necessary coursework to obtain a Master of Public Health (MPH) degree. A handful of four-year combined residency programs lead to board eligibility in preventive medicine and either internal medicine, family medicine, or pediatrics. Many physicians complete preventive medicine training as a second residency to augment their current practice or in anticipation of a career pivot.

Internal medicine, pediatrics, family medicine, OB/GYN, infectious disease, pathology, and emergency medicine are other specialties commonly held by doctors at health departments.

Public health training

Many positions, especially in larger departments, require or prefer public health training or experience. Several public health degrees are available, although an MPH is the most popular among physicians. Full-time MPH programs span one to two years, and many have part-time tracks available.

Excellent non-degree training opportunities are available in public health, including several offered by the CDC. The Epidemic Intelligence

Service, for example, is a competitive two-year fellowship that trains physicians and others in public health-related fields to investigate and intervene on public health threats. Others include the CDC Experience Applied Epidemiology Fellowship and the CDC Evaluation Fellowship.

Finding opportunities at health departments

State and local health department websites are a primary resource to find job openings, especially if you are looking within a specific geographic area. Job boards and newsletters from the American Public Health Association, the American College of Preventive Medicine, the National Association of County and City Health Officials, and the American Association of Public Health Physicians are other sources. Federal public health jobs are posted on USAJOBS.

COMPENSATION AND BENEFITS

The average annual salary for a public health physician was $255,993 in 2023.[102] State health agency employees earn higher salaries, on average, than employees in local health departments;[103] however, large city health department salaries often rival those of state departments. As government employees, physicians in health departments at all levels receive good benefits packages, regular working hours, weekends off, and generous paid time off.

Compensation for federal positions is usually based on the federal pay scale, supplemented by allowances and adjustments for specialized roles. Compensation for USPHS Commissioned Corps officers is similar to other uniformed services branches; base pay increases with promotions and years served. Various incentive pays, special pays, and bonuses contribute significantly to overall compensation. Benefits include free or low-cost healthcare, retirement contributions, housing allowances, and more.

Many health departments have loan repayment programs. You may be eligible for loan repayment through the National Health Service Corps if you work for a health department in an underserved area.

Jeffrey Alvarez, MD

Chief Medical Officer of NaphCare

Practice setting

NaphCare, Inc., is a privately-owned company providing comprehensive healthcare services to correctional facilities— both jails and prisons — across the country.

Employment type and schedule

I am a full-time employee. I mainly work during regular business hours. As the chief medical officer, though, I am always on call.

Patient population and clinical work

Correctional populations have a large percentage of patients with substance use disorders, chronic medical disease, and mental health disorders. Many patients have little to no treatment of their conditions when not in custody. Most patients are of a low socio-economic background and lack housing, employment, or family support.

At this point, I spend less than 5% of my time doing face-to-face patient encounters. I spend 10% to 15% of my time on clinical administrative tasks. The rest is spent on chart reviews, peer reviews, utilization management, clinical policies, and corporate meetings.

The amount of time I spend on direct patient care has decreased as my career has progressed. I spent nearly a decade practicing family medicine in community health centers. Then I took a staff physician job at a county jail, which was 100% clinical care. I transitioned to the medical director position at that facility and began splitting my time between patient care and administrative responsibilities. My next position was as the director of correctional health services for the county and was entirely administrative. I was in that role for about four years before taking my current position with NaphCare.

A typical day at work

I attend many virtual administrative meetings with clients, regional and facility clinical leadership, quality improvement staff, accreditation staff, and training staff. I review the charts of complex patients as needed or requested by onsite providers, regional leadership, facility leadership, or patient advocates. I travel to NaphCare's contracted sites once a month or more frequently to meet with onsite health staff and facility administration.

Unconventional aspects

The physical environment of jails and prisons is an obvious unconventional part of the job. There are a lot of security and safety measures in place, which can make it difficult to move around freely and easily. You need special clearance to get into the building, and your orientation includes security training.

Another one of the most unconventional aspects of this work is dealing with requests about the care of a patient from attorneys, courts and judges, and the American Civil Liberties Union or other patient advocacy groups. I never had to respond to an attorney or judge before I began working in corrections.

Best parts of the job

Prior to working in correctional medicine, my entire career was in community medicine at county clinics and community health centers. The correctional patient population is the most underserved group I have ever worked with. It is a very fulfilling job knowing you are making a difference in a patient's life when they are likely at one of the lowest points in their life and see very little hope in their situation. Helping them during their incarceration can have a huge impact.

Challenges faced

There are two main challenges. One is recruiting health staff to work in correctional facilities. Many people have a biased or misinformed view of what it is like to work in a jail or a prison. The second is dealing with provider burnout and compassion fatigue. Although the personal satisfaction of helping incarcerated patients can be high, it can also be very deflating seeing many patients come back into custody repetitively without a change in their health status secondary to a lack of compliance with healthcare follow-up after release.

Qualifications and skills needed for this career

You need compassion and dedication to assisting underserved populations, along with a nonjudgmental attitude toward healthcare delivery. Experience treating medical conditions with a high prevalence among incarcerated populations, such as substance use disorders, is helpful; however, many skills are easily learned.

Advice for students and physicians

Don't be afraid to try it out. Many people think jails and prisons are dangerous, yet I have found them to be the safest environment in which I've worked.

I feel we have a responsibility in our profession to develop the next generation of health staff. The correctional environment can be an excellent training ground for new nurses, mental health staff, and medical and psychiatric providers. I wish more facilities would reach out to schools to champion student rotations in correctional health-care. If your school or program doesn't offer a rotation at a jail or prison, work with your administration to set one up so you can get a feel for correctional medicine.

CAREERS WITH LIMITED PATIENT CONTACT

Medicine revolves around seeing patients, but the pace of patient visits can be grueling, and building patient relationships can be exhausting. Jobs with limited or negligible patient contact can be a welcome relief. Such opportunities are not all nonclinical; many merely take a step back from direct patient care, shifting the focus from patient interactions to overseeing, managing, directing, or consulting on patient care from a distance. They still require you to leverage medical expertise and clinical skills and your decisions and recommendations still affect patient management and clinical outcomes.

These jobs can sometimes blur boundaries regarding physician-patient relationships. When you are not directly seeing patients but still hold responsibilities for their care, it can raise questions about the nature of your obligation to the patient, the need for a medical license, and potential legal liabilities.

Despite the challenges, these roles have a lot to offer. They are low stress, well-compensated, flexible, and interesting. You can pursue them as a side gig while maintaining a full-time job for extra income and experience. Or they can help you stay connected to medicine during a career transition, raising a family, or preparing for retirement.

Advanced practice provider supervision

There are more than 355,000 nurse practitioners (NPs)[104] and 168,000 physician assistants (PAs)[105] licensed in the United States, and these numbers are rising rapidly.

Major legislative efforts have aimed to broaden APP practice scopes and lessen requirements for physician oversight. Contrary to popular belief, this has not resulted in a decrease in APP collaboration with physicians.[106] APP supervision benefits the APP, their patients, and also the supervising physician by helping to ensure high-quality patient care and improved outcomes. It allows physicians to extend their capabilities and expand their reach. It offers flexibility, enabling physicians to continue practicing medicine while taking a step back from direct patient care.

APP TRAINING AND SCOPE OF PRACTICE

APPs were introduced to expand access to care, respond to a growing physician shortage, promote team-based care, and contain healthcare costs.

NPs form the largest subset of advanced practice registered nurses (APRNs). They undergo a two- to three-year master's program with 500 to 1,000 clinical hours. Training emphasizes health promotion and education. Other APRN types are nurse anesthetists. nurse midwives, and clinical nurse specialists.

Becoming a certified PA (PA-C) also requires a two- to three-year master's program and includes between 2,000 and 2,500 clinical hours. PA education is based on a medical model with a stronger foundation in basic sciences.

APPs can practice across a variety of settings and specialties. They are more frequently found in rural and underserved regions than are physicians.[107] A high percentage of NPs are certified in primary care; more PAs work in surgical subspecialties and emergency medicine.

APPs can diagnose, treat, and prescribe, although their precise scope of practice varies by state, including which procedures they can perform and which treatments require special training. Regulatory oversight comes mainly from state medical boards for PAs and nursing boards for NPs. Payer and employer policies can further restrict scope of practice.

Practice authority and supervision requirements

Individual states have laws governing the level of physician supervision for APPs. Supervision refers to physician oversight of activities and decisions, balancing autonomy with access to medical expertise. Many healthcare professionals advocate for the use of the term *collaboration* instead of supervision to emphasize the teamwork between APPs and physicians.

As of 2023, 28 states permit NPs to practice independently;[108] the remaining states mandate some form of physician supervision. Few states allow PAs to practice unsupervised, but efforts are underway to change this. Some states have more stringent supervision requirements than others, requiring varying degrees of physician onsite presence, chart co-signing, and face-to-face meetings. All states allow for indirect supervision in many situations, in which the physician is available for remote consultation.

Liability and risk in APP supervision

Supervising physicians have legal responsibility for the APP's practice. Deficient supervision, poor communication, or delayed interventions can increase liability risks, including potential malpractice claims. If there are allegations of improper supervision or negligence, the state's medical board can investigate the physician, potentially leading to fines, practice restrictions, or license revocation.

Some physicians avoid APP supervision out of concern of the risks; however, APP supervision is a valuable and necessary component of our healthcare system. Do not dismiss supervision positions solely because of the inherent risks involved. Instead, take time to mitigate risks by forming a supportive relationship with the APPs you supervise. Establish clear communication lines, document supervision activities, maintain professional liability insurance, and stay current on applicable laws, regulations, and standards of care.

UNCONVENTIONAL APP SUPERVISION JOBS

APP supervision, in a broad sense, is not unconventional; it has a common and well-established role within the healthcare industry. In fact, a majority of physicians routinely work with APPs.[109] Nonetheless, there are many less traditional APP supervision jobs. Many of these check the boxes for doctors seeking flexibility, remote work, and a less busy schedule.

Supervising physician for healthcare corporations

Some healthcare organizations rely heavily on APPs to provide patient care services. Common examples include occupational health clinics, urgent care centers, and healthcare chains operating under a single management structure. Telemedicine companies are increasingly utilizing APPs as the main point of contact for straightforward patient visits.

In APP-centric care models, APPs deliver the core services of the business, but they still need physician supervision if required by the state. In many cases, the physician's primary role is supervisory, with minimal direct patient care.

Supervising physician for APP-owned practices

Another option is supervising an NP or PA in a practice they own and operate. In an APP-owned practice, the absence of a corporation or third-party entity allows the physician and APP to tailor their collaboration to their work preferences and the practice's needs.

Some states have rules regarding the conditions under which an APP can own a practice, such as having a certain amount of experience.

Supervising physician for healthcare payer home visit programs

Many commercial insurance companies, including Anthem, Humana, and Optum, operate home health evaluation programs in which NPs conduct in-person medical assessments to gather health information and coordinate care for insurance plan members. In states requiring supervision, physicians review member assessments, offer phone consultation when needed, and conduct other oversight work as required by the state. They do not personally conduct visits or evaluate patients.

In states restricting independent NP practice, these programs offer contracted roles for physicians that require as little as an hour or two of work per month. NPs focus on patient assessment and care coordination, rather than prescribing medications or providing treatment, which minimizes time and risk for the supervising physician.

APP supervision as an adjunct role

Physicians in hospital and healthcare system leadership roles often supervise APPs. The supervision portion of the job is a distinct component of the overall position, so compensation can be separate from salary in the form of a stipend.

BECOMING A SUPERVISING PHYSICIAN

APP supervising positions for licensed physicians of all specialties are available. It is not always necessary to have the same specialty as the APP, but you must have sufficient knowledge and experience related to the services the APP provides and conditions they treat.

There are multiple ways to find supervising jobs. National or multi-state healthcare corporations, telemedicine platforms, and insurance companies commonly post on job boards. Networking can identify opportunities with healthcare practices in your community. APPs in solo practice often rely on existing relationships and word of mouth. You can contact intermediary matching services, such as Collaborating Docs and Supervising MD, which act as facilitators to connect APPs with supervising physicians.

After securing a position, you need to establish a supervision agreement with the APP and submit state-specific documentation. Companies may provide standard agreements, though you still need to review these to ensure they are in line with your practice preferences and state rules.

Do not confuse your supervision agreement with your employment agreement; they are separate but need to align with one another. The supervising agreement describes the supervisory relationship, including the APP's scope of practice, how the physician and APP will communicate, and a quality assurance plan. The employment or contractor agreement governs your relationship with the practice or company hiring you.

COMPENSATION AND FINANCIAL CONSIDERATIONS

Compensation for APP supervision roles varies; each model has its merits and limitations. The most common and straightforward arrangement is a flat fee, which provides a set amount regardless of the actual hours spent supervising. An hourly rate or a fee per chart review or per consultation will compensate you for your time but may not account for the responsibility and risk you assume. In some arrangements, compensation is tied to the practice's profit or the APP's billing, calculated as a percentage. While potentially lucrative, this can introduce conflicts of interest and could create an incentive for overutilization of unnecessary services.

Limited data are available on how much physicians are being paid to supervise APPs. A large national survey of primary care NPs in 2017 reported a median fee of $500 per month, with a range up to $4,167 per month.[110] Monthly fees as high as $5,000 were reported in a study of psychiatrists.[111]

Physicians employed full-time by hospitals or healthcare systems who are asked to supervise an APP in addition to their regular duties may receive a stipend ranging from a few thousand dollars to tens of thousands of dollars per year.

APP billing and reimbursement

APPs employed by a healthcare system or corporation usually are not involved in the compensation for their supervising physician; however, APP practice owners should bear in mind their practice's bottom line when negotiating a supervising physician fee. In this context, it can be helpful to understand how medical billing and reimbursement work for APPs. Medicare, for instance, reimburses APPs at 85% of the physician rate for comparable services.

Billing structures differ between NPs and PAs. While NPs can bill Medicare directly, PAs must route their billing through their supervising physician. Private insurers have varying policies — some may reimburse APPs at the same rate as physicians, while others offer a lower rate.

Billing practices also vary based on the APP's licensure and work setting. Independent billing is common, with APPs using their own National

Provider Identifier (NPI) numbers. Split/shared billing occurs when the supervising physician and the APP are both involved in patient care, billing separately for distinct services rendered. Incident-to billing is less common and involves billing for the APP's services under the supervising physician's NPI, typically in scenarios where direct supervision is involved.

Independent medical exams (IMEs)

Have you ever made an important decision based on biased information or unreliable data? Chances are you regretted that decision.

Access to reliable, impartial information can be the difference between fair and unfair outcomes. This is especially pertinent when a decision will significantly affect an individual's life. Third-party evaluations, such as IMEs, provide a neutral perspective and ensure decisions are based on accurate data and objective evidence. For doctors, conducting IMEs can be a stimulating and lucrative side gig or full-time career.

EXAM PURPOSE AND PROCESS

An IME is an assessment requested by a third party (most commonly an insurer, employer, court, or lawyer) when they need an objective opinion about an individual's health status, rehabilitation potential, or functional abilities. It is performed by a physician or other healthcare professional who has no prior relationship with the individual. Because the purpose is to provide an assessment of a medical condition, most often in the context of a legal or insurance-related matter, physicians involved in IMEs serve both the medical profession and the legal profession.

The evaluation focuses on issues like the nature and extent of injuries or disabilities, causation, and potential treatment options. It informs decisions in legal or insurance cases but does not replace medical care or offer treatment to the examinee. There is no continuity of care or follow-up with the evaluating physician.

A bulk of IME work revolves around disability assessment, including its presence, cause, type, severity, and impact. In some contexts, IMEs are dubbed "disability exams" and are key in determining eligibility for disability benefits, such as from the Social Security Administration or the Department of Veterans Affairs.

Conducting an IME begins with reviewing the exam's stated purpose and expectations. There may be specific questions pertaining to the examinee's current health status, work-related conditions, expected medical improvement, or preexisting conditions. The physician then reviews the examinee's medical history and records, which the client provides. In some cases, a physical exam is conducted. Findings are written up in a report, which is forwarded to the party that ordered the IME.

Physician-patient relationship in IMEs

Even though doctors do not provide treatment during IMEs, they still have ethical principles to uphold, such as confidentiality and informed consent. In the setting of a third party requesting the IME, this can raise some concerns. For example, you may come across new clinical findings that require diagnostic testing or treatment, which introduces questions about whether to inform the examinee. Even the American Medical Association has admitted that the physician-patient relationship formed through an IME is difficult to define.[112]

Despite the limited relationship, there is a malpractice liability risk and patients have won lawsuits against doctors who performed their IMEs.[113]

You should approach IMEs with the same professionalism, care, and attention to detail you would when examining a patient with whom you have a full, long-standing relationship.

TYPES OF IMES

The purposes and components of IMEs vary depending on the industry and specific use case.

Insurance IMEs

Insurance entities use IMEs to assess claims and decide compensation levels for disabilities ranging from joint and spinal injuries to brain trauma and mental conditions. Claims may arise from long- and short-term disability insurance, workers' compensation, and auto insurance policies. Long-term care insurers also use IMEs for policyholder assessments. Life insurers may request IMEs during underwriting or renewal. Health insurance plans occasionally use them to verify the need for particular treatments. Even homeowners' insurance personal injury claims can necessitate IMEs.

Litigation IMEs

Litigation IMEs provide objective medical evaluations in legal disputes concerning medical causation, prognosis, or damages. The court or judge usually selects the physician to perform an IME. In personal injury cases, IMEs assess the degree of injury when the defendant challenges the plaintiff's claims. For medical malpractice, IMEs determine whether professional negligence led to harm. In the realm of product liability, manufacturers and their insurers may commission an IME to gauge the extent to which a product caused injury.

Employer IMEs

Employers use IMEs to get an independent assessment of an employee's job fitness, the need for accommodations, or the cause of an injury for liability and workers' compensation cases. Legal prerequisites for employer-initiated IMEs can vary. Generally, there must be a valid business rationale for the IME, adherence to medical privacy laws, proper notice given to the employee, and opportunity for employee objections or input.

Life care planning IMEs

IMEs used in life care plan development resemble litigation IMEs in that litigation is usually involved; however, the purpose of the evaluation is different. Life care planning IMEs focus on assessing the long-term needs of individuals with catastrophic injuries to better project future care needs and costs. They are used in decisions related to fund allocation by insurance firms, managed care organizations, and workers' compensation boards, as well as in personal injury cases, estate planning, and the discharge planning process for facilities.

A life care planner, who typically has a background in nursing or rehabilitation, develops the bulk of a life care plan by evaluating the individual's medical condition, functional abilities, limitations, and quality of life. Much of this is done using written documentation and records. However, the medical records available to them do not always provide a complete picture and can be ambiguous, incomplete, or have discrepancies. IMEs provide physician-level expertise through observations, reviews, exams, and interviews.

GETTING INTO IME WORK

IME work aligns well with specialties related to physical injuries and disabilities, including PM&R, neurology, and orthopedics. Physicians in most specialties can find IME opportunities. For example, occupational medicine is relevant for workplace injuries and psychiatry is fitting for cases involving mental health issues.

Qualifications for IMEs

To conduct IMEs, you must be familiar with the particular medical conditions or injuries being evaluated. Clients and IME companies usually require specialty board certification and an active medical license in the state in which the IME is conducted; some states require a certain amount of practice experience.

State-specific laws dictate IME protocols for workers' compensation cases, including who is qualified to conduct them.

Though not required, certification as an independent medical examiner can be helpful. This is offered by the American Board of Independent Medical Examiners.

Physicians who perform life care plan IMEs can become certified life care planners through the International Commission on Health Care Certification. PM&R specialists are eligible to pursue the Certified Physician Life Care Planner (CPLCP) designation from the CPLCP Certification Board.

Our medical education system does not train us on how to conduct IMEs. Take the time to ensure you have a thorough understanding of the concepts, terminology, procedures, and reporting requirements involved in the IME process. The International Academy of Independent Medical Evaluators is a good resource.

Finding IME opportunities

You can get started with IMEs by either establishing a specialized IME practice or incorporating IMEs into an existing medical practice. You can market your services directly to potential clients, such as insurance companies and legal firms, or source work through professional networks and referrals. You can also sign up as a provider for one or more IME companies, which maintain a panel of qualified physicians whom they link with clients. These companies handle logistics like scheduling and payments, which can result in lower compensation per IME, but allows you to concentrate on medical evaluations rather than marketing or administrative work.

COMPENSATION

Compensation for IMEs varies dramatically depending on medical specialty, case complexity, location, and factors related to the requestor, such as the entity type and their policies. In most cases, physicians can set their own rates, subject to negotiation with the insurer or party requesting the IME. In other cases, the fee is set by state workers' compensation programs, courts, or state agencies. Insurance companies and third-party IME companies may establish their own fee schedules for physicians performing IMEs on their behalf.

Average IME fees in a 2020 survey ranged from several hundred dollars to over $10,000, depending on specialty, although sample sizes were small for many specialties surveyed. Two prevalent IME specialties — orthopedic surgery and PM&R — had average IME fees of $1,778 and $2,004, respectively. The average time spent was about three to four hours per case.[114]

When setting your rates for IMEs, be mindful of the time and effort involved as well as the associated expenses, such as liability insurance, office space and equipment, and administrative costs. When possible, look at local market rates for IMEs and similar services. Some medical associations have ethical guidelines stating that IME fees should be not excessive, though they do not specify what constitutes a reasonable fee.

Interprofessional eConsults

Consulting on the side has always appealed to physicians. It is intellectually stimulating, flexible, and offers autonomy. Historically, consulting done by doctors was limited to nonclinical engagements. This is changing as the use of technology and the internet in healthcare delivery grow. There are now opportunities for clinical consulting gigs that offer all the draws of being a consultant: engaging work we can do when and where we want to do it. Interprofessional eConsults are a prime example of this.

THE eCONSULTS CONCEPT

An eConsult, or electronic consultation, is a web-based method for healthcare providers to seek quick advice from specialists. The conventions in this space are still developing, with terms like *remote specialist consults* and *provider-to-provider consultations* also used.

eConsults take place asynchronously through secure platforms or shared EHR systems. Specialists offer their expertise on diagnosis, treatment, or management but do not assume care for the patient. Typically, consults are initiated by primary care physicians who need specialist input for outpatient issues, but specialists also request them.

An eConsult starts when a provider identifies a complex case needing specialized input. They submit a detailed question through a designated platform, attaching pertinent patient data such as medical history or test results. A specialist reviews the data, writes a recommendation, and sends it back to the requesting provider, who then reviews it and decides how to integrate the recommendation into the patient's care plan.

eConsults offer advantages to providers, specialists, patients, and healthcare systems. They give providers easy access to specialist expertise, aiding decision-making without significant workflow disruption. Primary care providers face the challenge of staying up to date with evidence-based care and guidelines. With eConsults, direct access to specialist expertise helps them make informed decisions while still retaining patients under their care.

In many cases, an eConsult eliminates the need for a formal specialist referral. Unlike formal consults, they do not require scheduling in-person appointments, so access to specialist advice is faster. Documentation requirements are less burdensome, reducing both administrative work and turnaround time. eConsults offer advantages over curbside consults, too. Curbside consults are informal and can lack adequate information and documentation. The digital nature of eConsults ensures that consulting specialists have the data they need to give detailed advice — and get paid for it.

eCONSULT OPPORTUNITIES FOR PHYSICIANS

eConsults are atypical as far as clinical jobs go. Barriers to entry are low and licensing requirements are more relaxed compared to telemedicine practice.

Most physicians begin doing eConsults by joining the panel of a third-party eConsult company. These companies contract with healthcare entities, serving as an intermediary between the requesting provider and consulting specialist. They also provide the platform and infrastructure for communication.

The market currently has few players but is expected to grow. RubiconMD and AristaMD, both established in 2013, lead in size and recognition. Both have quick, straightforward onboarding processes for licensed physicians wishing to join their specialist panels. Another nationwide platform, ConferMED, focuses on partnerships with federally qualified health centers. Some companies, like Included Health, include eConsults as just one of several virtual healthcare services that they offer. Platforms with limited partnerships and geographic reach include Sitka and Converge.

A major selling point for eConsult companies is fast turnaround time, with consults completed in less than a day and often within a few hours. Therefore, physicians who have some flexibility to address consults as they become available are more likely to be successful in working for third-party eConsult panels.

Some healthcare systems (particularly large, academic institutions) have internal eConsult programs for their own clinicians that integrate eConsults into their affiliated specialists' regular workflows; others establish specific schedules or dedicated time slots for specialists to address eConsult requests. Examples include the CARE Line at Cleveland Clinic and AskMayoExpert at Mayo Clinic.

Physicians in private practice can offer eConsults as an independent service, assuming they have the necessary technology and communication channels.

GETTING INTO eCONSULTS

Board certification and a few years of practice experience suffice to join an eConsult panel. Specialty demand varies, with the highest volumes seen in hematology/oncology, cardiology, endocrinology, rheumatology, and dermatology.[115]

One thing that distinguishes eConsults from direct patient care and traditional telemedicine is that eConsults generally do not constitute practicing medicine. As such, some platforms require their consultants to hold only a single state license to complete consults in multiple states. Whether this is technically allowable is a gray area and can differ by state. For example, Maine mandates an active Maine license if the consulted patient resides in Maine. Rhode Island stipulates an existing physician-patient relationship or the presence of a Rhode Island-licensed physician for consultations but does not specifically mention eConsults in their rules. Many states' rules do not directly address consult services or eConsults.

The concept of a physician-patient relationship is also important when it comes to malpractice risk. Medical malpractice lawsuits are based on two key elements: the establishment of a physician-patient relationship and an accusation that the physician caused harm to the patient by deviating from the recognized standard of care. As a new area in healthcare, eConsults do not have a body of case law. However, legal precedents from other indirect patient interactions like curbside consults suggest that eConsults can form a physician-patient relationship.

Third-party eConsult platforms try to minimize legal exposure by labeling their services as educational rather than as a diagnostic or treatment service. Regardless, we are accountable for our own actions as doctors and should operate under the assumption that a physician-patient relationship exists when giving specific, actionable advice. Hence, malpractice insurance is advisable and some platforms offer this to their network physicians.

The eConsult Workgroup is a collaborative effort between payers, providers and policy leaders that offers advocacy and helpful resources.

FINANCIAL CONSIDERATIONS

Most independent eConsult platforms pay a flat fee per consult in the range of $30 to $50. At the time of this writing, one platform's specialist job postings list an average $20,000 per year earning potential as supplemental income for several specialty types.

In healthcare systems with in-house eConsult programs, compensation structures range from flat fees to time-based pay and even stipend arrangements tiered by eConsult volume or other metrics.

Private practice physicians can form agreements with other medical practices and healthcare systems with predetermined service fees. Or they can directly bill patients' insurance companies. There are five codes that can be used for eConsults within the current procedural terminology (CPT) medical coding system. Four of these require both verbal and written reports and one requires only a written report to the requesting provider.

Medicare reimburses eConsults between $24 and $48 per consult, depending on time spent. There are restrictions such as the allowable eConsult frequency for a given patient and whether there is a subsequent referral to a specialist. State Medicaid programs and a growing number of commercial insurers also reimburse eConsults.

Medical directorships

Most physicians have been in a situation in which they had responsibility without authority — and it is usually frustrating. Feeling like we lack control over clinical decisions can lead to burnout and disengagement.

Enter the medical director.

Medical director roles allow doctors to exercise their professional judgment while retaining authority. Hospitals, healthcare systems, and other medical facilities and programs — which are often led by non-physician executives — hire medical leaders to ensure quality of patient care and act as intermediaries between clinical and administrative teams.

MEDICAL DIRECTOR ROLE AND RESPONSIBILITIES

Medical directors are responsible for the overall clinical care provided by a healthcare organization, including administrative services, guidance, and leadership. The precise responsibilities vary depending on the organization type, although many involve activities related to quality improvement, cost containment, clinician training, performance improvement, and revenue cycle management. They may direct activities of other physicians, perform chart reviews to maintain care consistency, attend meetings with medical staff and organizational leadership, and participate in strategic planning.

Most positions include clinical decision-making on some level. Complex cases, emergency situations, adverse events, and circumstances with an ethical dilemma or patient complaint may require the medical director to get involved in patient management decisions. Ultimate responsibility for patient care and treatment decisions lies with the treating physician; however, medical directors may supervise APPs or have other clinicians functioning under their license.

The title *medical director* is not a standardized title across healthcare settings. The position is well-defined in some situations, such as when federal regulation mandates a medical director. This is the case with dialysis units and hospice agencies, for example. In other cases, it is simply a title used to differentiate the medical director role from that of an attending or treating physician. It is also commonly used for physicians working for companies outside of healthcare services delivery, such as with pharmaceutical and insurance companies.

Over time, medical directorships have increased in importance and broadened in scope with the heightened focus on quality in healthcare.

MEDICAL DIRECTOR JOBS IN CLINICAL SETTINGS

Medical directorships are found across the healthcare industry. Other chapters in this book discuss the medical director role for long-term and post-acute care facilities, medical spas, hospice and palliative care services, blood banks, and worksites. Several other medical director positions that are mainstream within clinical settings are described here.

Emergency medical services (EMS) agency medical director

The National Association of State EMS Officials, the National Association of EMS Physicians, and the American College of Emergency Physicians issued a joint position statement supporting the role of physician medical directors as an essential component of EMS systems. Paramedics and advanced life-support providers function under the medical director's supervision.

An EMS medical director oversees the medical operations for an entire EMS system and is responsible for establishing protocols for prehospital emergency medical care for ensuring competency and performance of the personnel who follow the protocols.

The minimum qualification for the position is a state medical license. Other criteria differ by state but generally include board certification in emergency medicine or equivalent competency. Advanced life support certification and completion of an approved medical director training course are usually required.

Dialysis medical director

Under Medicare regulations, dialysis centers must have a medical director who is a licensed physician and assumes responsibility for ensuring the center provides high-quality patient care. Since its inception, the role has evolved from having a clinical focus to being more of an administrative and leadership role.

Dialysis medical directors must allocate a minimum of 25% of their total work time to fulfilling Medicare-mandated responsibilities, which range from water quality oversight to approval of involuntary patient discharges.

Home health agency medical director

According to the Medicare Conditions of Participation for Home Health Agencies, every health agency that provides nursing care or other therapeutic services in patients' homes must have a medical director who is responsible for the implementation and ongoing evaluation of the agency's policies and procedures related to patient care.

Behavioral health medical director

Medical directorships are available for a variety of behavioral health facilities and programs, including inpatient psychiatric hospitals, residential treatment centers, intensive outpatient programs (IOPs), substance abuse treatment programs, and community mental health centers. Many states and the federal government have established specific licensure and certification requirements for medical directors in this field. The Joint Commission also requires that there be a medical director for accreditation of certain behavioral health services.

Hospital service line medical director

Medical directors in hospitals oversee clinical, operational, and financial aspects of a designated service line, focusing on improving patient care and outcomes within that specialty. They may also direct Centers of Excellence or other designated care centers established by government programs, specialty professional societies, or consumer advocacy groups.

Larger hospitals often hire medical directors who oversee cross-disciplinary functional areas such as quality improvement, case management, and graduate medical education.

GETTING INTO A MEDICAL DIRECTOR ROLE

Given the leadership nature of the role, medical directors must have significant experience or specialized expertise. Regulatory and legal requirements can dictate qualifications; organizations may have internal policies on qualifications, as well. You may need to engage in self-directed learning or participate in committees or work groups to develop necessary skills like organizational transformation and financial performance.

Because many medical director jobs are not advertised, networking can go a long way. Executive healthcare search firms sometimes fill positions. Before accepting a role, carefully review the responsibilities, time commitments, company culture, employment terms, and compensation structure.

Professional liability

Medical directors need comprehensive liability protection. Determine which activities fall under the organization's coverage policies and where separate coverage is needed. Although they do not directly treat patients, medical directors are accountable for regulatory compliance concerning patient safety and clinical administration. Standard medical malpractice insurance may not fully cover these responsibilities. Additional policies like errors and omission insurance or directors and officers coverage are worth considering.

Legal issues

Federal and state laws affect medical director roles, especially when services are covered by government programs like Medicare. Noncompliance negatively affects the organization, but also can put you and your medical license at risk if you are serving as their medical director.

The Stark Law restricts referrals to entities with which there is a financial relationship, while the Anti-Kickback Statute bans value exchanges for such referrals. The False Claims Act penalizes fraudulent billing, and the Civil Monetary Penalties Law restricts hospitals from incentivizing physicians to limit services to Medicare or Medicaid patients. For medical directors of nonprofits, IRS tax-exempt rules prevent personal financial benefit from the organization's earnings. State laws may be more restrictive than federal laws.

The legal aspects of being a medical director may seem daunting; however, most medical directors do not face any legal issues related to their role.

COMPENSATION AND FINANCIAL CONSIDERATIONS

Medical directors can be employees or contractors. Compensation can be an hourly rate, salary, stipend, or even an at-risk structure tied to objectives. Pay varies by facility size, number of facilities overseen, scope of responsibilities, and level of expertise required. Do not expect the same rate you would earn for direct patient care. The median hourly rate for medical directors ranged from $112 for palliative care specialists to $216 for cardiologists in 2022.[53] Many positions come with the perk of having a flexible work schedule.

Administrative payments to physicians have historically been the subject of scrutiny by Medicare and other entities. Track your time spent on medical director responsibilities, even if you are not paid by the hour. Avoid billing for clinical services during the time you are providing administrative services. If you hold multiple medical directorships, be sure the cumulative roles as described on paper can reasonably be carried out by one physician.

Many physicians in medical director positions are also employed by the same organization for clinical services. In this situation, separate compensation arrangements may be necessary for the clinical and administrative aspects for billing purposes and legal reasons.

Remote monitoring

As the demand for healthcare services grows, so does the need for innovative solutions that can bridge the gap between patient needs and available medical resources. One promising solution is remote monitoring, which makes for a few interesting and worthwhile career possibilities for medical doctors.

REMOTE MONITORING TYPES AND USES

Remote monitoring and its associated teleconsultation services allow physicians to provide medical advice and guidance from a distance, using technology to access patient data and communicate with other healthcare professionals. A range of processes, platforms, and data transmission and storage methods provide the framework to implement these technologies into existing healthcare delivery models and settings.

While these services fall under the umbrella of telehealth, they are distinct in that they do not involve direct encounters between physicians and patients. This is a major selling point for doctors seeking more autonomy and flexibility in their work.

Several types of remote monitoring have demonstrated improved patient outcomes and reduced healthcare costs. However, this domain is still young and is quickly evolving. There are challenges related to integration into clinical workflows, the sheer quantity of data generated, and the poorly defined oversight role of the FDA.

Forms of remote monitoring are commonly categorized by patient care setting, such as in the intensive care unit (ICU), surgical suite, or ambulatory office. Each category has different roles and demand for physicians.

Ambulatory care and chronic disease management

Diabetes, hypertension, heart disease, and other chronic disease management can be supported by technologies that remotely monitor patients' health status. Devices range from specialized home health monitors to consumer wearables like fitness trackers. Collected data are transmitted securely to healthcare providers and used to inform clinical decisions such as medication adjustments and treatment modifications.

Remote patient monitoring in chronic disease management can identify high-risk patients early, mitigating complications or exacerbations. It is associated with a 50% reduction in hospital readmissions, higher patient satisfaction rates, and higher patient engagement.[116] More than 50 million patients used remote patient monitoring tools in 2022, and projections indicate significant adoption in coming years.[117]

Critical care

TeleICU, also known as virtual ICU or eICU, enables intensivists to monitor ICU patients from a distance via real-time physiological devices, assisting onsite teams with treatment decisions. Benefits over conventional ICUs include decreased hospital mortality and reduced length of stay,[118] likely resulting from enhanced ability to detect patient status changes while monitoring multiple cases simultaneously.

TeleICUs can be hospital-owned and staffed according to institutional needs. Or they can be outsourced using other hospitals or firms that support ICU networks using proprietary tools, clinical algorithms, and notification systems. Physicians can oversee multiple ICUs from a centralized location, which is valuable for smaller hospitals lacking specialized ICU staff.

Remote telemetry monitoring, remote cardiac care units, post-procedure recovery units, and post-acute care settings use similar models.

Surgery

Remote intraoperative monitoring involves observing physiological parameters like electrophysiology, hemodynamics, and respiration during surgery. Although its success depends on availability of reliable equipment and a skilled monitoring team, it allows for real-time interventions when executed effectively.

Neuromonitoring is a subtype of remote intraoperative monitoring focused on neurologic function during surgery. It can involve somatosensory-evoked potentials, motor-evoked potentials, and electroencephalograms.

Surgical teleconsultation allows physicians to provide immediate guidance and support to surgical teams during procedures. This is particularly useful for complex surgical cases in small or remote hospitals. A remote physician can review data, weigh in on surgical techniques, and make recommendations for intra-operative care.

Wound care

Remote wound monitoring is a technology-based approach to chronic and acute wound management. It utilizes data-driven applications that assess wounds and monitor their progression, assisting remote physicians in fine-tuning treatment protocols that are then implemented by onsite clinicians. It offers convenience for patients in hard-to-reach locations, minimizes in-person visit frequency, facilitates early intervention for nonhealing wounds, and averts complications.

EMPLOYMENT AND PRACTICE OPTIONS

There is a range of a career options incorporating remote monitoring and associated teleconsultations. There are opportunities in many specialties, especially neurology, critical care, surgery, and internal medicine.

Full-time remote monitoring jobs are still scarce but becoming more common. Some healthcare organizations have created dedicated positions to meet the rising demand for remote monitoring services. Within large healthcare systems, physicians can be employed in specialized roles such as medical directors of virtual ICUs. These may focus solely on remote monitoring or be a hybrid with in-person patient care.

Third-party companies offering remote monitoring services to healthcare systems employ physicians as full-time staff or as independent contractors for more flexible, part-time work. Examples include Accurate Neuromonitoring, Hicuity Health, and RemoteICU.

Integrating remote monitoring into private practice is another option. To go this route, first identify which patients would benefit from remote monitoring services, such as those with chronic conditions requiring regular follow-ups. Decide whether to partner with a remote monitoring service provider or to create an in-house solution. Either option requires a commitment to infrastructure, including technology and staff time.

COMPENSATION AND FINANCIAL
CONSIDERATIONS

Compensation for employed positions in hospitals or with third-party remote monitoring service providers is comparable to conventional patient care roles in the same specialty.

Insurance reimbursement for practice owners or partners who provide remote monitoring is somewhat complicated. Medicare began reimbursing for remote patient monitoring services for chronic diseases in 2019 and then added reimbursement for acute conditions in 2021. Billing methods and reimbursement rates depend on the service type, complexity, and location. Many commercial insurance plans cover remote monitoring services, as well. Reimbursement for qualified programs can generate more than $150 per patient per month.[119] This amount may seem small, but consider that a practice enrolling a conservative 50 patients in a remote patient monitoring program could generate $72,000 per year in extra revenue. Expect reimbursement policies to evolve as this field grows.

Charging a fee-for-service or implementing a subscription-based model for remote monitoring services is another option for private practices, allowing you to set your own fees based on market rates and needs.

Gregory Schwaid, DO, MPH

IME consultant

Practice setting

I have built a network of clients that request me to perform IMEs. These organizations span from local independent entities to government municipalities to multinational Fortune 500 companies.

Employment type and schedule

I am an independent contractor and have multiple clients. Each client has different demands and expectations of me. One of them requires I work 10 hours per week, another allows me to pick up work at my discretion, and others schedule consultations based on my availability. Some randomly send me evaluations to complete. Unless I am performing an in-person exam, my IME work essentially allows me to work when I want and where I want.

Patient population and clinical work

The assessments I do include long-term disability, short-term disability, government pension disability, Social Security disability, Veterans Administration disability, workers' compensation, standardized testing accommodations, student loan discharge, and more.

Each IME is tailored to the case's specific requests. Some organizations ask me to only consider specific ailments, while others may limit the time periods relevant to the review. To prevent going outside the defined parameters of the case, some organizations send me limited files to review, while others ask me to sift through complete medical records.

The vast majority of my IME work performed is in my home office. Most cases do not require any face-to-face evaluation of the client; however, I have performed physical exams both in-person and virtually. I occasionally evaluate a client at an attorney's office. Exams, when required, are limited in scope and focus on the reported problem.

A typical day at work

My job assignments vary by the day. I complete evaluations mailed to me or sign into an online database to assign a claimant to review. Each review typically takes two to three hours.

Unconventional aspects

Although I still use my medical degree, a large portion of my work is not oriented toward patient care. While performing an IME, I do not provide treatment. Treating patients would imply I have a physician-patient relationship, which would potentially establish a duty to diagnose and treat. I commonly use the terms *claimant, injured worker,* or *beneficiary* to describe the person I am evaluating. I use my medical background to form an unbiased judgment based on the available medical evidence for the claimant.

As physicians, we often find ourselves in leadership roles; however, I have learned this is not always the case while performing IMEs. Sometimes I make a recommendation based on the supported medical evidence and my partners will act contrary to my recommendation due to external factors such as cost.

Best parts of the job

I enjoy the freedom, which allows me to set my own schedule. The work is mentally stimulating and I am exposed to all branches of medicine. My take-home pay is also higher than what I would earn practicing clinical medicine.

Challenges faced

The largest challenges are within the IME reports themselves. The decisions I make heavily impact people's lives. The medical evidence I use to make my determination is not always clear cut. Because the stakes are so high, I sometimes face pressure from the claimant's legal representation, but it is important to remain unbiased. If I don't formulate an opinion that is in line with legal representation, they may stop referring their clients to me.

Qualifications and skills needed for this career

There is a need for all disciplines of physicians to perform IMEs. A board-certified physician is regarded as an expert in their field. From a legal system view, this expertise outweighs one's experience performing IMEs.

There are some organizations offering courses and certifications to physicians who want to learn to produce IMEs. I never took a formal course or completed a certification process, but it didn't seem to matter. I mainly built my clientele through networking and contacting attorneys and corporate entities, such as disability insurance companies.

Although it may seem difficult to break into the IME industry, these services are in high demand. There is more need for IMEs than there are physicians available to perform them. We are in an enviable position as experts, and therefore there is less threat of encroachment by non-physician medical professionals.

The barrier to entry to build an IME business is extremely low. A brick-and-mortar office or clinic is not needed. Many organizations that request in-person evaluations are able to host you in their office space.

Some clients mandate that I actively practice clinical medicine. This is because my qualifications and experiences are reviewed and potentially questioned by opposing legal counsel. If I want to represent myself as a medical expert, I must maintain my medical credentials and experience.

Advice for students and physicians

There is a great need for physician expertise outside of traditional clinical confines. There are many professional settings that have trouble finding physicians to fulfill their needs. I encourage physicians to be aggressive in seeking out these unfilled needs.

UNCONVENTIONAL CAREERS ACROSS THE GLOBE

The daily grind. This is where most of us find ourselves day after day, catching up on charting, sorting through inboxes, and dealing with the same patient complaints. The daily grind makes us dream of being elsewhere, perhaps experiencing another country or just enjoying a change of scenery. For most doctors, these dreams take shape in the form of short vacations crammed between long stretches of daily work.

The stresses of medicine aside, it is common for medical students and practicing physicians to want to travel for work or to work while they travel. Many want to fully immerse themselves in new cultures and places without sacrificing the career they have worked so hard for. This can be accomplished through numerous specialties, job types, and career trajectories.

There are even ways to incorporate a passion for travel into your practice when you personally cannot travel or are in between trips. Practicing travel medicine or humanitarian medicine, for instance, can be a bridge between career and adventure.

Cruise ship medicine

Most cruise ship passengers do not realize the extent of behind-the-scenes operations that make cruising seamless and pleasurable: food preparation, laundry services, maintenance, wastewater treatment, navigation…and medical care. This makes for an exciting career option for physicians to embark on (pun intended).

Although the work is challenging, some doctors regard a cruise ship gig as "getting paid to travel." You get to see parts of the world you otherwise may not see without the planning and coordination usually required for traveling abroad.

THE PRACTICE OF CRUISE SHIP MEDICINE

Leisure ships that cruise with a doctor on board range from 100-guest expedition ships to 6,000-guest mega-ships. When you factor in crew members, this is the population of a small town.

Larger cruise ships have an extensive medical suite with waiting rooms, triage areas, exam rooms, procedure rooms, small ICUs, and administrative space. They have lab testing, EKG, and imaging capabilities. There are one to two physicians, possibly some APPs, supported by a team of three to six nurses and paramedics.

The work schedule and structure vary by cruise line, although a typical arrangement is four months of work followed by two months off. The months spent working require a seven-days per week commitment with back-to-back sailings and long workdays.

The work of the cruise ship doctor includes a range of clinical medicine, occupational medicine, public health practice, and administrative duties.

Clinical medicine

The medical team manages all acute medical needs of guests and crew members. A typical day includes holding scheduled clinics and responding to urgent and emergent issues as needed. Physicians are always on call, although calls are triaged by nursing staff.

Most visits to the medical suite are noncritical, with 88% related to medical problems and 12% to injuries.[120] In most cases, travelers book a cruise only if they are healthy enough to travel on a cruise ship. Many issues are comparable to those seen in urgent care practice, although there are higher rates of certain presentations, like motion sickness, hangovers, sunburns, and near-drowning.

In emergencies, cruise ship physicians must make decisions related to urgent aeromedical evacuation, sending patients to nearby land-based hospitals, and requesting specialist consults at ports. These consults may require coordination with local healthcare providers and port authority personnel who may not speak English. In some areas, the nearest hospitals may have little to offer beyond the medical capabilities on the cruise ship.

Occupational medicine, public health, and safety

There is a crew member for every one to three guests on a cruise ship. They work as deck hands, engineers, cooks, stewards, performers, and managers. The scope of work makes for a broad range of occupational medical issues that the cruise ship's doctor needs to address. Because it is not uncommon for a large ship to have crew members from over 50 countries, language barriers can make caring for crew difficult.

Cruise ships have been referred to as "floating petri dishes." While they are actually quite clean, the close quarters, contained spaces, and shared activities are conducive to spreading communicable disease. Doctors are involved in prevention, outbreak investigation, and management of outbreaks and exposures. They may conduct sanitation inspections, water quality testing, and other routine public health activities.

Administrative aspects

Cruise ship physicians perform many tasks that, in a conventional healthcare setting, other designated staff are responsible for, like calibrating medical equipment. Other nonclinical tasks include supervising healthcare staff and running mock codes and drills with the crew.

One unconventional aspect of cruise ship medicine is the regulation: No international body regulates the practice of medicine at sea. Cruise ships sailing from U.S. ports are exempt from U.S. standards and regulations due to the common practice of registering ships in other countries with less restrictive rules.

The Cruise Lines International Association (CLIA), the largest trade association in the cruise industry, requires its member cruise lines to follow healthcare guidelines developed by the American College of Emergency Physicians. These guidelines set the standard for physician-to-passenger ratios, physician qualifications, required stock medications, and infection control practices, among other things.

GETTING INTO CRUISE SHIP MEDICINE

Many cruise companies hire physicians directly, although some contract with third-party companies that provide staffing for cruise ships, such as Vanter Cruise Health Services. Most cruise lines have fairly strict qualifications for their on-board physicians, such as an active medical license and basic and advanced life support certifications.

CLIA-member cruise lines require board certification in emergency medicine, internal medicine, or family medicine, or at least three years of post-graduate experience in general or emergency medicine. A broad medical background is best, given the range of passenger ages and the breadth of medical problems aboard. Certain other specialties may also find opportunities on a part-time or intermittent basis. For example, specialty cruise itineraries run by companies like Dialysis at Sea contract with nephrologists to oversee dialysis management throughout the trip.

The American College of Emergency Physicians Section on Cruise Ship Medicine is a resource for networking and CME.

COMPENSATION

Cruise ship medicine pays significantly less than a U.S. land-based practice. Many cruise lines allow their on-board physicians to have international equivalents of an MD (such as an MBBS or MBBCh) and can employ them more cheaply than a U.S. physician. U.S. primary care physicians (who earn roughly $100,000 less than per year than emergency medicine physicians for land-based work),[25] may find the compensation palatable. Physicians typically work as independent contractors, although there are some employed positions. Most companies cover malpractice insurance.

For those who enjoy life at sea, this career has many perks. Living expenses are covered while on board, including housing, meals, utilities, and entertainment. Doctors get a private, ocean-view cabin. Most employers cover travel to and from the ship's port. Unlike most crew members, physicians can use the ship's guest amenities, such as restaurants, pools, and theaters.

Small ship cruise lines like Lindblad Expeditions sometimes utilize physicians on a volunteer basis. The doctor cruises at no cost in exchange for their professional service during the trip. Given the limited number of passengers, the time spent providing medical care is minimal.

24. Expeditions and the wilderness

"Men wanted for hazardous journey. Small wages, bitter cold, long months of complete darkness, constant danger, safe return doubtful." According to legend, this was an advertisement placed by renowned explorer Sir Ernest Shackleton for his Imperial Trans-Antarctic Expedition in 1914. Despite the risks, he managed to assemble a 27-person crew that included two surgeons.[121] Clearly, humans have a thirst for adventure, challenges, and discovery.

Adventure travel, expeditions to remote locations, backcountry activities, extreme sporting challenges, and endurance events are attracting more participants than ever. With this comes the need for medical professionals to address the injuries, illnesses, and medical needs that can accompany these activities.

THE SCOPE OF EXPEDITION AND WILDERNESS MEDICINE

Wilderness medicine requires physicians to adapt medical care to the challenging conditions of remote and extreme settings that lack easy access to medical facilities. Expedition medicine focuses on medical support during organized, time-limited trips arranged by travel companies, schools, the military, or charities, and may involve mountaineering, trekking, or research. In practice, the terms wilderness medicine and expedition medicine are used interchangeably.

Although health issues in wilderness settings depend on the location, common conditions include fractures, sprains, cuts, hypothermia, heat illnesses, and altitude sickness. Also of concern are wildlife encounters, allergic reactions to plants or insects, and exacerbations of chronic conditions like diabetes or asthma.

As with practicing medicine in ordinary settings, wilderness medicine requires excellent history-taking, examination, and clinical reasoning skills. What sets it apart from conventional medical care is the lack of access to advanced medical facilities and equipment. The work depends heavily on clinical judgment and resourcefulness and requires medical personnel to make critical decisions under tough conditions like adverse weather and limited communication.

Medical support for expeditions

Medical support personnel required for an expedition depends on the activity's scale and complexity. Larger expeditions include a medical officer or medic who may be a physician, nurse, or paramedic. There are no universal qualifications medical officers, although some organizations do have guidelines.

Pre-trip work for the medical officer involves assessing team members' health, identifying potential health risks, preparing a medical kit, and working with team leaders to develop emergency plans and evacuation protocols.

During the expedition, the medical officer is always on-call. A review of hundreds of expeditions that included a physician found that 94% of medical incidents were minor; only 1% were severe enough to require medical evacuation.[122] The primary aim in severe cases is to stabilize the patient for transport to an equipped medical facility. Medical officers spend most of their time participating in expedition activities, with patient care taking up a minority of their time.

Post-expedition medical evaluations and follow-up care for injuries or illnesses sustained during the trip may also be a component of the physician's role.

JOBS AND GIGS ON EXPEDITIONS AND IN THE WILDERNESS

Physicians incorporate wilderness medicine into their professional trajectory mainly as a secondary focus or professional side interest. Full-time jobs concentrating on wilderness medicine are rare; most opportunities are short-term, intermittent, or part-time.

Integrating wilderness medicine into your career usually requires financial stability and a "day job" with ample schedule flexibility. For example, an emergency medicine physician may batch their shifts, or a hospitalist with a rotating schedule might swap weeks on service with a colleague to participate in a trip. Some trekking companies may need a physician for just a couple of weeks at a time, so the physician can use banked paid time. Longer expeditions might require taking a leave of absence.

Finding trips as an expedition physician

Expedition medical officers are often recruited or invited through connections or colleagues with experience in this field. You may want to reach out to the larger organizations that organize expeditions, including commercial adventure travel companies, mountaineering associations, and conservation and research groups. Notable examples include Choose a Challenge, National Geographic, Outward Bound, World Expeditions, and Raleigh International. Universities with expedition groups or outdoor education programs may offer opportunities, as well.

The online magazine *Adventure Medic* and the educational provider World Extreme Medicine post both paid and volunteer expedition medical officer position on their websites.

Seasonal work in wilderness medicine

Seasonal work in wilderness medicine is possible due to the fluctuating demands and activities in outdoor settings throughout the year. Although a medical degree is not usually required, some physicians join a ski patrol for perks like free skiing. The U.S. Antarctic Program employs around 3,000 people annually, including doctors, through the University of Texas Medical Branch's Center for Polar Medical Operations. Temporary medical camps in popular outdoor areas are options during peak activity months. Organizations like the Himalayan Rescue Association operate high-altitude medical clinics in the Himalayas, relying on volunteer physicians for staffing.

Advisory and consulting positions

Of all the opportunities in wilderness medicine, the greatest demand is for physicians to serve in advisory positions. These positions can be with commercial adventure travel companies, healthcare services providers in remote settings, or field rescue groups. Nearly all are part-time and can be compensated with hourly fees or stipends.

Companies like Global Rescue and SkyMed, as well as telemedicine firms like MedCall Assist and Emed Rescue 24/7, use medical directors to develop protocols and guidelines. They may also hire doctors for client consultation or clinician oversight.

Organizations that teach wilderness medicine and outdoor safety courses, such as the National Outdoor Leadership School and Wilderness Medical Associates, hire medical professionals to help develop and teach courses.

Many physicians with expertise in wilderness medicine get involved in search and rescue operations through local emergency management agencies and public safety departments, although usually on a volunteer basis.

FULL-TIME OPTIONS TO SUPPORT YOUR WILDERNESS MEDICINE WORK

Academic practice is a popular option among wilderness medicine doctors. Some academic medical centers are actively involved in wilderness medicine education, programming, and research. Physicians on faculty have access to resources, financial support, and protected time for research and teaching on the topic of wilderness medicine while also practicing clinically. The academic schedule can allow for extended periods off to participate in expeditions or wilderness medicine activities.

Working for a community hospital or healthcare system is another avenue. You may want to opt for a position in a rural area where elements of wilderness medicine frequently come into play.

The military appeals to many doctors who have an interest in wilderness medicine because it affords them the opportunity to use their skills in challenging and remote environments. Other government positions can also align with work in this field. For instance, the Department of Veterans Affairs recently established Clinical Deployment Teams and is seeking physicians with wilderness medicine or disaster medicine experience to join them.[123] When not deployed, team members work as hospitalists or in outpatient practices and are involved with deployment team training and preparedness.

GETTING INTO EXPEDITION AND WILDERNESS MEDICINE

Wilderness medicine expert Howard Donner, MD, wrote that "the most important single attribute that an expedition doctor can possess is common sense; everything else can be learned."[124] There are several ways to learn "everything else" at various stages of your medical training and professional career.

Wilderness medicine shares many qualities with emergency medicine. All emergency medicine training programs incorporate principles of wilderness medicine to some extent, making it a good specialty choice for students with an interest in this field. Some jobs are fitting for internal medicine and family medicine doctors. Given that many medical issues involve either trauma or infection, anesthesiology and infectious disease are also suitable options.

A growing number of medical schools offer wilderness medicine elective rotations and field experiences for students and trainees, with most ranging from one to four weeks in length.

There are fellowship programs in wilderness medicine, many of which are certified by the Wilderness Medical Society. Most are affiliated with emergency medicine departments and are financially sustained by having fellows work regular shifts in emergency departments. There are exceptions, however, such as the programs at Idaho State University and RiverStone Health in Montana, which target family medicine physicians.

Advanced life support certifications are a must.

Wilderness medicine courses and other training

Wilderness medicine courses are available on a variety of topics, some of which are specifically designed for physicians. Reputable educational providers include AdventureMed, Adventure Travel CME, National Outdoor Leadership School, and Wilderness Medical Associates. The Wilderness Medical Society offers a diploma in mountain medicine through a partnership with the University of Utah.

The American College of Emergency Medicine, the Society for Academic Emergency Medicine, and the Emergency Medicine Residents' Association have wilderness medicine sections or interest groups.

FINANCIAL CONSIDERATIONS

Physicians who pursue wilderness medicine do so out of a deep love for adventure, the outdoors, and adrenaline, rather than for financial gain. Medical officers are usually not paid, although occasional expeditions offer a stipend. Trip costs and travel expenses may be covered or discounted. You may be able to write off certain travel expenses as income tax deductions, depending on your tax and employment situation.

With careful planning, practicing wilderness medicine can be a means to travel for free or inexpensively and visit areas that are otherwise challenging to access.

Foreign affairs

International relations and national security are often seen as synonymous with political science and military strategy, but they also extend to medicine, introducing a career path for medical professionals. Many jobs in this field require traveling internationally or living abroad long-term, although it is not just the travel that makes these careers unconventional. The work may take place in high-security environments and politically sensitive areas and is an opportunity to apply your medical expertise while supporting national efforts.

CAREERS IN GOVERNMENTAL DIPLOMACY

Diplomacy shapes international relations by establishing communication channels and fostering trust between countries, thereby preventing conflict and promoting economic and cultural development. The U.S. Department of State executes foreign policy, including through treaty negotiation, global representation, embassy management, and consular services such as passport issuance. The department includes 11,000 civil service and 13,000 foreign service members in over 270 offices worldwide.[125]

Physicians in the foreign service primarily work as medical officers at embassies or consulates within the Bureau of Medical Services. Most work under the chief medical officer in the clinical programs section, delivering direct medical care, emergency services, and preventive health to U.S. government employees and families overseas. They also offer medical guidance during crises.

Primary care physicians are often in the role of regional medical officer, responsible for a range of healthcare services in a specific geographic area. Their clinical roles can differ based on location and needs. A team of APPs within the assigned region supports patient care duties. Each region also has a psychiatric regional medical director who provides mental health services, crisis support, and assistance with lifestyle adjustments and work stress for foreign service staff.

Getting into a career with the U.S. Department of State

Regional medical officers must be board-certified in family medicine, internal medicine, emergency medicine, or psychiatry and have at least five years of post-residency experience. Experience in public health, occupational medicine, travel medicine, or tropical medicine is beneficial. Proficiency in a foreign language is not a requirement but can be highly desirable and may increase the likelihood of being hired for certain positions.

The selection process for foreign service physicians is rigorous. Candidates undergo multiple rounds of interviews, an oral assessment, a background investigation, and a medical clearance process. Once accepted, they receive agency-specific training and orientation before being assigned to a post abroad.

CAREERS IN IMMIGRATIONS

People born outside the United States make up more than 13% of the U.S. population.[126]

The CDC outlines the requirements for immigration medical exams, which are overseen by U.S. Citizenship and Immigration Services (USCIS). The exam includes a history, physical, mental health screening, vaccination assessment, and lab tests.

Two categories of physicians conduct these exams. Panel physicians authorized by the U.S. Department of State perform exams for prospective immigrants overseas, submitting results to the local U.S. embassy or consulate. There are approximately 760 panel physicians around the world.[127] Within the United States, civil surgeons conduct exams required for adjusting immigration status, such as moving from a visa status to permanent residency.

Starting a career as a panel physician or civil surgeon

Any physician who has experience in general practice, family medicine, internal medicine, infectious diseases, or occupational health can qualify to conduct immigration exams.

To become a panel physician, you must be appointed by the local U.S. embassy or consulate. This requires holding a license in the country of operation and meeting other qualifications, which vary by country. Civil surgeons must hold a U.S. license, have a minimum of four years' practice experience, complete a training program, pass an exam, and pay a fee. Panel physicians and civil surgeons must adhere to USCIS's comprehensive technical instructions.

CAREERS IN NATIONAL SECURITY

The Central Intelligence Agency (CIA) is responsible for gathering and analyzing intelligence to safeguard U.S. national security, conducting counterintelligence activities, and executing covert operations. We tend to associate the CIA with secret agents, but it actually employs a wide range of personnel, including physicians.

Roles in the CIA are broadly classified as operational or analytical. Operational roles involve fieldwork for intelligence gathering, human source recruitment, surveillance, and paramilitary operations. Analytical roles focus on dissecting information to advise policymakers.

Physicians within the CIA's Office of Medical Services deliver medical and mental health services to agency staff, conduct pre-deployment health evaluations, and may offer ongoing care during field assignments. They also contribute to medical policy, emergency response planning, and medical technology development.

The CIA also employs medical analysts within its Medical and Psychological Analysis Center. These are psychologists, epidemiologists, physicians, and other professionals tasked with assessing global health issues and analyzing the health of foreign dignitaries.

Getting a job with the CIA

Becoming a physician with the CIA is a highly competitive and arduous process. Candidates must have completed residency in a pertinent specialty like emergency medicine or psychiatry, hold a medical license, and have at least three years post-residency experience. They must pass a stringent security clearance and background check. Once hired, they undergo extensive training.

The CIA Office of Medical Services employs doctors in primary care specialties and psychiatry, as well as other specialties as needed based on mission context, such as trauma medicine or surgery during conflicts. They may also look for physicians with expertise in infectious diseases, public health, and global health issues.

Physicians work at the CIA headquarters in Virginia or at one of the agency's overseas locations, depending on agency priorities.

COMPENSATION AND FINANCIAL CONSIDERATIONS

Compensation for foreign service physicians is based on the federal government pay scale. The Department of State provides relocation assistance, temporary housing, and travel expenses for overseas assignments; they also may offer recruitment and retention bonuses.

Most panel physicians and civil surgeons work in private practices, and their volume of immigration exams depends on local demand and practice size. Physicians can set their own fees for immigration exams, which are paid directly by immigration applicants.

The CIA is exempt from the federal pay scale due to being an independent agency. In 2023, the CIA website listed a starting salary for physicians of $306,600, plus government benefits, sign-on incentives, and moving expenses if you relocate.[128]

26. Humanitarian relief, disaster medicine, and displaced populations

The desire to help others is consistently reported as one of the top reasons for pursuing medicine.[129] Many doctors carry a humanitarian mindset throughout their careers, regardless of specialty or patient population.

Practicing humanitarian medicine takes this mindset a step further, adapting it into a focused career caring for patients in crisis situations.

THE SCOPE OF HUMANITARIAN MEDICINE

Humanitarian medicine includes all medical services and practices carried out in any number of circumstances concerned with human welfare. It can involve addressing the urgent medical needs of affected communities as well as providing long-term healthcare interventions. Much of the work is in resource-limited and volatile environments where situations and priorities can change quickly.

Disaster medicine — a subset of humanitarian medicine — focuses on providing medical care during and after natural disasters such as hurricanes or wildfires, and human-made disasters like terrorist attacks, industrial accidents, or civil unrest. In these situations, healthcare systems may become overwhelmed, infrastructure damaged, and large numbers of people require medical attention. Doctors may be involved in individual patient treatment and stabilization as well as efforts to develop and implement larger disaster response.

Treating refugees, asylum seekers, and displaced persons is another aspect of humanitarian medicine. At the end of 2022, the number of forcibly displaced individuals worldwide reached 108.4 million.[130] Access to healthcare is a significant concern, with many refugees lacking resources, facing language barriers, or encountering discrimination. Overcrowded living conditions, inadequate sanitation, and limited access to clean water can contribute to infectious disease spread.

JOB OPTIONS IN HUMANITARIAN MEDICINE

The job options for doctors in humanitarian medicine are diverse. A career with a multilateral organization like the World Health Organization (WHO), for instance, has a very different flavor than one with a small nonprofit.

Global and multilateral organizations

Most global and multilateral organizations are associated with the United Nations (UN) and international bodies. Although their work spans beyond healthcare, they recruit physicians to varying degrees to address humanitarian crises and global health challenges.

The UN engages in humanitarian medicine through its specialized agencies, including WHO, the UN Population Fund, the UN High Commissioner for Refugees, and the UN Children's Fund. Independent from the UN system, the International Organization for Migration supports migrants' health and well-being. The International Committee of the Red Cross focuses on providing humanitarian assistance and protection to victims of armed conflict and other situations of violence. The World Bank plays a significant role in global health by financing health projects and supporting healthcare systems in low- and middle-income countries.

Employment with these organizations requires specialization, significant prior work experience, and a knowledge of public health, business, economics, or social and behavioral sciences.

Not-for-profit non-governmental organizations (NGOs)

NGOs operate independently of government control, aiming to address various social, health, and humanitarian needs. Increasing demand for humanitarian aid has led to recent growth in NGOs. Some have a specific target group, health condition, or geographic location they prioritize.

NGOs fill gaps in assistance where central governments may be lacking, but rely heavily on public funding, with the U.S. federal government directing billions of dollars to NGOs each year.[131] They can also be funded through private foundations, corporate sponsorship, and individual donors.

Several prominent humanitarian NGOs actively recruit physicians. Médecins Sans Frontières (known in the United States as Doctors Without Borders) provides medical care in more than 80 countries and conducts nearly 10 million outpatient consultations and over 100,000 surgical interventions each year.[132] Others include CARE International, International Medical Corps, MedGlobal (which was founded by physicians!), Relief International, and Save the Children.

These organizations offer both long-term and short-term assignments for physicians, with some focusing on clinical work and others being more administrative.

Faith-based organizations are a subset of NGOs whose work is heavily influenced by their religious values. Catholic Relief Services, Samaritan's Purse, and Mercy Ships are a few examples of NGOs that depend on physicians for conducting their humanitarian clinical work.

U.S. governmental organizations

Several U.S. government agencies, including the U.S. Agency for International Development (USAID) and the CDC, employ physicians in roles that may involve coordinating medical relief, planning emergency responses, and delivering healthcare services in crisis settings.

Although their primary mission is not humanitarian work, the uniformed services also become involved in relief operations. The USPHS Commissioned Corps deploys medical personnel in response to emergencies and disasters to provide medical care and public health services.

The Peace Corps recruits medical professionals as advisors and educators for 12-month volunteer assignments.

Industry, consulting firms, and academic institutions

Private industry and consulting firms. which have increasingly become involved in humanitarian medicine and post-disaster reconstruction, may hire doctors for medical expertise and guidance in humanitarian contexts.

Schools of medicine, nursing, and public health also offer opportunities to contribute to humanitarian efforts by providing technical assistance and data to inform the UN, government agencies, and NGOs about humanitarian needs and implementation strategies.

FITTING HUMANITARIAN MEDICINE INTO YOUR CAREER

Some physicians opt for full-time field humanitarian work. This is most feasible with the larger NGOs like Doctors Without Borders who have an ongoing need for physicians at multiple locations and offer financial incentives. A typical initial assignment is six to nine months, followed by options to extend or move to another location. The more work you have done for an organization, the more likely they are to offer flexibility in terms of assignment timing, length, location, and other preferences.

Dividing time between humanitarian work and U.S.-based practice is a common approach to a humanitarian medicine career. This can be achieved with locum tenens when not deployed, finding an employer who will accommodate extended periods of absence, relying on a spouse for steady income, or other approaches. Academic roles can be well-suited due to semester-based schedules and summer breaks.

There are also options if you prefer shorter or more intermittent humanitarian assignments. Some organizations offer doctors in high-demand specialties or who have humanitarian experience deployments as short as one to two weeks.

PREPARING FOR A CAREER IN HUMANITARIAN MEDICINE

The decision to pursue humanitarian work should start with some soul searching and self-reflection. You need to have the adaptability and tolerance to work in high-stress, disorganized, and uncertain environments. You need to be capable of making difficult decisions with limited information.

You also need to accept risk. The work can be difficult physically and emotionally. It might be dangerous, depending on the location. The opportunities most appealing to you may be inconvenient due to professional commitments or family obligations, requiring you to shift your priorities or compromise to integrate humanitarian work into your career.

Medical training and experience

Many humanitarian organizations require physicians to have at least one or two years of practice experience.

No single medical specialty will fully prepare you for all clinical scenarios and conditions you may encounter in humanitarian medicine, although emergency medicine is highly applicable. One- to two-year fellowships in disaster medicine and international emergency medicine are available. Although not widely recognized, the American Board of Physician Specialties offers specialty certification in disaster medicine, with eligibility gained through either a fellowship, field experience, or a combination of relevant training.

Family medicine, internal medicine, and pediatrics offer broad skill sets ideal for low-resource settings and community health. Surgical specialties and anesthesia are also in high demand. Some physicians find value in completing a rural medicine fellowship because of the emphasis on healthcare provision in low-resource settings.

Humanitarian and location-specific training

A career in humanitarian medicine requires a broad understanding of humanitarian aid and its related disciplines. Various certificate, diploma, and degree programs focus on disaster relief and humanitarian assistance, ranging from brief, online self-study modules to in-depth, in-person programs. One notable free option is the four-week Health in Complex Humanitarian Emergencies course offered by Emory University. Several universities offer a two-week course funded by WHO on Health Emergencies in Large Populations. Many humanitarian organizations provide their own training courses as part of the onboarding for volunteers and staff.

It is possible, although unlikely, that you will have dedicated interpreter services during an international assignment. You may want to learn new language skills. Language immersion programs, university language courses, online or app-based language learning platforms, and language exchange programs are options. In the same vein, do your best to learn about local politics, economics, customs, and cultural practices.

Public health and global health training

Formal public health training is not necessary for short-term assignments focusing on clinical work. On the other hand, a public health education can be invaluable for physicians in full-time roles with government agencies or in academia. MPH programs, CME courses, and nonclinical fellowships such as USAID's Global Health Fellows Program, are all options for learning about public and global health.

Finding and evaluating opportunities

Finding job opportunities in humanitarian medicine that meet your needs may be tough. Full-time positions are relatively scarce and may require an extensive search. The UN careers page and USAJOBS are good places to start.

Limited-term assignments are easier to come by, but the process of applying and preparing is time-consuming and in-depth. Some NGOs, such as Doctors Without Borders, allow any qualified physicians to express interest and apply for general consideration. Others post ads for specific positions or specialties they have a need for. Many are open to physicians calling to speak with a recruiter and may allow you to join a standby roster.

There are job boards focused on nonprofits, international development, and humanitarian work, including Impactpool, DevNetJobs.org, and Reliefweb. You'll want to thoroughly examine the organization you are applying to and the specific project you would be involved in. Research their mission, funding sources, and track record. Be cautious of small organizations or humanitarian "mission trips" that may be poorly planned or uncoordinated.

FINANCIAL CONSIDERATIONS

The choice to pursue a career in humanitarian medicine cannot be driven by financial gain. Most doctors who take humanitarian work assignments rely on their compensation from U.S.-based work in between trips to cover their living expenses and savings goals.

Some NGOs provide modest pay to physicians; Doctors without Borders, for example, offers compensation which considers prior experience and assignment length and location. In 2023, their starting gross monthly salary was $2,209, plus benefits and all living expenses.[133] Unfortunately, compensation from most NGOs doesn't rival this. For many organizations, physicians are unpaid volunteers.

Physicians who are employed by healthcare systems or academic institutions and plan to retain their jobs can check into the availability of department or discretionary funds to help cover the costs of a humanitarian deployment. Using a CME allowance is another option. You can also seek medical school loan deferment during humanitarian work.

Full-time jobs with U.S. government agencies or multilateral organizations offer salaried positions with full benefits, however, the salary may be less than what you could earn in private practice.

27. Living and practicing medicine abroad

Mark Twain eloquently claimed, "Nothing so liberalizes a man and expands the kindly instincts that nature put in him as travel and contact with many kinds of people." Too often, we limit our travel to brief vacations or reserve it for retirement. This is unnecessary. With careful planning, it is possible to live in another country while simultaneously practicing and sustaining your medical career.

PRACTICING WITHIN A FOREIGN HEALTHCARE SYSTEM

Some physicians who move abroad choose to stop practicing medicine, or they take a nonclinical job that doesn't require a medical license; however, many countries make it feasible for U.S. physicians to get credentialed and practice in their healthcare system.

Every option for practicing in a foreign country has advantages and disadvantages. Working in a private hospital or clinic often provides the greatest autonomy and financial rewards, but it is challenging to establish a patient base and familiarize yourself with regulations and reimbursement systems. Employment with a foreign government-operated hospital or clinic can provide more stability but can be fraught with bureaucratic processes.

Finding a job abroad

The best approach to finding a job abroad depends on the specific country, its healthcare infrastructure, and its cultural norms. U.S.-trained physicians are highly sought after in some countries, which simplifies the job search process.

Opportunities are found through job boards, healthcare associations, networking, and directly contacting potential employers. The job search process can differ between the public and private sectors, much like it does in the United States. There are recruiting firms and job boards specializing in medical jobs abroad, such as Global Medical Staffing, Hippocratic Adventures, and NZDr Medical Careers.

Several U.S.-based healthcare systems have foreign sites, many of which primarily serve the healthcare needs of Americans living or traveling overseas. They tend to follow standards and practices used in the United States. Many have hiring and onboarding processes geared toward U.S. citizens. Examples include the Cleveland Clinic Abu Dhabi, Johns Hopkins Singapore, and various Mayo Clinic Global network sites.

Medical licensing and registration

Researching and understanding a country's medical licensing system takes time, starting with identifying the regulatory body responsible for medical licensing.

Some countries readily accept American medical credentials and training. This can drastically decrease the time it takes for the licensing process. As a result, countries with reciprocity are popular among U.S. physicians. Examples include Australia, Belize, Canada, New Zealand, Singapore, United Arab Emirates, and United Kingdom. Going to a U.S. territory makes things even simpler — the U.S. Virgin Islands, Northern Mariana Islands, and Guam accept U.S. credentials.

Obtaining a license may be contingent on showing proof of a job offer, malpractice insurance, and a clear background check. Many countries require that foreign physicians pass a licensing exam. You may need to complete an approved training program or period of supervised practice. A language proficiency test may be required. There may be multiple pathways for licensing even within a single country, depending on specialty, intended practice duration, and other factors.

PRACTICING UNDER A U.S. LICENSE WHILE LIVING ABROAD

There are a few ways to continue to practice with a U.S. state license while living abroad.

Telemedicine is the most feasible way to practice under a U.S. license, as long as you are in a country with access to reliable, high-speed internet, although there are some challenges and restrictions. You must have a license in every state that your patients are located and you must be a resident of the United States to get a DEA license to prescribe controlled substances.

With a few exceptions, Medicare and Medicaid do not reimburse providers located outside the United States. Some commercial insurance companies require doctors to have an office in the United States, while others do not. Similarly, telemedicine companies are split as to whether they allow their contracted physicians to work from outside the United States.

Another approach is living or taking extended trips abroad, interspersed with periodic locum tenens assignments in the United States. Most locum assignments run from a few weeks to several months and may provide adequate income to cover living expenses during the periods living abroad.

Two other options covered in other chapters of this book are working abroad at a U.S. military base or embassy.

CHOOSING WHERE TO LIVE AND THE IMMIGRATION PROCESSES

The choice of where to go might be an easy one for you. If not, begin by thinking about things from a personal — rather than professional — perspective. Any place in which you would not enjoy your time outside of work should quickly fall off the list. Language proficiency is another easy way to narrow down potential locations.

Immigration and visas

There are multiple visa categories, each with eligibility criteria, requirements, and allowable duration. Some countries have visa programs specifically designed to attract foreign healthcare workers; for other countries, the process is long and onerous even for qualified physicians.

Obtaining a work visa in most countries requires having a job offer and sponsorship from an employer. The employer provides supporting documentation, such as an employment contract, and will help you submit the necessary documentation.

For those without an employee sponsorship, a spousal visa can be an option for married couples in which only one spouse is employed locally. A business visa may allow the physician to engage in telemedicine or work as a consultant for a U.S. company while living abroad. Freelancer visas are acceptable for working as an independent contractor in certain countries, including Germany, Netherlands, and Spain. Several countries, such as Barbados, Bermuda, and Croatia, have introduced digital nomad visas to attract remote workers.

Immigration and visa regulations and requirements can be complicated. Even with support from a prospective employer, many physicians seek professional help from lawyers or immigrations consultants who assist with document preparation, ensure compliance with immigration laws, and advocate for them.

FINANCIAL CONSIDERATIONS

Full-time salaries in many countries are lower than U.S. salaries. Whether the finances of living and working abroad make sense for you depends on more than just salary, though. The cost of living may be lower, work hours may be less demanding, and experiencing another country and its culture may be priceless.

Familiarize yourself with currency exchange rates. The value of the currency you earn in your host country can fluctuate over time in relation to the U.S. dollar, meaning that your earnings may have greater or lesser purchasing power when you convert them to U.S. dollars.

Compensation structures and negotiation practices vary across countries. Benefits and allowances for travel, housing, and transportation may be part of your compensation package, but they are not a guarantee. Your eligibility for local health insurance coverage will depend on the country's laws and healthcare system.

Income tax

You will likely need to pay taxes to the country in which you are working, in addition to filing a U.S. income tax return. You may also have tax requirements in your former U.S. state of residence after you move abroad. Fortunately, there are systems in place to prevent double taxation. The U.S. has tax treaties with many countries allowing for tax reductions and exemptions. The Foreign Tax Credit offsets taxes paid to the country you are living in.

Other tax-related requirements include filing the Foreign Bank Account Report and complying with the Foreign Account Tax Compliance Act.

Depending on your situation, expenses related to your job abroad may impact your tax liability, so track your expenses carefully.

Taxes are tricky. Hire a professional to assist you if you decide to take your career abroad.

Travel medicine

In 1958, Pan American Airways marked a new era in travel, operating the first jet-powered, commercial transatlantic flight, taking 111 passengers from New York to Paris on a Boeing 707. Since then, global travel has steadily grown faster and more accessible.

One billion people take international trips each year[134] for purposes ranging from vacation to business to medical tourism. Travel promotes cultural exchange and economic growth and it's fun, but it comes with risks. International travelers face increased morbidity and mortality; between 43% and 79% of travelers to developing countries become ill,[135] demanding the expertise of physicians to address travelers' medical needs.

THE SCOPE OF TRAVEL MEDICINE

Travel medicine encompasses health promotion, disease prevention, and management of medical issues while taking into consideration specific characteristics of the geographic region and the traveler's specific health needs. Common medical issues include diarrhea, respiratory infections, skin infections, and injuries. Insect-borne and other infectious diseases are a concern, especially in areas with inadequate sanitation, poor hygiene, or limited healthcare infrastructure. Travelers can experience exacerbation of pre-existing medical conditions due to changes in environment or access to medical care. Travel-related stressors like jet lag can also aggravate medical and mental health conditions.

Appropriate vaccination and preventive medications mitigate the risk of becoming sick while traveling; the personal behaviors of a well-informed traveler can reduce risk even further.

Pre-travel consultations assess the health risks associated with a traveler's planned trip and provide appropriate care and guidance. Treatment plans are based on the patient's history and their destination, planned activities, lodging, and other trip details. Health management may include immunizations, chemoprophylaxis, and standby medications. Patient education includes destination-specific guidance on water disinfection, insect protection, infection prevention, and general safety practices.

Post-travel consultations, although not conducted nearly as often as pre-travel consultations, are used for follow-up care and treatment of travel-related illnesses that present late.

TRAVEL CLINICS

Travel clinics are the most common practice setting for physicians in travel medicine. Travel consultations sometimes take place in primary care clinics, but there has been a shift toward specialized travel clinics that provide more comprehensive travel services. These clinics have grown in popularity in response to increasing demand for travel-related healthcare and recognition that travel medicine requires a depth of knowledge extending beyond what most primary care doctors can reasonably keep up with.

More than 1,000 travel clinics operate in the United States,[136] ranging from large corporations like Passport Health to small, independent practices. Most are staffed by a physician or APPs who are overseen by a contracted physician. Many academic medical centers and health systems run travel clinics within their internal medicine, preventive medicine, or infectious disease divisions. Some local and state health departments, university health clinics, and urgent care centers also operate travel clinics.

Incorporating travel medicine services into a broader practice is a feasible undertaking. Specialized vaccinations, such as for Japanese encephalitis and yellow fever, need to be stocked, but otherwise there is minimal need for new equipment or supplies. Some practices dedicate certain days or half-days to travel consultations, while others intersperse travel consultations with other visits. Many clinics operate on a fee-for-service basis, charging a flat fee for the consultation and extra fees for any required vaccines and lab tests. Although most health insurance plans do not cover pre-travel consultations, vaccinations may fall under preventive care benefits.

OTHER CAREER OPTIONS IN TRAVEL MEDICINE

Opportunities in other settings are available for physicians with an interest in travel medicine.

Travel insurance and assistance services

Travel insurance covers travel cancellations and delays, but also health-related travel interruptions, including trip cancellation for medical reasons, medical expenses during travel, and emergency medical evacuation. Given this, travel insurance plans must evaluate travel-related risks to determine appropriate coverage options and premiums. Medical directors review health-related claims and conduct medical risk assessments. They may provide guidance on pre-existing medical conditions and the appropriateness of medical treatments received by covered travelers.

Travel assistance services companies provide support to travelers during their trips, which can include emergency medical coordination. Increasingly, these companies offer medical advice and consultations for non-emergent issues and may employ or contract with physicians to conduct telemedicine visits with travelers, oversee medical helplines, and assist in coordinating care for medical evacuations and medical repatriation.

Medical services at resorts and tourist destinations

Travel medicine traditionally emphasizes international travel, but it also extends to travel within the United States. Some upscale hotels, resorts, and theme parks have medical facilities on their premises and employ medical professionals to provide onsite healthcare services. Physicians with medical practices in popular tourist towns and destinations can distinguish themselves by catering to the needs of travelers.

Global health and tropical medicine

Travel medicine can include aspects of global health and tropical medicine. Global health encompasses trans-national health issues on a large scale, while tropical medicine focuses on the prevention and management of diseases commonly found in tropical and subtropical regions. Physicians who are interested in these fields have career options focusing on population-level health. Job opportunities exist with government agencies such as CDC and WHO, non-governmental public health organizations, and research institutions to develop strategies for global disease prevention and control.

GETTING INTO A CAREER IN TRAVEL MEDICINE

Travel medicine is not a recognized medical specialty and there is no standardized training pathway. About 60% of travel medicine physicians come from an infectious disease background.[137] General internal medicine, family medicine, and preventive medicine are other appropriate specialties.

Most medical training lacks any focus on travel medicine. In fact, medical providers who do not have training specific to this topic often make errors in judgment and offer poor advice during pre-travel consultations.[138,139] There are a few options for learning more about travel medicine. The International Society of Travel Medicine offers a Certificate of Knowledge in travel health. Most MPH programs offer courses on topics related to travel medicine. There are master's, certificate, and fellowship programs in tropical health.

The CDC is one of the best sources of up-to-date information for travel medicine practitioners. Its Travelers' Health webpage includes current travel health notices and destination-specific health recommendations. CDC also publishes a reference guide on vaccine-preventable diseases and immunization recommendations. Travax and Tropimed are two online, subscription-based decision support tools for healthcare professionals who offer travel medicine services.

VaxServe, a subsidiary of the pharmaceutical company Sanofi, has a program to help practitioners begin offering travel healthcare. Travel Clinics of America offers a business opportunity for healthcare providers to incorporate travel medicine services into their existing practices, which includes training, clinical resources, operational support, and marketing.

COMPENSATION

Data is limited on physician compensation in this field. Infectious disease specialists earned an average salary of $262,000 in 2023,[25] which is likely in the range of most specialists who focus on travel medicine.

Suzanne Sweidan, MD, FACP

Regional Medical Officer for the U.S. Department of State,
Bureau of Medical Services

Practice setting

I work for the U.S. Department of State, Bureau of Medical Services. Our mission is to promote and safeguard the health and well-being of America's diplomatic community and to facilitate the diplomatic efforts of the Department of State. We practice in health units located in embassies and consulates overseas. As of May 2023, there are 206 health units around the world. Our services are in the outpatient setting, primarily in-person but also via telemedicine.

Employment type and schedule

I am a full-time, direct hire federal employee.

When assigned to a post abroad, I participate in a call rotation schedule with other health unit staff for first call, and also serve as second call when other health unit employees, such as nurses, are on first call. When assigned domestically in Washington, D.C., I participate in a call rotation as the MED duty officer for any emergencies at post, such as a death of a patient or political unrest affecting the embassy or consulate community in some way.

Patient population and clinical work

My patients are U.S. federal employees with various foreign service agencies, and their family members, including pediatric patients. We provide primary and urgent care services to them when they are assigned to posts overseas. We also provide occupational health services to locally employed staff who work in embassies and consulates abroad.

Approximately 50% to 75% of my work when abroad is clinical. We also advise the embassy's or consulate's senior leadership on any issues related to the medical field and serve as medical diplomats in evaluating local medical resources and building bridges with our foreign counterparts.

A typical day at work

Every day truly is different. When assigned overseas, a typical day may include walk-in hours for urgent patient care, scheduled patient care appointments (well checks, chronic disease follow-up, acute issues), senior leadership meetings with other embassy and consulate sections about various issues, overseeing a training course in basic life support for community members, providing other relevant training to the health unit nurses, or visiting a local provider to review their facility and resources. Responding to medical emergencies is also always a possibility.

Domestically, work depends on your particular assignment. Washington, D.C.-based assignments tend to be leadership positions that include crucial program and people management, such as bureauwide quality management or managing the program that oversees all of the medical evacuations returning to the United States.

Unconventional aspects

I am a foreign service medical specialist, meaning that part of my work is about being a diplomat — building bridges with medical providers in nations around the world so my patients get the care they need. Along the way, I learn incredible new things about different cultures and medical systems and support the crucial work that Americans do abroad.

Best parts of the job

I never get bored. I get to move to a new place, work assignment, and/or country every one to three years, so I am also challenged in new ways. This keeps it exciting. This job feels like the one I will retire from. It changes enough that I feel like I have a new job every so often even though I'm with the same organization. I reach retirement eligibility with a pension after 20 years of service.

As a small group of clinicians, physicians, APPs, psychiatrists, and lab scientists, there is a lot of comradery.

Challenges faced

Working for a federal agency sometimes means that making necessary change takes longer than you would like. Moving frequently is adventurous and fun but also a challenge. It affects your spouse's employment options, your children, and other aspects of your life.

Qualifications and skills needed for this career

At least five years of post-residency experience is required to work as a physician with the Bureau of Medical Services. You need the ability to care for women, children, and pregnant patients. You must be internal medicine, family medicine, or emergency medicine trained. The full list of requirements is included on the U.S. Department of State careers website.

Flexibility, resilience, and patience are important traits. You need a desire to have new experiences and challenges. A sense of adventure and valuing meaning in the work you do are important, as is a desire to see, learn about, and impact communities around the world.

Advice for students and physicians

The federal job application process takes some time so if you think it's even an option, apply. You'll have time to learn more and reconsider before ever having to commit to starting.

CAREERS ADDRESSING
THE MEDICAL NEEDS
OF THE WORKFORCE

The average adult spends nearly a third of their time at work. This amounts to a substantial chunk of our lives. Work environments vary from office spaces to construction sites to offshore oil rigs. For many, occupational roles come with inherent health risks, whether potential exposures or physical hazards. These risks can lead to a range of occupational injuries and illnesses. Work demands often do not stop when employees clock out. Work-life boundaries are blurred and it is increasingly challenging to disconnect from work-related stressors.

There are plenty of opportunities for physicians to address workers' health and medical issues. These opportunities go beyond the traditional roles we associate with medicine, extending into preventive care, industrial hygiene, and even industries like aviation and maritime. They provide physicians a chance to fuse their medical expertise with an understanding of workplace dynamics and demands.

A growing recognition by employers of the value held by workplace health and wellness is prompting them to provide healthcare services onsite and dedicate resources to safety and prevention. Much of this effort requires physicians for program development, oversight, review, and hands-on patient care.

The unconventional careers described in this section allow you to treat individual patients while simultaneously contributing to the broader health and capabilities of our nation's workforce.

Aerospace medicine

The term *aerospace* might evoke a clichéd mental image of a pilot in an instrument-filled airplane cockpit or an astronaut bouncing around in a space suit. Flight and space capture our imaginations from a young age and offer seemingly limitless possibilities and potential for exploration.

These possibilities and potential extend to physicians. A career in aerospace medicine is a blend of adventure and expertise, combining the thrill of flight with the critical skills of a medical professional.

MEDICAL NEEDS OF AEROSPACE PERSONNEL

Aerospace medicine addresses the health and safety concerns of individuals involved in aviation and space operations, including pilots, astronauts, and other personnel, and spilling over into the medical concerns of airplane passengers. It incorporates elements of many clinically focused medical fields, including cardiology, pulmonology, neurology, and psychiatry, but also requires an understanding of physiology, psychology, environmental factors, and technology.

Much of aerospace medicine aims to prevent medical issues in flight and space by ensuring a medically fit workforce. According to the Federal Aviation Administration (FAA), "There are literally thousands of ways to crash an aircraft"[140] but the pilot's medical condition shouldn't be one of them. Potentially disqualifying medical conditions for pilots include uncontrolled epilepsy, insulin-dependent diabetes, certain types of heart disease, hearing or vision loss, and drug or alcohol abuse.

Some medical issues are related to or exacerbated by the aircraft and flying environment rather than the underlying health of the pilot or crew. Exposure to high altitudes, changes in atmospheric pressure, and prolonged weightlessness significantly affect the body.

CAREER OPTIONS IN AVIATION
AND FLIGHT MEDICINE

Despite its importance, aerospace medicine remains a relatively unknown career option. Despite several clinical career paths in this field, nearly half of medical students have never heard of aerospace medicine as a specialty.[141]

Aviation medical exams

Becoming an aviation medical examiner (AME) is the most straightforward and attainable route for most physicians interested in incorporating aerospace medicine into their career. AMEs determine if pilots meet the medical certification standards. This requires assessing overall health and evaluating any medical conditions affecting the pilot's fitness to safely operate an aircraft, which can differ based on specific job or role.

The FAA sets the standards for medical certification. Employers may also have their own, more stringent requirements for pilots and crew members.

Employment options may be found with the FAA, flight medicine clinics, commercial airlines, and corporate aviation departments. Independent flight medicine clinics operate in various settings such as in hospitals, airports, or standalone offices. Some private flight medicine clinics are affiliated with a specific airline or aerospace company. Along with aviation medical exams, physician services might include medical clearance exams for air traffic controllers or specialized testing for conditions such as sleep apnea that could affect pilots' performance.

Commercial aviation and medical evacuation

Corporate employment and consulting present additional opportunities. Commercial airline medical directors may conduct medical screenings of potential pilots and provide telemedicine and care coordination for pilots and crew.

In the case of an in-flight medical event, diverting the airplane for a passenger or crew member needing medical attention costs between $3,000 and $100,000, depending plane size and rerouting details.[142] An increasing number of airlines are using remote emergency medical response services, which are staffed by physicians who offer consultations.

Medical evacuation companies also employ physicians to provide clinical care and oversight during evacuation flights. These physicians address emergencies that occur during air transport of a patient, and they coordinate with ground medical teams to transfer care upon arrival.

Careers in the military

All military branches need physicians with expertise in aerospace medicine to work in military medical clinics, flight test centers, and research facilities. The military's aerospace medicine specialists and flight surgeons provide medical care to aviators and aircrew members.

CAREERS WITH SPACE PROGRAMS

Space is a hostile environment, with microgravity, high radiation exposure, isolation, and other extreme environmental factors that present medical risks. As with pilots, astronauts can have exacerbations of chronic conditions or have new medical issues arise during spaceflight.

Space agencies and programs such as the National Aeronautics and Space Administration (NASA) have physicians on staff. The International Space Station has a dedicated and complex health medical system designed to ensure crew member health. The establishment of the U.S. Space Force and the emergence of private space agencies such as Axiom Space, Blue Origin, SpaceX, and Virgin Galactic created additional options for physicians in space medicine. Physicians working for these private companies are often given the title of flight surgeon, although the scope of this role has broadened from its original use for doctors providing care to military aviators.

Employment with a space program involves supporting all phases of space missions. Preflight, physicians may be responsible for medical screenings, crew training, and aspects of flight planning. The inflight phase requires monitoring for routine and urgent crew medical needs via teleconferencing. After a mission, doctors are involved in crew reconditioning and debriefs.

In rare cases, physicians may be selected to go on space missions themselves. Out of several hundred NASA astronauts, a small percentage have been doctors. Looking to the future, space tourism may provide potential new opportunities in this field.

GETTING INTO AEROSPACE MEDICINE

Board certification in aerospace medicine requires a two-year residency after internship. Some programs prefer or require that applicants complete a full residency in another specialty beforehand. Occupational medicine, preventive medicine, internal medicine, emergency medicine, and surgery are highly fitting.

Of the five accredited aerospace medicine residencies, two are military programs. Although these residencies have relatively few applicants, those applicants tend to self-select and programs can be competitive. Elective rotations in sports medicine, wilderness medicine, dive medicine, critical care, and other relevant areas can strengthen your application.

There are only about 700 aerospace medicine diplomates.[143] Physicians who are not board-certified in aerospace medicine can still have a career in this field by gaining experience or training in aviation or space-related industries and understanding e basics of flight operations, aircraft systems, and aviation regulations. The National Transportation Safety Board and the International Society of Air Safety Investigators offer courses in aircraft accident investigation, for example.

Working as an AME requires a U.S. medical license and a background check. Physicians must complete a multi-day AME training course, pass a test, and undergo a simulated patient exam.

Having flight experience or being a pilot can be beneficial. Becoming a pilot involves completing ground school training, logging a certain number of flight hours, and passing the necessary exams and practical tests.

Being open to living in areas where there is a strong aerospace industry presence can increase the chances of finding employment. Houston is a major hub for the aerospace industry and is home to NASA's Johnson Space Center. Several private aerospace companies are headquartered in Southern California.

COMPENSATION

Salaries for civilian physicians working for FAA, NASA, or other federal agencies are based on the government pay scale. FAA medical officer positions posted to USAJOBS advertised a salary range of $145,286 to $212,100 per year in 2023.

As they would for other services provided in private practice, physicians conducting AME exams can set their own fees. The pilot seeking certification usually is responsible for the cost of the exam.

Compensation for military aerospace medicine physicians is based on the military pay scale. As of 2023, U.S. Department of Defense (DOD) incentive pay for military physicians who have completed an aerospace medicine residency is $43,000. They are also eligible for a retention bonus up to $35,000 for four years of service[144] and loan repayment. Depending on duties, physicians may qualify for various incentive and special pays, such as hazardous duty pay and aviation incentive pay.

Employee health and occupational medicine

There is increasing recognition among corporations, government agencies, and other organizations that health must be prioritized in the workplace. As a result, there is a growing demand for physicians to practice occupational medicine in various settings and locations, with many jobs offering an attractive combination of clinical and nonclinical responsibilities.

Also enticing is the fact that occupational medicine residencies are short and uncompetitive. Because most jobs in this field boast an excellent work-life balance and solid pay, occupational medicine is truly a hidden gem for physicians desiring a career outside of the ordinary.

THE EXTENT OF WORKPLACE ILLNESS AND INJURY

Occupational medicine focuses on the prevention, evaluation, and management of work-related injuries, illnesses, and disabilities.

Workplace injuries range from basic lacerations to traumatic brain injuries. They can be the result of accidents, repetitive movements, or overexertion. Illnesses arising from exposure to hazardous substances, poor air quality, and other environmental factors in the workplace include occupational lung diseases, noise-induced hearing loss, and mental health conditions, to name a few. There were nearly 3.5 million work-related injuries and illnesses reported by employers in 2021,[145] although underreporting is likely.

JOBS IN OCCUPATIONAL HEALTH CLINICS

Occupational health clinics provide services to workers in various industries. Many clinics are hospital-based, structured as a division of the family medicine or emergency medicine department. Others are standalone clinics, operating as a single-location practice or a chain of clinics. They are also onsite clinics in industrial work settings like manufacturing facilities or refineries.

Most occupational health clinics provide acute care for workplace injuries and illnesses, medical evaluations for workers' compensation cases, and preventive care such as immunizations. They perform pre-employment physicals, fitness-for-duty evaluations, drug and alcohol testing, and rehabilitation services. Onsite clinics may also provide emergency response services.

Certain job types and industries have specific pre-employment exam requirements. Commercial motor vehicle drivers, for example, must undergo exams conducted by certified healthcare providers that meet the requirements of the U.S. Department of Transportation (DOT), commonly referred to as "DOT physicals." Given the precise requirements and certification standards, occupational health clinics are often used for these exams.

Fitness-for-duty evaluations

Fitness-for-duty evaluations are used in industries that require workers to operate heavy machinery, work at heights, or perform other high-risk tasks. They determine whether an employee can perform their job duties safely and competently given the condition of their health. The core of the evaluation is a medical history and exam, although it may also include diagnostic testing.

Any situation in which there may be concern about an individual's ability to perform their job can prompt a fitness-for-duty evaluation, including returning from a medical leave of absence or after a safety-related incident. The employer is typically responsible for covering the cost.

Workers' compensation cases

Physician involvement in workers' compensation ensures an injured worker receives appropriate medical care and that their employer provides any necessary work accommodations. It is often the physician who keeps the injured employee, their employer, and the insurance company on the same page regarding the worker's work restrictions and progression of their recovery.

CORPORATE MEDICAL DIRECTOR CAREERS

Occupational corporate medical directors are hired by corporations in industries where employees are exposed to work hazards, such as manufacturing, construction, mining, and transportation. Larger corporations may have an entire medical department with a full-time physician in this role, while smaller ones have a part-time physician who acts as a consultant through the human resources department.

Many corporate medical directors spend time on the same patient care activities as physicians in occupational health clinics. They are also responsible for the administration of health and medical programs company-wide. This includes developing and overseeing health surveillance protocols for occupational exposures, identifying health hazards in the workplace, and implementing strategies to minimize exposures and safety risks.

WORKING AS A MEDICAL REVIEW OFFICER

A medical review officer (MRO) reviews and interprets lab test results from employees and others undergoing drug testing. In occupational medicine, MROs help ensure workplace safety and compliance with drug testing regulations, most commonly in the transportation, healthcare, and aviation industries.

This role is unconventional in that the physician is not responsible for providing medical care to patients or determining treatment. Instead, they act as an impartial expert in reviewing lab results from urine, saliva, blood, or hair samples. This may require an interview with the donor (for example, to determine whether there are any legitimate medical explanations for a positive result), but the MRO provides their interpretation and recommendations directly to the employer.

Although their work relies on an understanding of pharmacokinetics and lab testing procedures, MROs also need to be knowledgeable about regulations governing drug testing. DOT regulations and other federal laws describe how drug testing is conducted, how the results should be interpreted, and how employees are notified of the results. Private companies with drug-free workplace programs may also use internal policies for drug testing.

Beyond the workplace, MROs review test results for substance abuse treatment programs, family law and custody cases, and other situations.

OTHER OPPORTUNITIES IN OCCUPATIONAL MEDICINE

Certain government agencies, including the National Institute for Occupational Safety and Health and the Environmental Protection Agency, have opportunities for physicians in occupational medicine. All military branches employ physicians for their occupational medicine programs as well.

Union physicians provide medical care for members of a labor union; they may be employed directly by the union or work for a healthcare provider contracted by the union. In addition to patient care, union physicians may be involved in negotiating healthcare benefits for union members.

Many occupational medicine specialists also offer their expertise as independent consultants and expert witnesses in legal cases related to workplace injuries and illnesses.

GETTING INTO OCCUPATIONAL MEDICINE

Certification in occupational medicine is through the American Board of Preventive Medicine. Training requires an internship and a two-year residency program. There are only 23 residency programs; the majority accept only a few residents per year, although most do not get many applicants. More than half of physicians complete training in another specialty before pursuing an occupational medicine residency.[146]

Occupational medicine certification is not a requirement for all jobs in employee health clinics or as a corporate medical director. Some employers accept internal medicine, family medicine, emergency medicine, and other specialties.

Obtaining an MPH or Master of Science in occupational health and safety is a way to learn the relevant principles of public health, epidemiology, occupational safety management, and regulatory compliance. Most residency programs provide one of these degrees tuition-free.

To become a certified medical examiner for commercial motor vehicle drivers, you must complete a training, pass a test, and join the DOT's National Registry of Certified Medical Examiners.

Licensed physicians can obtain certification as an MRO from either the Medical Review Officer Certification Council or the American Association of Medical Review Officers. Both organizations require applicants to complete a short training course and pass an exam.

The American College of Occupational and Environmental Medicine is a resource for CME, clinical practice guidelines, and networking opportunities.

COMPENSATION

Occupational medicine specialists earned an average of $292,814 in 2023.[33] The reported compensation for corporate medical directors ranged from $270,000 to $725,000 in 2018.[147]

The compensation structure for independent physicians who provide fitness-for-duty and workers' compensation exams is negotiated with the employer. Some states set limits on the amount that can be charged. For example, in California, the Division of Workers' Compensation sets a fee schedule based on the complexity and duration of the exam.

MROs for third-party administrators earn an hourly rate or a flat rate per case reviewed. Compensation for MRO work can be low — in the ballpark of $75 per hour or $15 per case reviewed. Some physicians may find this acceptable because the work is interesting but not difficult, and they can do it on their own time and from the comfort of home.

31. Maritime, undersea, and hyperbaric medicine

About 90% of global trade is carried by sea[148] and a sizable volume of cargo is transported by inland waterways. Fishing and harvesting aquatic life generates more than $200 billion in sales annually.[149] Sport fishing, recreational diving, yachting, and passenger water transport comprise a significant percentage of the tourism industry. Offshore installations, including oil and gas extraction and wind farms, rely on maritime support services to operate. Ports, marinas, and shipyards provide infrastructure for all of these activities and undertakings.

Clearly, the marine industry is a substantial source of employment worldwide. Maritime work environments come with unique features that give rise to some interesting career options for physicians.

MEDICAL NEEDS IN THE MARITIME INDUSTRY

Maritime medicine encompasses all possible health concerns of seafarers and other workers in the maritime sector. It draws on principles of clinical medicine, occupational medicine, environmental health, emergency response, mental health, and public health — all within a maritime context. Physicians in this field need to be knowledgeable about the relevant clinical topics and also about navigation, ship types, and marine and underwater environments.

Ships and other maritime worksites are dangerous places to work. Accidents are common and can be life-threatening or deadly. Among the many medical conditions encountered are acute cardiac conditions, anaphylactic reactions, hypothermia, and drowning. Mental health issues and excessive work-related stress are widespread. Maritime workers also require preventive care, such as prophylaxis for infectious disease. Treating mariners and divers presents logistical difficulties related to accessing care from sea and arranging onshore medical services.

The international nature of maritime work also adds unconventional aspects to practicing medicine in this field. Multiple international organizations regulate the industry and it has a highly multicultural workforce.

MARITIME MEDICINE PRACTICE SETTINGS

The opportunities in maritime medicine vary widely in acuity, practice setting, and responsibilities. There are both U.S.-based and international jobs available.

Medical clearance evaluations

One practice option in maritime medicine is conducting evaluations for medical clearance of seafarers and merchant mariners. To evaluate medical fitness to work at sea, physicians review a patient's medical history, conduct an exam, and complete required paperwork. They need to consider the worker's assigned tasks and overall safe ship operation.

The U.S. Coast Guard, through its National Maritime Center, operates a Merchant Mariner Medical Certification Program. Physicians need to complete an approved training program to become a designated medical examiner. Exams can be offered in any medical practice setting but are usually done at maritime medical clinics.

Ship medicine

Some ships require an onboard physician, depending on the vessel type and crew size. Shipboard doctors work for the Navy, the Coast Guard, or private organizations, providing medical care to crew members and performing administrative duties such as training crew members in basic healthcare, overseeing the ship's medicine chest, conducting ship assessments for sanitation, and preparing for inspections.

Telemedicine is an increasingly important aspect of shipboard medicine, especially for ships that don't have an onboard doctor. Maritime Tele-medical Assistance Services, also known as RADIOMEDICO services, offers remote medical expert consultation to ships.

Port medicine

Medical care is also needed at port locations. This includes managing acute and chronic medical problems for crew members, helping patients access secondary care, and conducting fitness-for-duty exams. Occupational health clinics, maritime medicine institutes, travel clinics, and general practices can provide these services. Physicians in private practice near ports can contract with shipping companies, vessel management firms, and other maritime corporations to provide services to their employees.

JOBS IN UNDERSEA AND DIVING MEDICINE

Undersea and diving medicine is concerned with the challenges presented by the underwater environment and its impact on the human body. Diving poses unique health risks, including barotrauma, hyperoxia, nitrogen narcosis, and decompression illness. There are also long-term effects, such as changes in bone density and loss of lung function.

Physicians in this field work to mitigate these risks through both prevention and response to urgent medical situations during diving. Patients can be recreational divers or professional divers who work in underwater construction, sea life harvesting, rescue diving, underwater oil rig operations, and marine research.

More so than in other medical fields, physics principles come into play with diving medicine, such as the effects of changing pressure, gas pathophysiology, buoyancy, and energy flow. You need to think about demands and dangers like tidal currents, entrapment, and diver panic and fatigue. Knowledge of diving trip planning and coordination, equipment, safety precautions, and warning signals is essential as well.

Fitness-for-diving evaluations

Fitness-for-diving evaluations assess a diver's physical and psychological health to determine suitability for participation in diving activities.

The requirements and process for physicians to conduct fitness-to-dive evaluations vary across organizations and diving types (military, commercial, scientific, or recreational). Some evaluations must follow established diving medical standards, such as the South Pacific Underwater Medicine Society Medical Format. Most can be performed in either primary care or specialty practices, with patient referrals coming through networking with dive shops and diving schools and by establishing relationships with diving-related organizations.

Jobs in the military

Undersea medicine is a specialized field within Navy medicine. Undersea medical officers provide medical care to Navy divers, submariners, and special operators, as well as general operational medicine tailored to the needs of a unit. Other military branches have divers, too, and therefore need physicians with expertise in this field.

Hyperbaric medicine

Hyperbaric medicine is commonly associated with diving and undersea medicine; however, its applications extend beyond diving. Hyperbaric oxygen therapy involves administering pure oxygen to a patient at increased atmospheric pressure, which can accelerate the body's healing processes. It is the primary therapeutic modality for decompression sickness and arterial gas embolism and an adjunctive therapy for about a dozen other conditions, including carbon monoxide poisoning, necrotizing infections, crush injuries, and skin ulcers. Off-label use is also quite common.

Doctors work in all settings in which there are hyperbaric oxygen therapy chambers. These can be hospital-based hyperbaric centers, wound care centers, independent free-standing centers, and military facilities.

GETTING INTO MARITIME AND UNDERSEA MEDICINE

Physicians interested in a maritime medicine career must decide whether to join the military or work in the civilian sector. A Navy physician can pursue assignments as a shipboard medical officer or as a land-based medical officer in a naval hospital or clinic. Civilian physicians have the option to work in private practice, a corporation, or a maritime medical center. Most opportunities are in major port cities.

Occupational medicine and emergency medicine are fitting for a career in maritime medicine, although primary care specialties and general surgery are also options.

Subspecialty certification in undersea and hyperbaric medicine requires a one-year fellowship. Although some programs are geared toward emergency medicine physicians, they accept any primary specialty.

Specialized training on topics such as shipboard medicine, diving emergencies, and fitness-for-diving exams are available through several sources. Reputable organizations for education and professional development include the International Maritime Health Association, the Undersea and Hyperbaric Medical Society, and the Divers Alert Network.

COMPENSATION

This field is small and the positions held by doctors are highly variable, so compensation data is limited. Physicians specializing in hyperbaric medicine earned an average salary of $307,241 in 2021.[10] Salaries for military physicians are based on the military pay scale.

Most medical clearance and fitness-for-diving evaluations are fee-for-service. Physicians can set their own price point, with the fee being charged to the employer or directly to the patient, depending on the situation.

Military personnel

Just as many doctors feel called to care for the sick, some feel called to serve our country. A career in military medicine is a way to do both.

Physicians play an important role in the nation's defense strategy — both as members of the military and as civilians — managing the medical needs of more than 2 million military personnel[150] and their families.

HEALTHCARE IN THE MILITARY

The military healthcare system operates within the Department of Defense and is comprised of hospitals and clinics staffed by both military and civilian clinicians. They are permanent facilities that function similarly to civilian hospitals in many ways. Some physicians are surprised to learn that military medicine is an opportunity to practice in state-of-the-art facilities and with the use of advanced medical technologies. The DOD is on the forefront of robotic surgery, prosthetics, and telemedicine, among other technologies.

Each military branch has an organization that manages its healthcare activities. These include the Army Medical Department of the U.S. Army, the Air Force Medical Service, and the Bureau of Medicine and Surgery for the Navy and Marine Corps. Included in the military healthcare system is the Defense Health Agency, which operates the military health coverage plan TRICARE.

PRACTICING AS A MILITARY PHYSICIAN

There are approximately 11,000 active-duty and 3,000 reserve physicians.[151] Physicians enter the military as officers and practice in a variety of environments. Medical officers spend much of their time providing care to military personnel and their families at military healthcare system hospitals and medical offices. They may also be assigned to an operational unit as a secondary duty and accompany that unit as it trains in the field.

Deployment is arguably the most unconventional aspect of a career as a military physician. Deployments are defined as any activity in which service members and supplies are moved to a specified destination to carry out a mission. Most deployments are overseas, although some are domestic. Mission types include active combat, peacekeeping and diplomatic activities, and embassy security. Resources and infrastructure are limited during deployments. There may be suboptimal conditions and high acuity medical needs. Willingness to deploy is a necessity; however, on average, physicians face less deployment than other military career fields.

Medical officer roles share many similarities between service branches, although there are some important differences. Most physicians in the Navy spend a portion of their service practicing shipboard medicine. Service in the Army or the Marines is more likely to take a physician close to combat. Branches also differ in the locations of their major bases, the duration of deployments, types of training opportunities, and general culture.

Part-time military service

Reserve physicians maintain a civilian career while committing to part-time military service requirements, which are as few as two days per month and two weeks per year, with the potential for additional paid service opportunities. As with active-duty physicians, reservists can be deployed.

PRACTICING AS A CIVILIAN PHYSICIAN

There are options for physicians to care for military personnel without joining the military themselves.

Civilian physicians can find jobs at most military hospitals and clinics doing similar work as an active-duty physician in the same facility, but without the risk of deployment.

Military entrance processing is another option. The U.S. Military Entrance Processing Command program is responsible for screening and processing enlisted applicants into the military. There are 65 processing stations throughout the United States that put applicants through a series of clinical exams and lab tests to ensure they meet the standards to serve. Physicians review assessment findings, order necessary additional testing or consults, and make a final determination about each applicant's qualification. Each station has a chief medical officer overseeing the program and may contract with other physicians to conduct screenings.

PATHS TO A CAREER TREATING MILITARY PERSONNEL

The military takes a two-pronged approach to gaining medical officers; they target students before and during medical school and they recruit physicians during and after residency.

Pre-med students can apply to the Uniformed Services University of the Health Sciences (USU), which is the only federal medical school. Its mission is specifically to develop health professionals to support military units. Students begin as commissioned officers and commit to seven years of active duty within their selected service branch. Alternatively, pre-meds can elect to attend a civilian medical school through the Armed Forces Health Professions Scholarship Program and commit to three to four years of active-duty service after post-graduate training.

Students on both paths are free to choose their specialty, although military needs and available slots play a role. Through the military match process, students are matched to a military residency program or deferred to apply through the civilian match.

Medical training for military medical officers is not always a linear process; some doctors receive further graduate medical training after they have practiced for a period. In the Navy, for example, many doctors complete a tour as a general medical officer between internship and residency.

The process of joining the military for those who have already completed medical school begins by contacting a recruiter from your service branch of interest, since each branch recruits, trains, and retains physicians separately.

For civilian physicians wishing to treat military personnel, the USAJOBS website lists job openings with the DOD. Healthcare provided within the military health system encompasses the entire spectrum of healthcare from prenatal to end-of-life care, so there are opportunities for all specialties. The government uses a numbered system for grouping similar occupations; look for jobs in the Medical Officer–0602 series.

COMPENSATION

Salaries for military personnel follow a standard pay schedule. Basic pay depends on years of service and rank. Special and incentive pays address various qualifications or events, such as hazardous duty incentive pay and assignment duty pay. Special pay is based on specialty, board certification, and service agreement or deployment length. Incentives include bonuses such as sign-on bonuses for in-demand specialties.

Taking basic pay and all types of special pay into account, active-duty physicians earn between 32% and 58% less than nonmilitary physicians in the same specialty[152]; however, several factors mitigate this.

Medical trainees in military programs have a leg up when it comes to pay and expenses. USU students attend medical school tuition-free and receive the full salary and benefits of a uniformed officer while in school. The Armed Forces Health Professions Scholarship Program pays for tuition, fees, and living expenses throughout the duration of medical school. The Financial Assistance Program offers supplemental income during residency in exchange for a service commitment upon completion.

Military residents earn significantly more than those in civilian residency programs. Given the high debt burden of most U.S. medical school graduates, this can make up for a lower salary after training.

Military benefits are substantial; they include generous vacation time, housing and subsistence allowances, health and life insurance, retirement plans, malpractice coverage, education benefits, and student loan repayment programs. Active-duty physicians and their families are eligible for recreational and travel benefits, such as free space-available flights and use of military exchange stores.

Physicians retiring from active duty receive a variety of benefits, including health insurance through TRICARE.

Reserve members are paid for their training and medical duties; they receive full benefits during deployments and qualify for certain loan repayment programs.

Salary for civilian physicians is largely determined by government pay scales, with negotiation focused on adjusting the starting step within a given pay grade. Benefits often surpass those in the private sector.

David Almario, MD, MSPH

Occupational Medicine Specialist

Practice setting

I work for an integrated multispecialty organization that provides occupational medicine services. It is a national nonprofit with healthcare facilities across the United States.

Employment type and schedule

I am a full-time associate and partner. My work schedule is Monday through Friday, 9:00 a.m. to 5:00 p.m. There are no weekends and no call.

Patient population and clinical work

I spend all my time on outpatient clinical work, both in-person and virtual. This includes 80% workers' compensation injuries, 10% pre-employment physicals, and 10% DOT physicals. The workers' compensation portion comes from state and federal programs. Injuries primarily involve musculoskeletal injuries ranging from acute sprains and strains to repetitive strain injuries.

A typical day at work

I arrive approximately 15 minutes before the first patient is scheduled to check my virtual in-basket and respond to queries from patients, business and nursing staff, and other physicians. Clinic officially begins at 9:00 a.m. Our clinic functions as a hybrid of regularly scheduled outpatient visits intertwined with walk-ins who present with adult urgent care type injuries, such as lacerations, dog bites, sprains and sprains, and eye injuries. There is an official lunch break from 12:00 to 1:00 p.m., although frequently this time is devoted to catching up on notes and seeing walk-ins. Clinic then resumes, lasting until 5:00 p.m. However, any walk-in patients can still check in up to 4:59 p.m. and they still need to be properly evaluated and treated.

Unconventional aspects

Workers' compensation requires use of specific forms for documentation. There is a detailed history of present illness, including mechanism of injury and causation analysis. There is an emphasis on providing appropriate work restrictions, such as light duty, rather than taking patients completely off work. There is more visibility with our documentation, with oversight from workers' compensation insurance carriers and utilization review physicians who may agree or disagree with our care.

Ordering studies and treatment (for example, an MRI or physical therapy) is not as straightforward, as orders are processed as "requests for authorization" to the workers' compensation insurance carrier. More complex requests, such as for surgery or epidural steroid injections, are forwarded to utilization review, where an independent physician reviews the requests and approves or denies them.

Best parts of the job

Many patients in our clinic do not have private health insurance. Thus, when they are hurt on the job, their only means of medical care — as well as financial benefits when they are unable to work — come solely from our medical department and the workers' compensation carrier. Examples of these patients include laborers, often in agriculture, construction, or similar industries. It can be quite challenging, yet rewarding, caring for these patients' injuries to the point of them returning to full duty. If it were not for workers' compensation care for these patients, it is possible they would live the rest of their lives with a permanent disability and not be able to return to work.

Challenges faced

Managing patients with possible nonindustrial-related motives during their care can be a challenge. It is also challenging to align expectations of the patient with those of workers' compensation guidelines, particularly with expected timeframes for returning to work.

Qualifications and skills needed for this career

This field demands abundant patience, as optimizing workers' compensation care relies on multiple parties coordinating to provide timely care. These can include insurance carriers and outside facilities like physical therapy offices, for example. Apart from simple acute injuries, many cases last at least several months. The occupational medicine provider serves essentially as the primary treating physician during the entirety of a workers' compensation claim.

Almost all occupational medicine providers need to be certified to conduct DOT physicals. Another certification many occupational medicine providers have is MRO certification, although I do not perform any MRO duties in my current position.

Advice for students and physicians

Occupational medicine is a relatively small field. Many fourth-year medical students (including me at the time), have not heard of this specialty or had the opportunity to rotate in the field. Many attending physicians in other specialties do not know what occupational medicine entails. There is often a negative connotation associated with the phrase "workers' comp doc."

Nevertheless, outpatient occupational medicine provides a regular, stable work schedule, without call or weekend responsibilities. Clinic days are often dynamic, with a wide variety of acute and chronic injuries to manage. The field can certainly provide the work-life balance often desired by graduating medical students.

CAREERS AT THE INTERSECTION OF CLINICAL MEDICINE AND INNOVATION

A career in medicine has always been synonymous with healing and patient care, but increasingly, it is also about playing a role in advancing medical science and breaking new ground in healthcare.

Being both a doctor and a trailblazer is not as difficult as you may think. It doesn't require working in academia or applying for grants. It doesn't mean spending your days in a lab pipetting. Rather than conducting research, physicians in clinical roles can serve as conduits between the lab and the bedside. They can translate scientific advancements into tangible benefits for patients. By keeping current with the latest medical literature, attending relevant conferences, and collaborating with researchers and experts in cutting-edge domains, you can integrate innovation into your everyday practice.

Similarly, this does not necessitate leaving your clinical job for a career in industry. Evaluating and implementing new treatment approaches or interventions in clinical practice strengthens the body of evidence that legitimizes those treatments, thus paving the way for broader acceptance among medical professionals, patients, payers, and regulators.

If you are willing to learn, adapt, and explore, then your medical degree opens doors for you to be at the forefront of a wide variety of medical subfields.

Cannabis and psychedelic medicine

The U.S. Controlled Substances Act of 1970 placed psychedelics and cannabis in the most restrictive Schedule I category. This impeded research opportunities and relegated the substances to countercultural use. The government's War on Drugs intensified these challenges.

But the tides are turning. We have seen a shift in the public perception and legal climate surrounding psychedelic compounds and cannabis. There is more recognition of their therapeutic potential than ever before and their value in medicine is being reconsidered. Increasingly, the medical field views these compounds as beneficial, especially as adjunctive measures and later-line treatments.

However, psychedelics and cannabis remain tightly regulated, stigmatized, and misunderstood — even by much of the medical community. For physicians willing to take an unconventional path, this creates a few exciting career options.

PSYCHEDELICS AND THEIR MEDICAL USE

Psychedelics are a class of psychoactive substances that alter perception, cognition, and emotions. They can stimulate intense sensory experiences, vivid hallucinations, and altered thoughts. Classical psychedelics, such as psilocybin, are best known for inducing mystical experiences and spiritual insights. 3,4-Methylenedioxymethamphetamine (MDMA) promotes feelings of empathy, emotional openness, and connectedness. Ketamine and other dissociative psychedelics produce a sense of detachment from one's body and surroundings. Each type offers both a window into altered states of consciousness and therapeutic potential.

Ketamine is one of only a few psychedelics approved for medical use and is classified as a Schedule III drug. Initially developed as an anesthetic, it gained recognition as a rapid-acting and potentially transformative treatment for severe depression. In 2019, it was approved for treatment-resistant depression and depression with acute suicidal ideation, which led to the emergence of ketamine-assisted therapy for mood disorders.

Psilocybin and MDMA are still Schedule I substances but have displayed potential in treating a range of mental health conditions. Research is so encouraging that the FDA gave breakthrough therapy designations to both substances. Several jurisdictions have been reevaluating their drug policies as well. In 2019, Denver became the first city to decriminalize psilocybin. Soon after, Oregon was the first state to legalize medical use of psilocybin.

Ketamine clinics and ketamine-assisted psychotherapy

Ketamine clinics specialize in treating depression, anxiety disorders, and other conditions whose symptoms can improve with ketamine. Treatment can be with IV infusion, intranasal, or oral formulations. Many clinics incorporate psychotherapy before, during, and after administration. Physicians conduct medical evaluations and oversee medication administration; therapists typically provide the supportive therapy sessions.

The number of ketamine clinics in the United States increased five-fold from 2015 to 2018,[153] and continues to grow. As the country warms up to the idea of using psychedelics in medical practice, we will likely see this type of medical practice extend to other substances. In Oregon, for example, the first psilocybin treatment center received a license in early 2023.

CANNABIS AND ITS MEDICAL USE

Cannabis has a history of human use for various purposes dating back thousands of years. It contains over 100 different cannabinoid compounds, with delta-9-tetrahydrocannabinol (THC) and cannabidiol (CBD) being the most well-known and studied. THC is responsible for the psychoactive effects and acts as an analgesic, antiemetic, anticonvulsant, and appetite stimulant, among other effects. CBD offers therapeutic benefits without inducing euphoria or intoxication. While not traditionally classified as a psychedelic, cannabis has some psychedelic-like properties, including heightened sensory perception, altered time perception, and changes in mood and cognition.

Evidence supporting the benefits of cannabis in treating medical conditions has been growing steadily. We have the strongest evidence of its benefit for chronic pain, spasticity, nausea and vomiting, and treatment-resistant epilepsy.[154] Studies suggest effectiveness in managing many other medical conditions, including HIV, cancer, glaucoma, and cachexia. There is also encouraging data for use in a range of psychiatric conditions, including anxiety disorders, mood disorders, psychotic disorders, and PTSD.[155]

Cannabis legal landscape

Thirty-eight states have implemented medical cannabis programs, which allow patients with certain medical conditions to access medical cannabis, despite it remaining federally illegal. The government has chosen not to strictly enforce federal cannabis laws in states that have legalized it.

State programs require patients to obtain a recommendation from a licensed healthcare provider confirming they have a qualifying medical condition. Patients can then apply for a medical cannabis card through the state and purchase medical cannabis from licensed dispensaries.

The role of physicians in medical cannabis programs

Many Americans depend on having a medical cannabis card to manage their symptoms, and they depend on physicians to get that card, but many physicians choose not to participate in their state's medical cannabis program. In Florida, for example, fewer than 2% of licensed doctors provide medical cannabis certifications. Some doctors are concerned about legal risks, lack the necessary knowledge about the risks and benefits of cannabis, are barred by their employer from providing cannabis certifications, or simply wish to focus their time on other treatments and clinical services. This translates into significant opportunity for doctors who wish to get involved with medical marijuana programs.

Most patients seek out specialty practices for cannabis evaluations and recommendations. Establishing such a practice can be simple and inexpensive. A consult for medical cannabis includes taking a history and providing an examination, coordinating with other clinicians who may be involved in treating the patient's condition, providing education about medical cannabis, and having a frank discussion about the risks and expected benefits of its use.

Unfortunately, doctors who open such practices must compete with multi-state corporations that exist exclusively to hand out medical cannabis certifications for essentially anyone who will pay their fee. Some states have tried to constrain this commercialization by requiring physicians to have a bona fide doctor-patient relationship with anyone they certify.

GETTING INTO PSYCHEDELIC AND CANNABIS MEDICINE

Physicians in nearly all fields of medicine have found ways to effectively incorporate psychedelics and cannabis into their practices, although some specialties lend themselves particularly well to these treatments. Psychiatry is a natural fit, given the applications to mental health conditions. Anesthesiology is well-suited for treating patients with ketamine, especially as an infusion. Oncologists face challenges in effectively managing cancer-related symptoms and chemotherapy side effects with conventional treatments, and therefore may want to carve out a place for medical cannabis in their practice.

No specific training is required to prescribe ketamine, as long as you are licensed to prescribe controlled substances. However, some states do have specific requirements for ketamine infusion centers. The extent of laws and requirements pertaining to psychedelics will probably increase as states take steps to decriminalize or legalize these substances for medical use.

Each state has its own process and requirements for physicians to register for medical cannabis certifications. Most require a fee and completion of a state-approved training course.

The Center for Psychedelic Therapies and Research at the California Institute for Integral Studies offers an eight-month certificate program for medical professionals. Several academic institutions with psychedelic research centers offer CME, webinars, and other educational programs for clinicians. The Center for Psychedelic Psychotherapy and Trauma

Research at the Icahn School of Medicine at Mount Sinai is a notable example.

We are also beginning to see clinical practice guidelines emerge, which can be an asset when practicing in this field. The American Psychiatric Association, for instance, has published a consensus statement on the use of ketamine for treating mood disorders.[156] A number of professional associations and private educational providers offer courses and resources on medical cannabis as well.

FINANCIAL CONSIDERATIONS

Many insurance companies cover the cost of ketamine for its FDA-approved indications. As most treatment at ketamine clinics is off-label, clinics earn most of their revenue from out-of-pocket payments. Most charge an initial consultation fee between roughly $100 and $500, and charge between $400 to $1,200 per ketamine infusion.

Insurance companies will not reimburse physicians for encounters specifically for medical cannabis evaluations. Most practices charge in the range of $150 to $250 for a consultation. Many states mandate that patients have periodic recertification by a doctor to renew their medical cannabis card, and most practices charge somewhat less for these follow-up visits.

Clinical pharmacology

There are over 20,000 prescription drugs available to consumers in the United States,[157] and new drugs and new indications are continuously being approved. Many have complex actions, interactions, and potential adverse effects. New post-marketing studies, black box warnings, and withdrawals abound. It is hard to keep pace with developments and physicians often lack resources for clear, impartial information to guide our decision-making when prescribing drugs.

The field of clinical pharmacology aims to address these challenges.

THE SCOPE OF CLINICAL PHARMACOLOGY

The jobs of a cardiologist, pediatrician, or radiologist are widely understood, but few people can describe the day-to-day responsibilities of a clinical pharmacologist. A recurring joke in medicine is that perhaps clinical pharmacologists themselves are unsure of their role.

Broadly defined, clinical pharmacology delves into the relationship between drugs and humans. It encompasses the evaluation of drug safety and efficacy, optimization of drug dosing regimens, identification of potential drug interactions, and provision of drug information. It is not a new field, but it is constantly evolving, driven by advances in science and technology. When applied to clinical practice, it improves the quality of patient care.

Clinical pharmacologists and clinical pharmacists are frequently mistaken for each other. Many physicians do not realize they are two types of professionals with different degrees and training paths. Clinical pharmacologists have an MD or DO and additional training in pharmacology; clinical pharmacists have a PharmD with additional training in clinical pharmacy.

The need for clinical pharmacologists

Many clinical pharmacologists have a career in drug development, usually working for pharmaceutical companies; however, this industry-based, nonclinical career path is only one option. The demand is growing for clinical experts in drug therapy who can optimize treatment plans in patient care settings.

Inappropriate drug prescribing affects more than one-third of all patients.[158] Inappropriate prescribing leads to emergency room visits, hospitalizations, adverse drug events, and functional decline.[159] Some errors are minor, but some can result in serious and even fatal outcomes. Given that inappropriate prescribing has financial ramifications, many hospitals are adding clinical pharmacologists to their staffing plans.

CLINICAL PHARMACOLOGY JOBS FOR PHYSICIANS

Clinical pharmacologists use their knowledge of drug development, therapy in special populations, adverse drug effects, drug epidemiology and statistics, and therapeutics to assist in patient management.

In large academic medical centers, most clinical pharmacologists are involved in patient care, with many holding faculty appointments in the department of pharmacy or department of medicine. Many are involved in inpatient and outpatient care. On average, they spend 15 hours per week on clinical work.[160]

Consultative services

In an effort to ease providers' burden of keeping up with the increasingly difficult task of prescribing drugs, hospitals offer clinical pharmacology consultative services. General practitioners and specialists both consult clinical pharmacologists for guidance regarding the selection, dosing, and monitoring of medications for patients. They may be asked to assist in managing a multi-drug regimen or a drug-related complication, for example. Clinical pharmacologists on a consult service are essentially the hospital's expert prescribers. Most consultations are in the inpatient setting, although clinical pharmacologists may follow up with their patients in an outpatient clinic after hospitalization.

Most clinical pharmacologists continue to practice in their primary specialty, conduct research, or both.

Staffing a drug information center

Some clinical pharmacologists have the opportunity to work in their institution's drug information center. These centers answer drug therapy and medication-related questions for healthcare professionals, organizations, and sometimes the public. They may also offer guidance to pharmacy and therapeutics committees, develop disease-specific treatment algorithms, provide continuing education programs for healthcare professionals, and develop drug databases.

Most drug information centers are found in academic medical institutions and are staffed by clinical pharmacologists and pharmacists. They may receive funding through the institution's budget as well as through government grants or contracts, private foundations, or pharmaceutical companies. Their traditional role is to provide drug information services internally within the institution's' affiliated hospitals and clinics; however, some may also charge fees for their services to external clients, such as such as healthcare insurance companies and public health departments.

The responsibilities, schedule, and employment model for clinical pharmacologists in a drug information center depend on its size, services, and funding sources. For most physicians, this role is just one component of their academic practice.

GETTING INTO CLINICAL PHARMACOLOGY

Clinical pharmacology is formally established as a medical specialty in Australia, Canada, Japan, and some European countries; however, it is not recognized by the ABMS in the United States. Certification through the American Board of Clinical Pharmacology is the most well-established pathway for this career. It requires board certification in any primary medical specialty as a prerequisite; internal medicine is the most common choice. A two-year clinical pharmacology fellowship is required.

It is possible to be recognized as a clinical pharmacologist via other routes. Several internal medicine residency programs offer a clinical pharmacology track, including the University of California San Francisco, the Mayo Clinic, and the University of Pennsylvania. Completing a Master of Science or other advanced degree program in pharmacology is also an option.

Despite the recognized need for clinical pharmacologists in hospitals and other healthcare facilities, their services are often underutilized and their role remains poorly defined at many institutions. So, if pursuing a career in this field, you may need to educate employers and colleagues about what you can offer.

Professional organizations in this field are the American College of Clinical Pharmacology and the American Society for Clinical Pharmacology and Therapeutics.

COMPENSATION

Compensation arrangements for clinical pharmacologists vary according to their employment setup. Given the small number of physicians in this field, there is no reliable information about average compensation. Most can expect to earn a similar annual salary to that of their primary specialty in academic practice.

Clinical research

Over the past half-century or so, there has been a shift from experience-based to evidence-based medicine. Research is at the core of this shift. Now more than ever, physicians need to be active participants in generating the evidence that clinical practice relies on.

THE PHYSICIAN-INVESTIGATOR

Clinical research is the systematic investigation of medical treatments and interventions in a real-world context. The careers described in this chapter focus on interventional studies, which involve testing in humans to evaluate safety and efficacy. These are usually clinical trials conducted to gain approval for a new drug or drug indication.

There is often a rigid division between clinical work and research; however, this does not need to be the case. There are opportunities to integrate the two as a physician-investigator. These types of jobs are primarily within the development component of drug research and development, where, due to our ability connect clinical insights with research data, physician involvement is invaluable.

The most striking difference between traditional clinical work and clinical research is the relationship with the individuals you assess and treat. In the context of clinical research, they are study participants instead of (or in addition to) being your patients.

The number of physician-investigators has stagnated over the past few decades,[161] despite growth of the pharmaceutical industry, the number of investigational drugs, and the overall physician workforce.

ROLES FOR PHYSICIANS IN CLINICAL RESEARCH

Clinical trial sites are selected by either a pharmaceutical industry sponsor or a contract research organization (CRO) hired by the sponsor. In evaluating potential sites, they look for healthcare professionals with expertise and experience in the therapeutic area or medical specialty relevant to the trial. Other selection criteria include institutional track records, availability of trained research staff, ability to recruit and retain trial participants, and necessary infrastructure and resources.

Most clinical trial sites are academic medical centers, but they can also be hospitals, private practices, research institutes, and government facilities. Staff involved in running the trial are typically employed by the institution. Some CROs, such as Covance, IQVIA, Parexel, and PPD, have their own research centers to use as clinical trial sites for their own investigator teams and research staff.

The primary job for a physician is as a site investigator. Many physicians take on an investigator role in parallel with their existing clinical work or academic appointment.

Principle investigator and sub-investigator

The principal investigator oversees the clinical trial process at a single trial site, from recruiting patients to executing protocol execution while ensuring adherence to regulatory standards, scientific quality standards, and ethical guidelines. In doing so, they interface with the industry sponsor or CRO on issues related to safety updates, protocol amendments, reporting, and the like.

The team assisting the principal investigator includes research coordinators, clinicians, patient recruitment specialists, data coordinators, pharmacy and lab technicians, and regulatory specialists. Most day-to-day tasks can be delegated to these staff members, including interactions with study subjects. However, the principal investigator holds ultimately responsibility, so may be personally involved with assessing eligibility, obtaining informed consent, performing exams, monitoring participants, and collecting data.

Sub-investigators assist the principal investigator in various study tasks. Many are physicians, but they are sometimes APPs or other healthcare professionals. Sub-investigators may work with other physicians within the institution to recruit patients to the clinical trial. They may assess and interpret clinical data, such as vital signs, EKGs, lab tests, and patient questionnaires. Depending on the nature of the investigational drug, they might perform medication administration and manage adverse events.

STARTING AND BUILDING A CAREER IN CLINICAL RESEARCH

A career incorporating clinical research requires a blend of clinical and research skills. Our medical education system focuses heavily on clinical proficiency. There is not a single, defined path for acquiring research skills, and doing so requires being proactive. This aspect can sometimes deter physicians from exploring clinical research jobs; however, there are no deadlines or rigid rules for becoming a physician-investigator.

Scientific degrees and research training

Most physician-scientists have an MD as their one and only professional degree, but a graduate scientific degree is worth considering. An MS in clinical research or an MPH concentrating on research, epidemiology, or biostatistics are options.

For students who have an early interest in research, an MD-PhD program offers advantages. NIH-funded Medical Scientist Training Programs cover full tuition and provide a stipend for living expenses, which ranges from $25,000 to $40,000 per year. MD-PhD graduates have the option of completing a clinical residency, a post-doctoral research fellowship, or both.

Aside from formal degree programs, there are structured research scholar programs and fellowships hosted by many academic institutions lasting for a few months to a full year. Examples include the Clinical Research Training Program at the NIH, the Doris Duke Research Fellowship, and programs offered by the Howard Hughes Medical Institute.

The NIH offers a series of free online courses on a range of topics in clinical research. Many colleges and independent educational providers offer certificate programs in clinical research and investigation, although these are unnecessary for most physicians.

The Association of Clinical Research Professionals and the American Physician Scientists Association are sources of professional support and networking.

Medical training and licensure

Pharmaceutical medicine is a recognized medical specialty with a formal training pathway in some European countries, but not in the United States. Physicians in any medical specialty can pursue a career in clinical research. Specializing in a field experiencing a lot of drug development may make it easier to become a physician investigator. Examples include oncology, rheumatology, and psychiatry.

Most clinical research positions require a medical license and many require or prefer board certification. Physicians without a license may be able to identify clinical research jobs that involve assessing and managing study participants within the confines of a protocol.

COMPENSATION

Clinical trial investigators are compensated for their time and contributions to the study. The amount can depend on the trial's therapeutic area, duration, phase, size, and other factors. Several payment models are used in the industry; the most common is a flat fee meant to cover the investigator's full involvement in the clinical trial. This fee is negotiated between parties, although pharmaceutical companies must adhere to fair market value standards.

In many cases, physician investigators are employed by the institution serving as the trial site. Large institutions have entire departments that oversee clinical research and manage research-related finances. They receive funds from the industry sponsor or CRO to cover research expenses and disburse payments to study personnel.

Some physicians who have been involved in research as part of their clinical jobs, at some point, transition their careers to the pharmaceutical industry. The skills used as a medical monitor or drug safety physician for a pharmaceutical company or CRO overlap with those used as a clinical trial site investigator. Average annual compensation for physicians employed by the pharmaceutical industry was $392,534 in 2023.[3]

Human enhancement and anti-aging

Humans have been searching for the fountain of youth for centuries. We have always been fascinated by the ideas of prolonging life and expanding what our bodies can do. The fields of human enhancement and anti-aging offer interesting career options for physicians who want to push the boundaries of what is possible in medical science.

THE SCOPE OF HUMAN ENHANCEMENT

Human enhancement refers to using any biomedical, pharmaceutical, or genetic intervention to improve an aspect of human existence beyond what is natural. Enhancements can be physical, with the goal of increasing strength, endurance, or speed. They can be cognitive or sensory, aiming to increase memory, attention, or intellectual capacity. Or they can aim to enhance resilience in unnatural or extreme environments. Approaches can be pharmacological or nonpharmacological, invasive or noninvasive, and permanent or reversible. Some techniques are passive while others require active participation from the individual.

No medications are approved by the FDA specifically for physical or cognitive enhancement in healthy individuals without any diagnosed disease, although they get used off-label. The use of stimulants for cognitive enhancement is an example. Other investigational approaches include deep brain stimulation to enhance mental function in healthy humans, brain-computer interfaces for direct neural control of machines or devices, and advanced prosthetics incorporating sensory feedback.

Implant technologies

Implant technology uses devices or chips that store information or perform specific functions within the body. Microchips, such as radiofrequency identification (RFID) and near-field communication chips, are small electronic devices inserted under the skin that can store personal information. The first RFID chip for humans received FDA clearance in 2004.[162] Other implant types include in-ear headphones, biomagnets, light sources and optical devices, and sensors for physiological monitoring. A notable mention here that is still in development is Elon Musk's Neuralink, which is a brain-computer interface technology to enable direct communication between the brain and computers.

ANTI-AGING MEDICINE

Anti-aging, a form of human enhancement, has developed as a separate field with its own therapies. Anti-aging medicine targets processes often considered to be normal elements of aging: memory loss, visual impairment, wrinkled skin, and slowed gait and speech, for example. Its goals are to maintain physical and mental health regardless of chronological age and ultimately to extend the healthy human lifespan. As such, the field relies on a wide range of preventive and therapeutic interventions including pharmacotherapy and behavioral interventions.

Regenerative medicine is one approach aiming to promote tissue repair and growth. The most-used in clinical practice today is PRP therapy, involving the injection of platelets into the body for wound healing, skin rejuvenation, hair restoration, and joint pain.

Hormone therapy in anti-aging medicine includes testosterone, estrogen, human growth hormone, and dehydroepiandrosterone replacement therapies. There is some evidence these treatments may be associated with improved energy levels, body composition, cognitive function, and overall quality of life.

Nutrition therapy, supplementation, and nutraceuticals are a common component of anti-aging medicine practices. IV vitamin therapy is a growing trend that involves administering a cocktail of high-dose vitamin C, B vitamins, acetylcysteine, and other vitamins and nutrients on a regular schedule. There is slim evidence to support this treatment for anti-aging, although it may improve symptoms associated with certain aging processes, such as fatigue.

Gene therapy, epigenetic therapy, telomerase therapy, and mitochondrial therapy all have the potential to address at the molecular level the underlying causes of aging. Although these treatments remain investigational, some are available for use in specialized clinics and clinical trials.

Nonmedical anti-aging services like cryotherapy, infrared saunas, and light therapy are touted as having anti-aging effects such as reducing inflammation, improving circulation, and promoting detoxification. Although scientific research on efficacy is limited, the associated risks are low. These services do not require a medical license or physician oversight but can be a good supplement to an anti-aging practice.

Various aesthetic health services get grouped with anti-aging medicine, although these services do not address the root causes of aging. Skin care treatments such as laser resurfacing, Botox injections, and microderm-abrasion can improve the appearance of wrinkles and age spots, and can promote the production of collagen and elastin in the skin.

PRACTICE OPTIONS

Despite the investigative nature of many aspects of human enhancement and anti-aging medicine, there are enough established treatments and sufficient public interest to make this a career focal point. Most physicians report receiving requests from patients for enhancement interventions at least monthly, but few actually prescribe them.[163] The demand will likely grow as new therapies become available and the evidence to support their use strengthens.

Thousands of specialty medical practices are devoted to longevity and anti-aging.[164] Starting a solo practice, joining a group practice, and entering academic practice are all career options. At the time of this writing, an integrative oncology center is advertising for a physician with a background in anti-aging medicine. A company called Fountain Life, whose mission is "to make age 100 the new 60," is looking to hire two doctors for the role of longevity physician. Human Longevity, Inc., is seeking a primary care physician and a radiologist as part of its membership care program.

Those with an interest in research should look to academic medical institutions for positions in labs and research centers investigating the therapies described above. The military offers another option, as the Department of Defense has shown great interest in human enhancement, primarily through the Defense Advanced Research Projects Agency (DARPA).

GETTING INTO HUMAN ENHANCEMENT AND ANTI-AGING MEDICINE

One challenge for students and trainees wishing to pursue this field is that the therapies span traditional medical disciplines. Because there are many mechanisms driving therapies and many types of technologies in this space, no single specialty will fully prepare you.

Of doctors currently practicing anti-aging medicine, 46% are in primary care or general medicine, 11% are endocrinologists, and the rest are an assortment of other specialties. Surgery is suitable for those wishing to offer microchip and biosensor implantation. Orthopedic surgery, plastic surgery, and dermatology are great options for anyone with an interest in PRP.

Several medical institutions offer unaccredited one-year fellowships in anti-aging medicine, including the University of South Florida and University of Miami schools of medicine. There are additional options for targeted training and education through several organizations. The American Academy of Anti-Aging Medicine offers several fellowship and advanced training programs in anti-aging medicine and regenerative medicine, ranging from a six-month certification program to a two-year fellowship program.

COMPENSATION AND FINANCIAL CONSIDERATIONS

Compensation for employment depends on the specific services offered. As usual, proceduralists such as those performing PRP or implant procedures can expect to earn more than those in cognitive specialties.

Many human enhancement and anti-aging therapies are regarded as investigational or medically unnecessary, and therefore not reimbursed by health insurers; however, patients seeking these services often expect to pay out-of-pocket.

Precision medicine

Much of clinical medicine is empirical or supported by limited evidence within a broad patient population. Precision medicine takes individual variability into account using data, algorithms, and molecular tools. It allows us to make treatment decisions based on a specific patient's individual features, genome variability, lifestyle, and environment. This emerging field allows us to customize prevention strategies, improve disease detection, prescribe more effective drugs, reduce overtreatment, and predict disease progression. It also creates new opportunities for physicians.

APPLYING PRECISION MEDICINE TO PATIENT CARE

We know genetic variation modulates disease susceptibility and treatment response. To successfully incorporate this knowledge into the clinical setting, we need patient-specific data. Our deepened understanding of genes and genetic mutations has led to advances in gene testing technologies and the widespread availability of genetic, genomic, and biomarker testing. With these test results, we can use pharmacogenetics and pharmacogenomics principles to anticipate a patient's likely response to treatment and to inform decisions about dosing and other aspects of care.

Precision medicine currently plays the most significant role in the fields of clinical genetics and oncology; however, its relevance is beginning to extend to other medical specialties.

Precision medicine in clinical genetics

Clinical genetics deals with the diagnosis and management of birth defects, dysmorphologies, developmental delays, metabolic conditions, and adult-onset genetic conditions. It is sometimes thought to be a research specialty; however, while most clinical geneticists work in academic medical centers and are involved in research, many spend significant time seeing patients. They conduct genetic risk assessments, determine genetic testing strategies, and make recommendations based on a patient's genetic diagnosis or risk. They work closely with genetic counsellors for patient education and with lab geneticists for test selection and interpretation.

A clinical geneticist might see a neonate with a positive newborn genetic screening test, a child with developmental delays or dysmorphic features, a couple with a history of multiple miscarriages, an expectant mother with abnormalities on prenatal ultrasound, and an adult newly diagnosed with a neurodegenerative disease.

Although single-gene inherited diseases previously comprised the bulk of their work, clinical geneticists are increasingly requested to consult on cases of multifactorial disease with a genetic component, such as Alzheimer disease, epilepsy, and schizophrenia.

Even in its traditional scope, clinical genetics is an unconventional career with several appealing features. There are few emergencies or after-hours calls. Appointments are long and unrushed. There is time to look up and synthesize information.

Precision medicine is, in many ways, a natural extension of clinical genetics, so opportunities in this field will expand as the applications for precision medicine increase.

Precision medicine in oncology

Much of the progress in precision medicine has been in developing cancer treatments, making medical oncology another suitable specialty for a career in this field.

Our understanding of how cells work at a molecular level has improved, leading to more effective therapies that can be selected based on patient- and tumor-specific features. This can minimize the trial-and-error treatment approach often used with standard chemotherapy agents. Additionally, an increasing number of cancer treatments are receiving approval for specific genetic or biomarker-defined cancer types. This can make treatment planning more complicated, but it also creates a growing need for oncologists who have developed proficiency in precision medicine and who stay updated on its advancements.

Focused precision medicine practice

Precision medicine is no longer confined to academia; it has emerged in niche private practices. Patient awareness and demand for precision medicine services are mounting. Direct-to-consumer genetic testing is rising in popularity, too, although consumers still rely on their doctors to help them interpret the results. Physicians in precision medicine-focused practices can help patients select and use these tests wisely.

A core service of a focused precision medicine practice is whole genome sequencing, along with physician consultation before and after testing. This can be offered alongside gene panels, single-gene tests, and whole exome sequencing. Medical management focuses on any actionable insights from testing in the context of other data and patient factors, such as addressing modifiable risk factors, recommendations for exercise and other lifestyle intervention, referral to other specialists, and medication customization.

Existing practices of this type tend to have a concentration on overall health and lifestyle. They may offer other types of targeted testing and management. This could be hormone testing and therapy, or microbiome and food sensitivity testing with associated personalized nutrition plans, for example.

GETTING INTO PRECISION MEDICINE

Medical genetics is one of the smallest ABMS-recognized specialties, with fewer than 1,500 board-certified physicians.[165] The increased demand for genetics services has created a shortage of specialists in this field.[166] Despite its small size, medical genetics is not a competitive specialty and historically there has been a high rate of unmatched residency positions.[167]

Training requires a minimum of a one-year internship followed by a two-year residency. About a quarter of medical geneticists are certified in a second specialty,[168] most commonly pediatrics. Four-year combined residency programs are also available.

Physicians in any primary specialty could theoretically obtain the necessary knowledge and training to apply precision medicine to their practice. A number of degree-granting programs, certification programs, and courses on the topic of precision medicine are offered by academic institutions and CME providers. Notable examples include the Massachusetts College of Pharmacy and Health Sciences Precision Medicine Graduate Certificate and Midwestern University's Post-Graduate Certificate in Precision Medicine.

There is already demand for physicians in this field. In 2020, there were well over 30,000 physician job postings mentioning precision medicine in California alone.[169] Right now, early adopters with an entrepreneurial spirit living in a large metropolitan area are best suited for precision medicine practice; however, the general applicability of genomic testing and precision medicine will continue to increase, creating broader opportunities.

The American Society of Human Genetics, The Teratology Society, and the American College of Medical Genetics and Genomics are sources of information for physicians with an interest in this field.

COMPENSATION AND FINANCIAL CONSIDERATIONS

The median salary for medical geneticists was $264,610 in 2021.[10] Compared to other specialties, medical geneticists are less likely to be compensated based on productivity or medical billing, due in part to the time required for research and education for each patient consult.

Physicians in private practice need to keep a close eye on health insurance policy changes, as the range of reimbursable services will continue to expand.

H. Samuel Ko, MD, MBA

Chief Executive Officer and Medical Director of Reset Ketamine

Practice setting

Reset Ketamine is an outpatient private practice in Palm Springs, California, founded in 2018. Our mission is to provide an innovative and rapid treatment utilizing IV ketamine infusions in a safe, therapeutic environment.

Employment type and schedule

I own Reset Ketamine and work for myself. I spend about 90% of my time on patient care and the rest on administration and management. I make my own schedule and see patients by appointment only. Since this clinic is my "baby," I can't set it and forget about it. I work on and think about the practice when I'm not seeing patients.

Patient population and clinical work

I treat patients ranging from age 17 to 80 who have various mood and chronic pain disorders, like treatment-resistant depression, PTSD, anxiety, fibromyalgia, post-herpetic neuralgia, trigeminal neuralgia, and migraines. Roughly 80% of our patients have a mood disorder and 20% of patients have a chronic pain disorder.

A typical day at work

I usually start my day around 10:00 a.m. and end between 4:00 and 6:00 p.m. I'm seeing anywhere from one to four patients per day and do my best to take a one-hour lunch break. Each patient takes about two hours per session. After the day is completed, I'll do phone calls, emails, scheduling, marketing materials, and other administrative work needed to run the practice.

Unconventional aspects

As a board-certified emergency physician, I've utilized IV ketamine for procedural sedation in the emergency room for over 10 years and transferred that skillset to my private practice. My paradigm of medical care includes a biopsychosocial-spiritual approach that supports patients in integrating lifestyle changes to improve their mental and physical health by using ketamine as a transformational medicine.

Ketamine is currently the only legal psychedelic available to treat patients who are suffering from various mood and pain disorders. It takes a significant amount of time and energy to treat each patient and to be present for them throughout their sessions. Working with

IV ketamine is on the cutting edge of medicine and it seems like a lot of physicians are not aware of the evidence supporting its off-label use for numerous conditions.

Best parts of the job

The thing I enjoy the most is seeing patients with jaw-dropping improvements in their lives. Also, how rapidly IV ketamine therapy can work for some patients who have "tried everything else" before. It's emotionally and spiritually nourishing to know I've made a difference in someone's life. I also believe in the "butterfly effect" and know that as our patients' lives are improved, they will further impact those around them as well.

I love the autonomy of having my own clinic and not answering to an administrator telling me how to practice medicine. I intend to maintain my practice for quite some time. It's very sustainable and the burnout I had suffered from the emergency department (before stopping emergency medicine work in 2021) is pretty much nonexistent.

Challenges faced

The stigma around treating patients with IV ketamine therapy is tough. Some doctors believe it's snake oil or some sort of scam. I aim to practice evidence-based medicine and stay up to date on the latest research. However, if another clinician isn't keeping up with the latest studies, their ignorance can be quite challenging.

I do realize medicine can be very slow to change. In medical school, I recall hearing the saying, "medicine changes one funeral at a time." After all, it did take over 50 years for handwashing to become accepted by physicians in the 1800s.

Qualifications and skills needed for this career

The ketamine space is really burgeoning now and there is no one specialty that dominates it. I've seen radiologists, family practice, anesthesiologists, psychiatrists, emergency physicians, OB/GYNs, and physiatrists who have opened up their own private practice ketamine clinics.

You need to be able to really connect deeply with patients and be willing to go the extra mile for them. Some other important qualities that come to mind are curiosity, courageousness, resourcefulness, patience, and open-mindedness. It helps to be thick-skinned and adventurous. Have a desire for life-long learning and develop good listening skills.

Advice for students and physicians

With the majority of physicians becoming employees of large healthcare organizations and corporate management groups, I believe it's crucial for doctors to take the lead again and become owners, creators, and entrepreneurs. As a group, physicians are talented, resourceful, and resilient, which means we have the power to make changes in the system. Of course, this can feel overwhelming, and a lot of it is out of your control. So, it's important to focus 100% on what you can directly control and take action on that.

What can you personally do to create something novel in medicine? It may be a new business, a direct primary care model, software app, consulting service, writing, creating YouTube video content, podcast, or something else entirely. There are so many opportunities in medicine and it doesn't have to be the traditional work your peers may be doing.

UNCONVENTIONAL CAREERS COMBINING MEDICINE AND WELL-BEING

Modern medicine emphasizes treating pathologic conditions and symptoms. It is reactive and frequently overlooks health promotion. COVID-19 highlighted the importance of wellness and self-care as we all sought ways to manage stress and anxiety during lockdowns. The increased demand for all types of services related to well-being persisted even after our lives largely returned to normal.

Physicians who choose to incorporate disease treatment and promotion of optimal health into their careers often end up in unconventional roles. The appeal for many doctors is the proactive approach. Instead of applying temporary fixes to complex disease manifestations, they get to work collaboratively with patients to prevent conditions and complications. For some physicians, this shift away from reactive care leads to greater job satisfaction.

As they pursue well-being, many individuals turn to cosmetology, aesthetics, and personal fitness services to help them look and feel their best. Though not required to provide these services, having a medical degree has its benefits. Whether through integrative medical approaches, medical spa treatments, or fertility support, physicians can offer a level of expertise, safety, and comprehensive care extending beyond what nonmedical practitioners can provide. We can diagnose underlying health issues that impact whether various services are safe or will be effective, for example. We can prescribe medications to complement other services. Our understanding of human biology helps us in offering tailored recommendations. Medical credentials tend to instill trust and confidence in our patients, as well.

Combining medicine and well-being, although unconventional, makes sense. It can mean healthier patients and a more fulfilled career.

38. Integrative, complementary, and alternative medicine

Doctors take pride in using scientifically grounded treatments to care for our patients. Alternative medicine is often viewed negatively and has been criticized as being inappropriately termed a type of "medicine."[170] However, we also recognize there are situations where evidence for medical management is lacking or inconclusive. We encounter patients who decline our recommendations or seek alternative therapies, yet still want a relationship and treatment from a credentialed medical doctor.

While some treatments may not be backed by solid data, they still have a place in our armamentarium for managing certain patients and conditions. For some physicians, alternative therapies and practices are at the core of their work.

TERMINOLOGY AND SCOPE OF THE FIELD

Complementary medicine refers to nonmainstream practices used alongside standard treatments, such as acupuncture, massage therapy, and yoga; *alternative medicine* replaces conventional treatments and includes modalities like homeopathy and naturopathy. These two categories overlap and are collectively known as complementary and alternative medicine (CAM).

Integrative medicine merges and coordinates conventional and CAM approaches, focusing on treating the whole person physically and mentally. Certain complementary treatments used in integrative medicine have amassed a body of evidence to support their use. Acupuncture, for example, is effective for treating chronic pain, nausea and vomiting, and anxiety; mindfulness meditation is effective for depression and anxiety; and chiropractic care is beneficial for certain types of back pain.

Interest and adoption of CAM

Many CAM treatments are not routinely available at U.S. hospitals; most are not reimbursed by health insurance. The classification of therapies evolves over time, though, and modalities are sometimes integrated into mainstream healthcare.

Over the past few decades, the scientific and medical communities have taken an interest in deepening our understanding of CAM. The federal government's budget for CAM research has been increasing,[171] and most medical schools now include CAM within their curriculums.[172] The public, too, has shown significant interest, with more than 30% of adults using CAM.[173]

Although nearly half of physicians have recommended CAM to their patients, few feel comfortable discussing it and most think they need to learn more about it to adequately address patient concerns.[174] This suggests that physicians who choose to focus on CAM or integrative medicine can help address a challenge their colleagues face.

JOB AND PRACTICE OPTIONS

There are possibilities for a career in CAM as an employed physician and in private practice.

Integrative medicine centers offer a range of conventional and complementary therapies, usually including some combination of acupuncture, chiropractic care, massage, herbal medicine, nutrition counseling, and mind-body therapies such as meditation and yoga. The largest centers are affiliated with medical schools or academic health centers; a number of these are supported by the NIH. Prominent examples include the Andrew Weil Center for Integrative Medicine, the Center for Integrative Medicine at the Cleveland Clinic, the Osher Center for Integrative Medicine, and the Duke Integrative Medicine Center. There are also many private, for-profit integrative medicine centers.

These centers employ healthcare professionals from various backgrounds, including physicians. A doctor's responsibilities are similar to those in a conventional outpatient setting, such as conducting patient evaluations, developing treatment plans, coordinating care, and providing patient education and support. The major difference is the use of CAM treatments and the availability of other practitioners to administer them.

Smaller private practices usually do not have the built-in patient referral network and support staff of integrative medicine centers but can offer greater flexibility and autonomy. A practice can focus exclusively on CAM; however, offering conventional medicine in addition to CAM modalities can help to differentiate your practice and increase revenue. Physician owners may choose to hire other practitioners to provide CAM modalities or they can get training and licensure to administer certain modalities themselves.

GETTING INTO INTEGRATIVE MEDICINE AND CAM

Any specialty can potentially be a fitting choice for physicians pursuing a career in integrative medicine and CAM, although some align more closely than others. Given the focus on holistic care, primary care specialties are great choices. PM&R specialists find CAM techniques valuable for managing chronic pain and improving functional outcomes in patients with various disabilities. Several subspecialties are particularly suitable as well. Many patients with cancer use CAM, making oncology and palliative medicine good options. Sports medicine physicians can incorporate CAM to help athletes recover from injuries and improve their performance.

Integrative medicine fellowships are available at a number of medical centers and institutions; most last one to two years. The American Board of Physician Specialties offers certification in integrative medicine to physicians who have a primary board certification and have completed an approved fellowship. Neither integrative medicine nor CAM are recognized as medical specialties by the ABMS or AOA.

There are numerous training and certification programs for many of the CAM modalities — some designed specifically for physicians. Programs vary widely in length, accreditation, quality, and cost, so research them carefully. Well-recognized certification bodies for the most popular CAM modalities include the National Certification Commission for Acupuncture and Oriental Medicine, the Yoga Alliance, the International Center for Reiki Training, and the National Certification Board for Therapeutic Massage and Bodywork.

CAM is not regulated in the same way as conventional medicine, and rules for its use differ greatly by state. A medical license does not necessarily give a physician the green light to practice all CAM modalities. All states require special licensure to practice chiropractic care; most require licensure to deliver acupuncture and massage. The practice of naturopathic medicine is regulated in roughly half the states. Some states have special licensing requirements or regulations for traditional Chinese medicine, homeopathy, herbal medicine, and other practice systems.

Resources for networking and continuing education include the American Holistic Medical Association, the Academy of Integrative Health & Medicine, and the American Society of Acupuncturists.

COMPENSATION AND FINANCIAL CONSIDERATIONS

The median annual salary for integrative medicine physicians was reported as $220,000 in 2023.[175] Based on anecdotal data and a review of advertised positions, physicians employed at integrative medicine centers are compensated similarly to outpatient primary care physicians.

CAM modalities can be a valuable additional revenue stream for a medical practice, although this requires strategizing and planning. Health insurance plans may cover certain types of CAM in specific clinical situations in which there is demonstrated benefit; however, many modalities are deemed experimental, investigational, or nontherapeutic and will not be reimbursed.

A survey of general practitioners in Germany found that those with a positive attitude toward CAM scored higher on a job satisfaction scale compared to those with a neutral or negative attitude toward CAM.[176] If you have a personal and professional passion for integrative medicine or CAM, you may find greater satisfaction in your work despite possibly earning less than you could by focusing exclusively on conventional medical practice.

Lifestyle medicine

Most adults having at least one chronic disease.[177] These conditions comprise a major part of what physicians treat and account for a majority of U.S. healthcare expenditures.[178]

Lifestyle behaviors are responsible for 80% of chronic diseases[179] and a majority of the morbidity and mortality that they cause. Despite this, physicians receive minimal training on lifestyle interventions. Our healthcare system falls short, too; lifestyle interventions and preventive care are not incentivized to the extent that other services are. When approached strategically, however, the practice of lifestyle medicine can be feasible, lucrative, and sustainable for physicians. For patients, it can be empowering, inexpensive, and can improve their quality of life.

LIFESTYLE MEDICINE OVERVIEW

Lifestyle medicine is the evidence-based practice of helping patients apply comprehensive lifestyle behaviors to prevent, treat, and even halt the progression of chronic disease. Nourishment, movement, resilience, and social connectedness are recognized as the four main pillars of lifestyle medicine. Within these pillars are the ways for patients to take control of their health, sometimes referred to as the lifestyle determinants of health. They include diet, physical activity, stress management, substance use, sleep, relationships, and social support, among others.

Numerous clinical practice guidelines from national bodies emphasize specific lifestyle treatments for lowering risk and assisting in management for a range of chronic diseases. Unfortunately, lifestyle recommendations provided by most physicians are vague or left out of patient encounters entirely due to time constraints, competing priorities, and reimbursement challenges.

In contrast, when patients see a lifestyle medicine specialist, lifestyle behaviors and modifications are central to the visit. Patients are given "prescriptions" for lifestyle interventions, which are specific recommendations comprised of a particular behavior along with the details needed to accomplish it, such as frequency, duration, process, technique, and logging or tracking instructions.

Publications and searches on the subject of lifestyle medicine have increased in recent years,[180] suggesting a rising interest in this field.

THE ROLE OF LIFESTYLE MEDICINE SPECIALISTS

Lifestyle medicine can be either the focus of a medical practice or incorporated into the services provided by a primary care or specialty practice.

Physicians in dedicated lifestyle medicine practices benefit from several factors. For example, there is a large patient market due to the prevalence of lifestyle-related conditions. In addition, lifestyle medicine practitioners can easily receive referrals from providers who lack the resources, time, or expertise to offer lifestyle interventions to their patients.

A new patient visit with a lifestyle medicine physician begins by evaluating how their lifestyle habits and choices may be affecting their health. This information is used to determine the necessary intervention and strategy for making changes. The visit might include a physical exam, screening tests, a nutritional assessment, lab work, and other studies. It also incorporates patient educating and coaching.

In most cases, the goal of lifestyle interventions is improving disease control or even reversing disease processes. As such, physicians need to know the diagnostic criteria and treatment goal indicators for a wide variety of conditions. They must be familiar with screening questionnaires, structured measures of disease activity for conditions, and other relevant measurement tools. Collaboration with other healthcare providers is important, as pharmacotherapy remains an important component of disease management for many patients.

Follow-up visits monitor progress, address roadblocks, and modify treatment plans. Patient self-reported diaries or mobile app data of physical activity, diet, and other behaviors are common.

SLEEP MEDICINE

Sleep medicine is not ordinarily considered a subfield of lifestyle medicine, although sleep is addressed in several lifestyle medicine competencies and plays a central in well-being and overall health. Sleep quality is a highly modifiable lifestyle factor. It can be thought of as the foundation of successful lifestyle interventions, since it is difficult for patients to adhere to a healthy diet, exercise programs, and other behaviors when fatigued.

Despite it being essential for health, sleep gets overlooked — especially from a medical perspective. Chronic poor sleep leads to a wide range of physical and mental health issues. Conversely, health issues can disrupt sleep, creating a vicious cycle if not addressed.

Sleep medicine specialists diagnose and treat sleep disorders and disturbances, including sleep apnea, insomnia, circadian sleep disorders, and narcolepsy. There is a great deal of opportunity right now for those who want to concentrate on sleep medicine. There has been a steady increase in the prevalence of sleep disorders, number of sleep studies conducted, and sales of over-the-counter sleep aids in recent years. The newer availability of at-home sleep testing is convenient for patients and an additional source of revenue for sleep medicine practices.

GETTING INTO LIFESTYLE MEDICINE

Physicians in any specialty can pursue a career in lifestyle medicine. Internal medicine, family medicine, PM&R, and preventive medicine provide particularly good foundations. Although not yet an ABMS-recognized specialty, board certification is available through the American Board of Lifestyle Medicine to doctors who have a primary broad certification, at least two years of practice experience, and completion of an approved lifestyle medicine course.

Sleep medicine certification is a joint effort between several ABMS member boards; specialization can be pursued after family medicine, internal medicine, psychiatry, pediatrics, neurology, or otolaryngology training. Certification requires a one-year fellowship.

The American College of Lifestyle Medicine is a respected resource for further information and guidance on a career in lifestyle medicine.

COMPENSATION AND FINANCIAL
CONSIDERATIONS

Lifestyle medicine specialists can earn a salary or revenue that rivals that of primary care physicians. Reimbursement for longer appointments, counseling, and lifestyle intervention can be a challenge. One way to address this is to approach your services as chronic care management, selecting standard billing codes based on the diseases resulting from the lifestyle behaviors you are addressing. Medicare and other insurers cover preventive services related to lifestyle medicine, such as tobacco cessation and alcohol misuse counseling, depression screenings, and annual wellness visits. Practices can make use of shared medical appointments and group therapy, which may also be covered.

The median annual salary sleep medicine specialists was $334,902 in 2021.[10]

Medical spas and aesthetics

As the name suggests, a medical spa combines the relaxing and tranquil atmosphere of a spa with the expertise and capabilities of a medical office. This combination appeals to patients and also offers an attractive job opportunity to physicians.

Many doctors entering this field are seeking a less chaotic clinical setting. Some wish to treat patients with less severe illness. Many want reprieve from health insurance companies. Others want an extra source of income. But, most importantly, doctors practicing aesthetic medicine are motivated by the belief that when we look good, we feel good. Improving patients' appearance can have a positive impact on their overall well-being.

MEDICAL SPA SERVICES

Aesthetic medicine uses minimally invasive procedures to improve or enhance a patient's physical appearance. It includes treatments to address visible signs of aging, enhance natural features, and protect younger skin.

Medical aesthetic practices — colloquially medical spas, medspas, and med-i-spas — offer a wide range of nonsurgical cosmetic medical procedures, most of which are performed by licensed professionals, which can include doctors, nurses, and aestheticians. Some services have been the cornerstones of medical spas for decades, but advancements in technologies and techniques have greatly increased the menu of options recently.

Injectables such as Botox and dermal fillers like hyaluronic acid are staples in medical spas, reducing wrinkles and adding facial volume. Biostimulatory treatments like Sculptra and Radiesse stimulate collagen production, improving skin quality for up to two years.

Laser and light-based treatments are nearly universal offerings, mainly aimed at removing unwanted hair, scars, tattoos, and wrinkles. Thermal and ultrasound treatments like Thermage and Ultherapy stimulate collagen for skin tightening.

Body contouring is a nonsurgical procedure to reduce localized areas of fat and improve body shape. The most popular technologies used for this are cooling, laser energy, and radiofrequency. Popular brands include CoolSculpting, SculpSure, and truSculpt.

More complex aesthetic procedures include laser-assisted lipoplasty, sclerotherapy, and thread lifting. These are less invasive than traditional cosmetic surgery and often used as an alternative to it.

Skin rejuvenation treatments, including chemical peels, microdermabrasion, and micro-needling, are also regularly offered at medical spas. They are performed by aestheticians and do not necessarily require a consultation with a doctor.

MEDICAL SPA OWNERSHIP, BUSINESS STRUCTURE, AND REGULATION

Aesthetic medicine services are in high demand. Most plastic surgeons have seen an uptick in requests for aesthetic procedures in recent years,[181] and more younger patients are receiving aesthetic treatments than ever before.[182] The number of medical spa practices has increased by more than 60% in the past five years.[183]

A physician-owned medical spa in which the physician is closely involved in the day-to-day operations and clinical care is the simplest way to meet requirements related to medical spa ownership, business structure, and clinical oversight. This is relatively uncommon, however; fewer than half are owned by doctors.[183] Physician-owned medical spas are predominantly found in states that restrict medical practice ownership to licensed doctors or limit business affiliations between doctors and unlicensed individuals or nonprofessional corporations.

Where allowed, aestheticians, entrepreneurs, or investors without medical training own and operate medical spas. Medical spa chains and franchises include Ideal Image, LaserAway, and Sono Bello, operating multiple locations under a centralized brand and management structure.

Medical spas are medical practices, regardless of their ownership and business structure. Licensed professionals with the necessary training and skills must perform and supervise treatments and procedures. Medical spas with non-physician owners hire a medical director or supervising physician to oversee medical care. In some states, this must be a licensed doctor; in others, APPs can take on the medical oversight role.

There is no industry-wide standard for the medical director's responsibilities and tasks. In most medical spas, the medical director spends time reviewing treatment protocols, training staff, conducting chart reviews, and monitoring care delivery. The time spent in direct patient care varies. Most medical directors delegate authority for performing treatments to other licensed clinicians and practitioners.

In many states, licensed staff can operate laser equipment and give injections without the supervising physician onsite, making it possible for most medical spas to have a part-time medical director. Other states require the medical director to be present for a certain percentage of business hours or to be immediately available when called.

GETTING INTO A CAREER IN AESTHETIC MEDICINE

Aesthetic medicine is not an ABMS-recognized specialty, so there are numerous paths to a career in this field. Plastic surgery and dermatology are the most well-aligned specialties; however, about two-thirds of medical spa medical directors are specialists in other fields.[183]

Although many medical specialties may be acceptable for a career in aesthetic medicine, most physicians need training beyond residency. Physicians who have completed a primary surgical residency, such as general surgery, otolaryngology, and OB/GYN, are eligible to pursue a one- to two-year fellowship through the American Academy of Cosmetic Surgery.

Many other aesthetics training programs are marketed as fellowships, although this term is used loosely. Some are comprehensive aesthetic programs lasting a year or more; others are as short as a few weeks and may focus on a specific treatment modality. They vary in their eligibility criteria, with some accepting APPs, dentists, and other non-physicians. They also vary in the quality of instruction and the amount of in-person, hands-on training provided.

Many are run by for-profit organizations and can be pricey. One attractive feature of most aesthetic medicine training curriculums is the inclusion of business aspects of a career in this field, such as owning and running a medical spa.

Several organizations, such as the American Board of Aesthetic Medicine, offer certification in aesthetic medicine, but there is no single certifying organization recognized as the standard in this field.

Qualifications for medical directors

The American Med Spa Association recommends that medical directors have an active medical license and "possess the appropriate education, training, experience, and competence to administer, delegate and supervise each aesthetic medical treatment at the medical spa."[184] Some states require that medical directors have training and experience specifically in aesthetic medicine, but most do not delineate the exact qualifications.

From a technical standpoint, medical directors must know how to give injections and operate lasers and other equipment. Medical spa procedures are not difficult to perform; the real expertise lies in assessing patient suitability, optimizing procedural technique, and managing complications.

Unfortunately, this is an industry is which business owners sometimes try to cut corners, occasionally hiring underqualified medical directors. Do not rely on a facility's job description to determine if you are truly qualified for the position. Protect your license and your patients by ensuring you have adequate knowledge, skill, and training for the job.

COMPENSATION AND FINANCIAL CONSIDERATIONS

The salary for a full-time medical spa physician depends on experience, specialty, and responsibilities, as well as on spa size, services, and location. Physicians in part-time positions are usually independent contractors and may be paid on an hourly basis, a fixed monthly fee for providing medical director services, or a combination of these. Some medical directors may also receive a percentage of the spa's profits or equity in the business.

Medical spas are a cash-pay business. The services offered are generally not covered by health insurance, so it is not worthwhile to contract with payers. That said, owning a well-run medical spa can be quite profitable. A single-location medical spa generates $121,632 in monthly revenue, on average, with patients spending an average of $536 per visit.[183]

The startup and operating expenses for a medical spa are substantial. A basic entry-level laser hair removal machine can cost around $30,000, while a more advanced machine with capabilities such as tattoo removal and skin rejuvenation can cost upwards of $100,000. Patients expect a comfortable and spa-like atmosphere, so owners cannot skimp on their office build-out.

Sexual and reproductive health

Recent events have shed light on the importance of sexual and reproductive health. The overturning of *Roe* v *Wade* disrupted access to safe and legal abortion. Several states passed laws restricting access to gender-affirming care for transgender youth. The COVID-19 pandemic impeded many women from obtaining contraceptives.[185] The consequences of these decisions and circumstances are significant.

The broad range of medical services addressing sexual and reproductive health affect individuals' and the public's health. Unfortunately, addressing these issues has been obstructed by stigma and political divisiveness. The importance of physicians in ensuring access to medical care of this type has never been higher.

PRACTICE SETTINGS AND SERVICES

The careers and practice scopes of physicians concentrating on sexual and reproductive health vary greatly. One doctor may see patients with a breadth of routine testing and treatment; another might have an entire practice dedicated to a select few services or a narrow patient population — hormone replacement therapy for menopausal women, for instance.

There is also diversity in practice settings, from large comprehensive sexual health centers to solo practices in rural areas. A handful of online care platforms for services like contraception and pre- and post-exposure prophylaxis such as Lemonaid Health and Nurx have entered the market in recent years.

Family planning and sexual health clinics

Family planning and sexual health clinics offer an array of sexual health services, usually without an appointment and sometimes without requiring health insurance. Services include contraception, pregnancy testing, screening and treatment for sexually transmitted infections, HIV testing and linkage to care, and counseling on reproductive health issues. Most of these clinics are run by nonprofit organizations or government-funded institutions and target individuals who cannot access affordable reproductive healthcare elsewhere. Nearly all employ at least one physician on a full- or part-time basis.

Planned Parenthood operates more than 600 centers across the United States.[186] They are funded through a combination of government funds, private donations, and fees for services. Programs like Medicaid and Title X allow them to provide affordable family planning services to low-income individuals.

Mobile reproductive health clinics are on the rise due to the increasing need for accessible services, especially in rural and low-income communities.

Employment with one of the several international organizations operating family planning and sexual health clinics in other countries is an option for physicians to work abroad.

Abortion services

Only 3% of family doctors provide abortion care,[187] so physicians who are willing and able to offer abortion services can meet that need in many communities. Abortion services are offered at some family planning clinics but are also provided at independent abortion clinics and healthcare systems, particularly in urban areas.

Laws and regulations related to pregnancy termination vary widely by state, and there is a limited ability to offer services in some areas. In states that have not banned abortion services, there may be specific licensing requirements for abortion clinics. A few federal regulations also apply, such as the Hyde Amendment, which prohibits the use of federal funds for most induced abortions.

Sexual minority health and gender-affirming treatment

Gay, lesbian, bisexual, and other sexual minority individuals have special healthcare needs and may face barriers to care. Several sexual and reproductive health issues disproportionately affect this population. For example, gay and bisexual men account for more than two-thirds of new

HIV diagnoses in the United States,[188] and lesbian women are less likely to receive cervical cancer screenings.[189]

Reproductive and sexual health-related services often comprise the bulk of the care offered in practices catering to sexual and gender minority patients. They offer hormone replacement therapy and other gender-affirming treatment, as well as referrals for gender-affirming surgeries. They provide pre- and post-exposure prophylaxis and HIV treatment. Many offer treatment for mental health conditions that are more common in this population and that may be related to sexual health issues, such as depression and substance use disorders.

Sexual dysfunction and intimate wellness

Sexual dysfunction can negatively impact quality of life, yet medical help may not be available, comprehensive, or comfortable for patients in primary care or conventional OB/GYN and urology clinics. By focusing on a narrower range of health concerns, physicians with specialized practices in this area may be better equipped to provide the latest and most effective treatments. Services offered can include treatments for erectile dysfunction, premature ejaculation, low libido, low testosterone, painful intercourse, and more.

Many menopause symptoms relate to sexual health, including vaginal dryness, decreased sex drive, and painful intercourse, and are often addressed in the same setting as sexual and reproductive health issues. Due in part to lack of health insurance coverage, compounded bioidentical hormone replacement therapy is one popular treatment option frequently offered in specialized practices.

Surgical and procedural treatment for sexual dysfunction issues is an option for doctors with the appropriate training. The O-Shot for women and the P-Shot for men involve PRP injections to improve sexual response. ThermiVa uses radiofrequency energy to alleviate symptoms of vaginal dryness, itching, and pain.

Nonmedical services can add value to these practice types. For example, sex therapy can help patients address psychological or emotional factors contributing to their issue. Pelvic floor physical therapy treats some causes of pelvic pain.

GETTING INTO A CAREER IN SEXUAL AND REPRODUCTIVE HEALTH

OB/GYN and urology naturally fit as foundations for a career in this field due to the benefits of specialized training on management of conditions directly related to reproduction and sexual function. Another benefit is surgical training, which expands the menu of services these specialists can offer to patients as well as improved reimbursement to the practice.

There are several suitable subspecialties of both OB/GYN and urology. The American Board of Obstetrics and Gynecology offers certification in complex family planning, gynecologic oncology, maternal-fetal medicine, and reproductive endocrinology and infertility. They also offer Focused Practice Designations in pediatric and adolescent gynecology and in minimally invasive gynecologic surgery. The American Board of Urology offers pediatric urology certification. Both boards offer certification in female pelvic medicine and reconstructive surgery.

Family medicine and internal medicine provide good backgrounds as well, although some physicians may need more education in certain areas, depending on the scope of practice they are pursuing. Internal medicine physicians wishing to treat gender dysphoria or menopause symptoms may want to subspecialize in endocrinology. Infectious disease subspecialization is an option for internists who have an interest in HIV and sexually transmitted infections.

Psychiatry is a pathway for anyone with an interest in the mental health components of sexual and reproductive issues. Some doctors may wish to obtain certification in sex therapy from the American Association of Sexuality Educators, Counselors, and Therapists.

There are numerous continuing education courses on topics related to sexual and reproductive health. The National Abortion Federation and the National LGBTQIA+ Health Education Center are reputable sources.

Educate yourself on the relevant laws and regulations in the state in which you practice. Laws regulating abortion access, parental consent for reproductive health services, contraceptive insurance coverage, and infection reporting vary and can be confusing.

COMPENSATION

Income varies greatly depending on the type of practice and services offered. In 2021, the average annual salaries for a few of the most relevant specialties were $280,912 for endocrinologists, $377,416 for OB/GYNs, and $522,211 for urologists.[10]

PHYSICIAN PROFILE

Myrdalis Diaz-Ramirez, MD

Functional Medicine Specialist at the SahaVida Institute

Practice setting

The SahaVida Institute is a comprehensive wellness center in Sarasota, Florida, dedicated to expediting profound transformations for patients so they can look and feel their very best. It provides both in-person and telemedicine visits.

Employment type and schedule

I am co-owner of the SahaVida Institute, where I work an average of four days per week. At the moment, about 20% of my time is spent on direct patient care.

I also do a lot professionally outside of the SahaVida Institute. I am a medical director for four personal injury clinics and provide direct patient care at another. I run the maxAllure Mastermind, which is a virtual six-month program for physicians, and host the Design Your Physician Life podcast. Both of these programs aim to empower physicians of all specialties to grow in entrepreneurship.

Patient population and clinical work

At the SahaVida Institute, I see patients who have tried everything, have gone to many different physicians, and haven't found the answer they need to get back to feeling like themselves. I also see patients who want to achieve higher levels of performance despite a great state of health and many who are simply looking for a physician who will take their time to listen, get to the root cause of any health problems, and provide a personalized exclusive treatment plan. I work with each patient to identify their needs and create a custom program that fits their lifestyle, health requirements, and wellness aspirations.

A typical day at work

In the morning, I meditate before or after taking my kids to school. Some days of the week, I exercise in the mornings before getting to the clinic.

Once I get into our wellness center, I review the tasks for the day and the week with my team. During the day, I see patients. I also do nonclinical chores like meeting with management, helping to optimize systems, meeting with vendors, and doing marketing. I work on social media at various points throughout the day. After the clinic work is over, I go home, eat, and spend time with my family. I work on the mastermind program in the evenings.

Unconventional aspects

Nowadays, more than 50% of physicians are employed and most accept health insurance. In my case, I co-own my clinic and don't accept insurance. This transition doesn't come easy. By accepting insurance, there is some certainty of payment and higher volumes of patients.

The concepts of wellness are applicable not just to patients, but to us as physicians, as well. There is a lot of overlap between the care I provide at the SahaVida Institute and the concepts and skills I teach in the mastermind and podcast.

Best parts of the job

I enjoy working with wonderful people, the amazing transformations of my patients, and the impact my team is making in helping physicians retake and remain in control of their lives.

Challenges faced

Having my local community see me transition from an interventional pain physician into a functional medicine physician after over 16 years has taken a lot of education. Finding reliable consulting companies has taken more than one iteration — for example, in the cases of marketing, website building, and in-house consulting. Entrepreneurial skills aren't widely known by physicians.

Qualifications and skills needed for this career

To become a functional medicine physician, you should have a deep interest in investigating what ails a human being. Be a good listener capable of spending 90% of the time listening and 10% talking. Be interested in exploring alternatives outside of what medical school, residency, and fellowship taught us as we grow into new therapeutic options.

Functional and integrative medicine skills can be learned through different societies providing programs or fellowships that are not ACGME-accredited

Advice for students and physicians

In life, our happiness is 50% genetically predetermined and 10% determined by our circumstances; but 40% comes from our actions. We can take control of our lives, especially if we are exposed to possibilities. Investing time in the 40% contribution to my happiness through entrepreneurship is what completes me in a very deep professional sense and is something any physician can do. I invite readers to not give control of that 40% to others.

Regarding entrepreneurship, be ready to plan and design the life of your dreams. Understand that opportunities for learning and growth might disguise themselves as failures and that nothing happens until you take action.

Follow your passion with knowledge and surround yourself with people who will support your growth. Help other physicians around you and learn to live today without waiting. Have fun.

CAREERS WITH UNCONVENTIONAL PRACTICE AND PAYMENT MODELS

The conventional outpatient medical practice is a familiar scene: a brick-and-mortar office where the waiting room has a stack of old magazines. It is humming with medical assistants, front desk staff, and patients. The doctor has a packed schedule and is running behind. The cycle of insurance claim denials and appeals is never-ending.

None of the elements described above are prerequisites for practicing medicine, nor are they mandatory for job security. There is no rule dictating your patient panel size or the grandeur of your office space. The concept of a nurse taking vitals on the patient in Room 1 while you see the patient in Room 2 is not cast in stone.

If you have a valid medical license, a means to connect with patients, and way to secure compensation for the care you provide, then you can shape the way you practice. The careers covered in this section are a fraction of the available options. There are hybrids and derivatives of these, and others that take entirely different approaches.

You can opt to a join a group practice or healthcare corporation that uses a model detailed in the upcoming chapters, working as an employee. You will feel less burdened by the familiar sources of aggravation that plague your peers in traditional practices. Or, you might be inspired to start your own venture.

One thing distinguishing these unconventional practice and payment models is they do not come with the major hurdles that accompany starting a practice from scratch or going through grueling credentialling processes with insurance companies.

Cash-only practices

For more than a third of U.S. doctors, insurance requirements are among the least satisfying factors about medical practice.[190] The requirements are complex and can limit autonomy in medical decision-making. They are also time-consuming — so much so that we spend our evenings at home catching up on insurance paperwork.[191]

Luckily, there is no law that states we must accept health insurance for the work we do.

THE BASICS OF A CASH-ONLY PRACTICE

In a cash-only medical practice, the patien-t pays directly for the services rendered (usually by credit card or check), at the time of service. The practice does not accept any form of insurance, does not bill health insurance companies, and typically does not collect any insurance information from patients.

Practice owners establish a straightforward fee schedule, outlining the costs associated with each service, procedure, and consultation. Most charge a flat amount for each individual service or for certain bundled services. Some use tiered pricing, with different price points based on the complexity or time required for services. A few establish sliding scale fees based on patient income or other qualifying criteria.

The terms *cash-only* and *fee-for-service* are often used interchangeably, but they are distinct. Fee-for-service encompasses a broader range of payment arrangements including payment from insurance companies and directly from patients for insurance cost-sharing. Fee-for-service can also involve billing patients later, as opposed to requiring payment at the time of service, which introduces the risk of nonpayment and the need for collection agencies.

Cash-only services within the U.S. healthcare system

Is a cash-only practice really unconventional? It doesn't seem like it should be. After all, we pay cash for nearly everything else in our daily lives. But, within the U.S. healthcare system, paying cash for medical care is indeed a departure from the norm. Out-of-pocket spending accounted for just 10% of expenditures for physician and clinical services in 2021,[192] and only 10% of private practice physicians do not accept insurance.[193]

Various experts and organizations have criticized the hassles of insurance network contracting and outdated payment systems. The American College of Physicians, for example, argues that the prevailing payment system has distorted the practice of medicine and undervalued its most foundational aspects while incentivizing expensive procedures and high patient volumes. In response, they put out a position statement in favor of physicians choosing how they charge for services.[194]

Advantages for physicians

Administrative simplicity is a major advantage of cash-only practices. By eliminating insurance companies from the equation, you can avoid the time-consuming process of waiting for payment and dealing with insurance-related tasks. You no longer must decipher billing procedures, wait for prior authorizations, or send in appeals for denied claims.

The cash-pay model offers the freedom to provide the type of care and services you want, rather than what's dictated by insurance coverage policies.

Since patients have a financial stake, they often are more engaged in their care, as well.

Patients welcome the cash-only experience

There is a misconception that only wealthy individuals are willing to pay cash for medical services; however, the population consuming cash-only healthcare services is quite diverse and it is growing.

One target market is insured patients facing out-of-pocket responsibility in the form of deductibles, co-pays, and drug costs. These costs can be hefty. On average, workers with employer-sponsored family health coverage pay more than $6,000 toward their medical care annually.[195]

Patients who do not anticipate reaching their deductible for the year are especially likely to seek out cash-only services.

Uninsured patients are another population of interest. More than 8% of Americans lack health insurance. Reasonably priced cash-only practices provide a way for them to access care and avoid emergency room visits.

Services meriting a cash-only model

The cash-only model is most straightforward for primary care doctors, although many specialty practices have been successful. The Surgery Center of Oklahoma and the Ear & Balance Institute are examples of two highly successful cash-only practices founded by physicians.

Patients are often willing to pay for interventions not covered by insurance, such as cosmetic procedures, fertility treatments, alternative therapies, and certain innovative diagnostics and therapeutics. Many will also pay for services going beyond the scope of their standard insurance coverage, such as enhanced preventive care and comprehensive chronic disease management programs.

Patients who want a high level of privacy or discretion for certain services, such as erectile dysfunction or addiction treatment, may be willing to pay out-of-pocket to avoid discussing these issues with their primary care doctor and to prevent services from appearing on their insurance records.

Apart from the specific medical services offered, numerous other factors weigh into a patients' decision about whether to pay out-of-pocket. They might value faster service and easier appointment scheduling, convenient office location, or increased face-to-face time with the doctor.

Challenges of a cash-only practice

Although a cash-only practice will relieve you of many administrative tasks, it presents a different set of responsibilities. You need to develop and maintain a patient base without being part of insurance networks. Since insurance companies will not predetermine them, you need to put more thought into selecting and pricing your services.

Federal, state, and medical board laws and regulations cannot be ignored simply because a practice does not accept insurance. Health Insurance

Portability and Accountability Act (HIPAA) privacy and security rules apply to all practices transmitting health information electronically. Thorough documentation is a necessity.

You may still need to be familiar with payer requirements for insured patients. Cash-only practices can see Medicare beneficiaries, for example, but this requires obtaining written consent for noncovered services. You can also choose to opt out of Medicare entirely.

FINANCIAL CONSIDERATIONS

There is the potential to earn more in a cash-only practice than you would by billing insurance. A higher income has been eloquently referred to as the "serendipitous byproduct" of running a cash-only practice.[196]

Setting your fees

There is no universal or standard list of retail rates for medical services, so you have a great deal of flexibility in setting the fee schedule for a cash-only practice. You are not bound by government or commercial reimbursement and therefore can charge more than insurance rates.

Avoid setting fees based on what you feel your time and expertise are worth. To determine optimal pricing, research the expected compensation by insurance companies for similar services to get a baseline. Look into the market demand and the fees charged by similar practices in the area. The Free Market Medical Association is a resource on market prices as well.

A sustainable fee structure figures into the financial needs of your practice, including rent, supplies, staffing, and other overhead expenses. Once you have calculated the actual cost of providing a certain service, factor in a margin for profit.

Educating patients on the cash-only model

Be able to articulate your practice's fee structure to patients. Explain in broad terms why the cash-only model makes sense for them and for the practice. Be prepared to discuss how cash fees are different from insurance reimbursement rates and provide a breakdown of various components contributing to the fees charged.

Make your fee schedule easy to access. Provide new patients with a clear policy on fees and payments, including payment expectations, accepted payment methods, potential discounts, and refund policies.

Conveying your practice's value proposition can be helpful to patients. Aspects that add value for patients might be extended appointment times, minimal wait times, access to specific services not covered by insurance, or a focus on customer satisfaction and individualized attention.

Assisting patients in minimizing their out-of-pocket costs

There are several ways to alleviate patients' financial concerns and make cash-pay services more affordable and accessible.

Patients with insurance may be eligible for reimbursement of out-of-pocket costs paid for certain services, but many will be unaware of this or not understand the process. You can provide patients with superbills and instructions on how to submit them to their insurance companies.

For patients with high-deductible health plans, offer guidance on utilizing Health Savings Account funds. You can also give patients the option of getting ancillary services, such as labs, completed at other facilities equipped to bill their insurance.

Offering financing or payment plans can be an attractive benefit for patients, particularly for more costly services. Several third-party financing companies offer loans or credit lines designed for healthcare expenses. In-house payment plans are another option, comprised of a customized payment schedule requiring an initial down payment and subsequent monthly installments.

Medical franchises

Fast food restaurants. Cheap haircuts. Ten-minute oil changes. These come to mind when we think about franchises. But food, personal care, and automotive services are just a few examples among the 775,000 franchise establishments in the United States.[197] Franchises exist in virtually every product and service business line, including the professional disciplines.

FRANCHISING IN HEALTHCARE AND MEDICINE

Healthcare's suitability to franchising has been overlooked and it lags behind other industries; but when done well, healthcare franchises help clinicians deliver care effectively, meet patient expectations, and streamline business operations.

Medical franchises encompass physician-directed urgent care, primary care, and specialty care practices. Some franchises offer healthcare services delivered by other licensed healthcare professionals like physical therapists and chiropractors. Medical support services, such as medical billing, lab testing, and healthcare staffing have also found a place in franchising. There are nonmedical franchises in the health and wellness space that may appeal to physician owners as well, including in-home senior care, fitness centers, massage clinics, and skin care services.

Franchising is sometimes labeled as a form of business investment, but this ignores the fact that the franchisee is a business owner. The owner is responsible for all parts of running the business, not just a financial contribution. It is more accurate to say that franchising is a business strategy that involves a contractual arrangement that permits the franchisee to use the franchisor's business format and to engage in selling goods or services under their set system and brand identity.

There is some evidence to support the value of franchising in healthcare. One study found that healthcare franchises perform as well or better than other healthcare businesses in terms of patient volumes, service quality, utilization, and physical accessibility.[198]

Comparison to independently owned and operated practices

Why not open your own medical practice and develop your own brand? This is a fair question. There are advantages to franchises and to business startups.

Starting a medical practice from scratch requires putting significant effort into planning your business structure, developing processes, and growing recognition from the ground up.

Our training as doctors concentrates on medicine, not business. Franchising provides owners with a proven business model and the independence of owning their practice, but with the assistance and safety net of the franchisor's developed systems and ongoing administrative and strategy support.

Franchises bring brand recognition, meaning that patients may be familiar with the business before your location even opens. Franchisors also engage in market research and pass along insights to franchise owners in the form of system changes, new services offerings, and promotions.

BECOMING A FRANCHISE OWNER

It takes effort to find a franchise with both a good track record and suitability to your location and situation. There is no comprehensive franchise registry, but there are online databases, such as Franchise Direct and the International Franchise Association directory.

As you investigate a franchise opportunity, review the franchise's history, including when it began, how fast it expanded, and how its brand and service offerings changed over time. Look at their geographic footprint. Review their fees, their requirements for new owners, and the training and support they provide. Developed franchise systems include much of this information on their websites.

Along with learning about the franchise itself, research the industry and market, even if you have experience practicing in it. Think about demand, current trends, and what existing businesses are servicing the area.

The next step after identifying a promising franchise is to express your interest. Franchisors will ask for information such as your background and financial situation. Just as you want to make sure the franchise is a good fit for you, they want to make sure you are good fit for the franchise.

They will provide a franchise disclosure document laying out the estimated initial investment, audited financial statements, information on current franchisees, total franchise revenue and profitability estimates, and other key data allowing you to perform due diligence.

To move forward, you will need to sign an agreement with the franchisor. Franchise contracts are complex and hundreds of pages long. They include the obligations and duties of both parties, fee structure, territory rights, trademark use permissions, performance and advertising standards, and service requirements. There are also confidentiality, noncompetition, security, and indemnity clauses.

With a signed agreement, you can take steps to open your business and participate in the training offered by the franchisor.

LAWS AND REGULATIONS IN MEDICAL FRANCHISING

As with healthcare, franchising is highly regulated. The Federal Trade Commission oversees franchising via the Franchise Rule, which aims to help prospective buyers make an informed decision about franchise ownership by requiring disclosure of certain information.

Some states have their own laws, including franchise filing requirements, rules regarding franchise offers and sales, warning periods prior to termination, and stipulations related to litigation that may arise from franchise ownership.

Healthcare laws that affect franchising

Franchising and medical law have a potential for conflict related to medical practice control by a party who is not a medical professional. However, being a physician owner makes it easier to avoid conflicts and mitigates risks to some extent.

In certain states, laws governing the corporate practice of medicine prohibit a business entity from employing licensed healthcare providers in a manner that could influence their professional judgment. Some franchises use a management services model in which one business entity (often a professional corporation) provides the franchise's medical professional services and another entity provides the administrative infrastructure.

A good franchise will have a strong handle on relevant state and federal laws and will help you ensure your business is compliant. Depending on the medical services offered, some franchises have requirements related to the professional licensing of owners and employees. For example, they may require a minimum of one licensed practitioner on staff to conform with state requirements.

INCORPORATING FRANCHISING INTO AN UNCONVENTIONAL CAREER

Besides owning and working in a franchise business full-time, physicians have other ways to incorporate the franchise model into their careers.

Franchise ownership as a side gig

Some owners hire employees to manage the business's day-to-day operations, even operating the franchise as a side-business while maintaining employment elsewhere. This passive type of ownership is easier with a franchise business that does not provide any services requiring a medical license. However, even if your franchise is a medical practice, such as an urgent care center, you can limit your personal involvement by hiring another physician or APP to provide patient care.

Turning your medical practice into a franchise

Physicians who own a successful medical practice must decide how to grow it. Bringing in additional providers, expanding their scope of services, and opening a new location are all options. So is franchising.

Organic growth requires continued capital investments and direct internal team management, whereas growing as a franchise means new business owners will provide the investments and resources to expand the brand.

The key characteristics that make a medical practice suitable for franchising are profitability, an ongoing demand for the healthcare services, and geographic adaptability. You need to have defined processes for all operational aspects. Thriving franchises have something setting them apart from their competition. In medicine, this could be a more afford-able treatment, an exceptional patient experience, or a unique service menu.

If done right, turning your medical practice into a franchise is a triple win. You win by growing your business. Your franchisees win by benefit-ing from the brand and systems you have already developed and proven. Patients win with improved access to the care they need or want.

FINANCIAL CONSIDERATIONS

The infamous fees associated with owning a franchise deter many aspir-ing business owners from franchise ownership; however, each franchise fee serves a purpose meant to help both the franchisee and the franchisor.

Startup costs

The franchise fee is an initial payment that awards you the right to oper-ate a business in compliance with the franchisor's system. It also allows the franchisor to train and support you. Although there is a wide range, average startup fees are between $25,000 and $50,000.

Other startup costs are the clinic or store build-out, furniture, equipment, supplies, and other expenses. Total startup costs for the least-expensive franchises are under $50,000, while the most expensive are well over $1 million. Franchisors will provide an estimate of total start-up costs to prospective owners. Many have a set minimum available liquid capital for new owners.

Fees and expenses

Owners pay the franchise an ongoing percent of their gross sales, known as a royalty fee. Royalties range from 4% to 12%. This is what generates a profit for the franchisor and allows them to innovate, refine their busi-ness systems in response to industry trends, maintain relationships with suppliers, and so forth.

Many franchisors charge an advertising fee. This comes as a percentage of gross sales (commonly 1% to 4%) or a flat fee. It goes toward creating and implementing marketing and advertising campaigns which will help drive your sales.

Most recurring expenses are the same as those incurred by independent businesses, such as rent, utilities, employee wages, insurance, and taxes.

Revenue and profits

Franchisors are prohibited from dictating prices charged by franchisees; however, they may offer recommended pricing. Franchisors also do not guarantee profitability to franchise owners. It is up to owners to take advantage of the franchise's training and support and to run their business well. That said, businesses become franchises because they found success with the franchise system.

MEDICAL FRANCHISE EXAMPLES

With more than 250 locations, American Family Care is among the oldest and largest medical franchise. Its flagship service is urgent care, although it also provides primary care and occupational health services. They are also among the most expensive healthcare franchises to open; startup costs are between $1 million and $1.4 million, which includes a $60,000 initial franchise fee and an estimated $500,000 clinic construction cost. To cover these costs, new owners must have a $1.2 million net worth and $550,000 in liquid cash. After startup, owners are responsible for a 6% royalty fee based on gross sales.

A less costly option is The DRIPBaR, which is an IV therapy clinic franchised in 2019 with over 200 locations. They have a $55,000 franchise fee, startup costs ranging from about $130,000 to $330,000, and a 7% royalty fee. Prospective owners must have a $300,000 net worth and $125,000 in liquid capital.

Other large medical franchise brands are OrthoNOW, Your Kid's Urgent Care, and Family Quick Care. Arcpoint Labs, Fastest Labs, and USA Mobile Drug Testing are successful lab test franchises. Franchising within the aesthetics industry is common; brands include Just Tattoo Removal, The Laser Lounge Spa, and Dermacare.

44. Membership medicine

Looking over your monthly credit card statements, you probably see at least a couple recurring charges for subscription services like Netflix, Spotify, HelloFresh, or Stitch Fix. If so, you're in good company — more than three-quarters of adults have subscription services.[199]

In a subscription-based service, the customer pays a recurring fee to access a particular service or product. This model is growing in popularity across industries and can even be applied to medical care.

MEMBERSHIP PRACTICE MODELS

Membership medical practices are growing 3% to 7% per year.[200] There is significant interest among physicians in transitioning to this model, with 9% reporting they plan to switch to a subscription-based practice in the next one to three years.[201]

Direct primary care

In a direct primary care medical practice, patients pay a flat fee on a monthly or annual basis to receive a range of primary care services. There are more than 2,100 such practices in the United States.[202] A typical patient fee is about $100 per month but can be as low as $70.[203] This fee ordinarily covers unlimited doctor visits, basic lab tests, and certain basic procedures such as skin biopsies and joint injections. Many practices offer other services for an additional fee.

The name *direct primary care* originates from the idea that patients have direct access to their primary care providers without involving a third party, such as an insurance company, to intervene. As a result, these practices can provide more personalized care to patients and decrease administrative burdens for physicians, possibly reducing reduce overhead expenses by more than 40%.[204]

Direct primary care practices can be solo or group practices with multiple providers and staff. The patient panel size also varies, but most practices aim to keep their panels small to allow for more individualized attention and care.

The typical direct primary care patent is a mid-life adult with an annual household income less than $100,000.[205] Although these practices usually don't accept insurance, most patients have insurance. Some have high-deductible plans and prefer to pay a membership fee instead of chipping away at their insurance deductible for the same services. Many feel the ease of accessing their doctor and covered services are worth the expense.

Concierge medicine

Concierge medicine, also known as *retainer medicine*, is a model in which patients pay a membership fee to access medical services beyond what is customarily offered in a traditional medical practice. The name comes from the concept of a hotel concierge who provides personalized service to guests.

Some concierge practices charge an annual or monthly fee for the physician's routine medical services; others offer a subscription for enhanced services, such as longer appointments or other specialized care. There are also hybrid models with tier fee structures.

The average monthly fee for concierge medicine is $200 per member.[206] This is higher than direct primary care practices, since most concierge practices offer specialty medical care rather than primary care, including 24-hour access to a physician. Although both models aim to provide personalized attention, concierge practices focus more on added-value and service-oriented care, such as private waiting rooms and other amenities. Not surprisingly, concierge practices attract a wealthier population than direct primary care practices, with a typical annual household income between $125,000 and $250,000 a year.[207]

Other, less common types of membership models include limited-service membership and employer-sponsored subscription healthcare services.

BENEFITS AND CHALLENGES

Membership medicine offers flexibility and reduced administrative burdens. With upfront effort, it is a more stable and predictable revenue source compared to the traditional fee-for-service model, which can have fluctuations in patient volume and insurance reimbursements.

The same benefits for physicians also lead to benefits for patients. In one study, concierge patients were more likely to report that their physician spent sufficient time with them in clinical encounters.[208] In another, a whopping 97% reported satisfaction with the care they received from their direct primary care doctor.[209] Patients also appreciate more tailored care without a focus on stringent insurance coverage policies.

Legal risks like compliance with healthcare laws may increase with this practice type. Subscription-based medical practices have, at times, been recognized as a type of medical insurance plan, leading to requirements for them to meet certain health insurance regulations.

Logistical challenges such as managing patient panels, scheduling appointments, and meeting patients' expectations may be more pronounced. The doctor must be more readily available during nonbusiness hours. Because it can be difficult for prospective patients to understand the membership payment model, marketing strategy may be tricky.

CAREER PATHS FOR MEMBERSHIP MEDICINE

Physicians of nearly all medical specialties can use a membership model, although primary care doctors may find it to be a more natural career path than others. In concierge medicine, roughly half of physicians are in primary care, yet many do not offer a full spectrum of primary care services. The lowest prevalence of concierge practices is among surgical subspecialties.[210]

You can build a solo or group practice from the ground up or transition an existing practice. One option to assist with the startup or transition is to partner with a third-party provider who offers a pre-set membership business model and support, in exchange for a fee or profit-share, similar to a franchise.

When transitioning a practice from a conventional model to a membership model, give patients ample heads up. Explain the new model and its benefits and be ready to address their concerns. Bear in mind that even with stellar communication, you will retain only a portion of your patient panel; however, you can generate a similar profit with a smaller panel size than a traditional practice.

Employment in a membership-based practice is an option for those without an interest in practice ownership. Expect to earn a salary equivalent to same-specialty physicians in a traditional practice.

The American College of Private Physicians and the Direct Primary Care Alliance are resources for more information.

Micropractice model

Bulky practices with large reception areas, multiple exam rooms, and numerous support staff are not the only path to success. Smaller, agile practices can offer job satisfaction and financial stability, while still providing high-quality, personalized patient care.

THE BASICS OF A MICROPRACTICE

A micropractice is an independent medical practice designed to be lean and patient-focused. The majority are run by one physician who has complete control over the work environment and the care provided. They focus on optimizing the smallest functional work unit capable of delivering good care.

Because limiting expenses is a priority, micropractices have few tangible assets. The office (if there is one) has one or two rooms. Most have no staff other than the physician. Any other staff have wide-ranging responsibilities involving both patient care and administrative tasks.

The doctor is responsible for many, if not all, business operations. Being personally responsible for scheduling, check-in, rooming, ancillary services, billing, and advertising — on top of patient care — is a lot of work, but this allows for ample control and flexibility. For example, there can be more variation in appointment lengths and clinic hours than is feasible in a standard medical practice.

The phrase *ideal medical practice* is used to describe this practice style. This comes from the belief that, for a medical practice to deliver care that is truly patient-centered, it needs to be free from any obstacles standing between the patient and the doctor.

UNCONVENTIONAL ASPECTS OF MICROPRACTICES

Micropractices challenge the traditional model of medicine in that they do not focus on treating as many patients as possible or offering a broad array of services that require support staff and equipment. In many cases, the streamlined nature of a micropractice allows the doctor to spend more time with each patient than would be possible in a typical outpatient practice, and remain financially afloat. This translates to improved patient relationships, a loyal patient panel, and a strong reputation.

The United States has seen a shift toward large healthcare systems and corporations buying out small physician-owned practices. By keeping costs low and maintaining efficiency, the micropractice offers a hedge against the risk of being swallowed up or driven out of business by large systems. Low overhead costs allow for care delivery at a fraction of the cost, making micropractices competitive in the current market.

Micropractices also benefit from their agility. Owners can make decisions without having to consult with higher-ups or tackle bureaucratic processes. They can quickly respond to changes in medical practice standards, regulations, and patient needs and adjust their operations accordingly. There is no need to train staff on how to implement changes because there are no staff members to train.

Another characteristic of micropractices is their reliance on technology rather than personnel to keep the practice running smoothly. Owners choose technologies with two goals in mind: to keep costs low and allow them to spend more time with patients. These tools can include scheduling apps, HIPAA-compliant patient communication solutions, and coding and billing software.

Physician satisfaction with this model is high. In a survey of micropractice owners, one respondent stated, "I would not trade this model for anything short of bankruptcy." Another remarked, "I have never been as happy practicing medicine as I am now."[211]

STARTING A MICROPRACTICE

Primary care specialties are the most suitable for starting a micropractice, although with creativity and careful planning, physicians of almost any specialty can use this model. Successful micropractices tend to have a narrow scope of services, since their minimal equipment and space makes it difficult to do procedures, labs, or specialized testing.

The ease of starting a micropractice is among its greatest benefits. There is far less to think about in terms of planning and implementation compared to a traditional medical practice. A barebones practice can operate as a sole proprietorship and be opened with merely an exam room, a few pieces of furniture, a computer, and a way to take payments. In one report, a micropractice owner went from concept to seeing patients within three months.[212]

Optional startup steps include registering as a formal business entity with the state (such as a limited liability company or professional corporation), credentialling with health insurance companies, and building a practice website.

The EHR is at the heart of a micropractice and is one of the highest recurring expenses. Look into several EHR options but avoid selecting the cheapest option. Other technologies, such as scheduling and billing software, can pick up where the EHR leaves off and support other processes. Determine how each technology will fit into your practice's processes or how your processes will adjust to fit with the new technology.

GROWING A MICROPRACTICE

Some micropractice owners have no desire to grow their practice beyond a certain patient panel size. There is nothing wrong with this approach, but others may want to accept additional insurance plans, move to a bigger office space, buy a piece of diagnostic equipment, or grow in other ways. Regardless of the goal, growth should take place in a way that maintains low overhead costs.

For a physician running a micropractice without any employees, everything falls onto their plate: copying and faxing medical records, spending time on hold with insurance companies, and placing orders for supplies. Unexpected situations inevitably arise, and someone needs to handle them. This is fine early on in your venture; however, as your patient panel increases, it may become challenging to manage everything. When the administrative and operational tasks feel like a burden, it is time to hire an assistant to allow you to spend more time providing billable services.

Collaborating with other micropractice owners is another way to grow while maintaining your practices' autonomy. Creating teams for backup and sharing resources such as an EKG machine or billing service can reduce costs without letting go of your status as an independent solo practice.

Exiting a micropractice can be difficult. In most cases, the physician *is* the business. Because there are few tangible assets to sell, prospects for finding a purchaser for the practice are limited. Some physicians may choose to simply dissolve their small business.

FINANCIAL CONSIDERATIONS

Low startup costs are a notable advantage of micropractices; reports have cited startup costs of less than $10,000. Others are in the range of $25,000 to $50,000,[213] which may seem hefty, but pales in comparison to the average medical practice startup expense of closer to $100,000.

Overhead expenses are in the range of 10% to 15%[214,215] on the lower end and 30% to 35% on the higher end. Compare this to an average overhead of 60% for a traditional primary care practice, of which staff salaries and physical office space are the largest expenses.

Revenue per patient varies depending on the services offered. Anecdotal evidence suggests micropractices can be financially successful while simultaneously being affordable for patients. One family physician micropractice owner who "does everything from running the website to answering the phone to cleaning the exam room," is able to charge $35 per appointment thanks to the micropractice model.[216] A financial benefit of micropractices is they can be profitable soon after opening; you won't wait years to see a return on your investment.

Most physicians who own micropractices earn less than they could in a traditional practice arrangement.[211,217] However, the income can be reasonable, especially when taking improved work satisfaction into account. Moreover, the inflation-adjusted average income for primary care physicians has actually decreased in recent years,[33] making the financials of owning a micropractice more appealing.

Virtual practices

In 1925, the cover of *Science and Invention* magazine pictured a doctor diagnosing a patient by radio .[218] This was the inception of telemedicine. Its uptake was slow; only 15% of office-based physicians were using telemedicine prior to the COVID-19 pandemic. But the pandemic catalyzed progress and, by 2021, this figure had risen to 87%.[219]

Today, having a good "webside" manner is nearly as important as having a good bedside manner. A career incorporating telemedicine is typical for physicians; but most telemedicine is integrated into existing healthcare systems or practices that also provide in-person patient care. Jobs in which doctors see patients only by telemedicine via a fully virtual practice are less conventional.

A CASE FOR THE MEDICAL VIRTUALIST

In some situations, telemedicine can replace, rather than supplement, care delivered in person. Its benefits to patients and to the healthcare system include effective management for a range of clinical conditions,[220] improved clinical outcomes,[221] and cost savings.[222] There are numerous advantages for physicians and their practices, as well, including flexible scheduling, the option to work from home, fewer appointment cancellations, low overhead expenses, and streamlined patient communication.

A practice that exclusively uses telemedicine can enhance these benefits through efficiency and the economies of scale. A handful of healthcare systems and insurers, including UnitedHealth Group and Firefly Health, share this outlook, as demonstrated by their "virtual-first" programs.

Internal medicine physicians, family medicine physicians, psychiatrists, and radiologists are in high demand for virtual practices, although many other specialties are suitable and sought after. Even physicians in procedural specialties can have a successful virtual practice by adapting which services they provide or which conditions they treat. The concept of a medical virtualist has actually been proposed as a cross-disciplinary medical sub-specialty.[223]

WORKING FOR TELEMEDICINE COMPANIES

Telemedicine companies provide a technological platform and healthcare services through virtual consultations. As such, they need physicians to evaluate, diagnose, and treat patients remotely.

Direct-to-consumer telemedicine companies connect patients directly with providers. They operate through real-time videoconferencing, phone calls, text chat, and other communication channels. The most prominent players in this space are Teladoc, Amwell, and Doctor on Demand, although there are many others. Each has its own approach to patient flow and other processes, each has its own target markets, geographic reach, and pricing models.

Once focused on primary care services, the telemedicine industry has expanded to include a growing number of specialties and clinical niches. Some companies offer online education resources, prescription delivery, online counseling, and other support services in addition to virtual doctor visits.

Rather than marketing their services to individual patients, some companies provide business-to-business services to organizations that purchase telemedicine on behalf of patients. An employer, for example, may offer telemedicine as an employee benefit, or a government agency may contract with the telemedicine company to service a specific population or region. Health insurance companies partner with telemedicine providers to offer virtual consultations to their plan members.

Telemedicine physician panels

Most telemedicine companies manage a physician panel, either through contracting or employment, to provide virtual care services. Many platforms are flexible in their scheduling options, allowing physicians to choose their own shifts or set their availability based on their preferences and commitments.

The number of patients each physician receives depends on patient demand, specialty, availability, and other factors. Many doctors join the panels of multiple telemedicine companies to increase their volume, making it possible to turn multiple virtual care contract positions into the equivalent of a full-time job.

Most telemedicine companies have a two-entity business structure for managing their operations and delivering patient care: One entity handles administrative tasks, insurance billing, marketing, and other support services, and a separate professional corporation or similar entity provides the actual patient care.

Finding jobs with telemedicine companies

For some larger companies, any qualified physician can join the panel through a streamlined onboarding process that starts by filling out an online form. Smaller companies tend to utilize a standard job application and interview process. Many post openings on their websites and on job boards, although they are increasingly relying on search firms and recruiters.

All telemedicine companies need clinical leadership. Chief medical officer, medical director, and other positions are options for those who want to get further involved in virtual care.

Other virtual medical services

Some healthcare services provided through virtual means do not involve direct communication with patients, but physicians are hired for prescribing, reviewing, and providing oversight.

In direct-to-consumer lab testing, such as that offered by LabCorp Ondemand and Everlywell, customers select and order lab tests from an online platform. The physician's involvement comes in the form of test requisition, as some states require a licensed healthcare provider to review and approve certain tests.

Telepharmacy and prescription medication delivery services sometimes offer certain medications to customers without an initial face-to-face interaction. These could include refills of legacy medications for well-controlled chronic conditions or common treatments for straightforward acute conditions. Physicians review and approve medication orders remotely and determine the need for a patient visit.

VIRTUAL PRIVATE PRACTICE

It is logistically and financially viable for individual physicians to establish and operate an entirely virtual practice. This means no brick-and-mortar office, onsite staff, large equipment, or commute to work. With 92% of adults owning a cell phone and 84% using the internet,[224] patients, too, are equipped to seek care from a virtual practice.

One key to starting a successful virtual practice is to gain clarity on the services to be offered and the patients to be served. Once decided, you need to choose from one of many available telemedicine platforms. They differ in terms of their pricing models, user interface, level of customization, and integration capabilities with EHRs and other systems. There are even free platforms, such as Doxy.me and Doximity Dialer.

Virtual practices rely on technology for all aspects of delivering medical services, not just the teleconferencing piece. You will need to select tools for scheduling, documentation, secure messaging, e-prescribing, and payment processing.

When choosing technologies, speak with other physician users about their experiences, ask for product demos, and sign up for free trial periods. Gauge the quality of customer support services. Verify that the vendor will help you maintain HIPAA compliance and will sign a Business Associate Agreement. In terms of cost, think beyond the monthly fee; there may be extra charges for customizations or added features, transactions costs, or price increases when your use reaches a certain level.

LICENSING, LAWS, AND LOGISTICS

There is no federal law governing the practice of telehealth. It is regulated at the state level with some states having specific rules about what is permissible while others remaining silent on the issue.

You must be licensed in the state where your patient is located. Therefore, multiple state licenses are necessary if you wish to provide telemedicine to patients in multiple states. This can be costly and time-consuming, but worth the hassle for the wider reach and larger patient volume. Some states have implemented special telehealth licensing provisions or reciprocal agreements facilitating cross-state practice. A handful offer specific licenses to physicians practicing only telemedicine in the state.

Insurance billing and reimbursement for telemedicine visits has some nuances. Many commercial and government payers reimburse telemedicine services, but they have different eligibility criteria and payment methodologies. There are 42 states with laws governing private payer telehealth reimbursement, with most states requiring payers to reimburse telemedicine visits at parity with in-person visits. All Medicaid programs provide reimbursement for live video sessions, and 28 reimburse for asynchronous telemedicine services. Medicare policies for telehealth are in flux at the time of this writing.

The American Telemedicine Association, the Society for Telemedicine and Telehealth, and various medical specialty societies are resources to assist in effectively and lawfully practicing virtually.

COMPENSATION AND FINANCIAL CONSIDERATIONS

A common compensation arrangement for contracted telemedicine panel physicians is a flat fee per completed encounter. In 2023, this ranged from about $25 to $40, with most visits taking between five and 15 minutes. Some companies pay an hourly rate. Compensation may vary by specialty, demand, or other factors, and may not be negotiable.

The profit potential for a virtual practice can be comparable to an in-person practice providing similar services. For self-pay practices, setting fees is no different from a cash-based brick and mortar clinic; however, virtual practices often have the advantage of reduced overhead costs, which can allow for more competitive pricing. The average price charged directly to patients for a telemedicine visit is about $79.[225] Most visits fall in the range of $40 to $100.

PHYSICIAN PROFILE

Subaila Zia, MD, MBA, FCCP

Founder and Chief Executive Officer of Telemedora

Practice setting

Telemedora is a healthcare startup with a mission to bring quality care to patients in multiple states by leveraging technology. It focuses on providing patients direct, personalized services via virtual care, including virtual sleep evaluations and home sleep testing. Through its business-to-business arm, it helps healthcare organizations to bridge gaps in pulmonary, critical care, and sleep medicine specialty care via a hybrid of onsite services, test interpretations, and virtual care.

Employment type and schedule

Telemedora is an early-stage start-up so, as the founder and chief executive officer, I wear many hats. My work schedule is adapted based upon where I am needed the most.

Patient population and clinical work

The demographics and medical needs of the patients I treat depend on what client I am working with. The patients who come to Telemedora directly are mainly adults with chronic sleep disorders like sleep apnea, restless leg syndrome, and insomnia. Consults from the hospitals and medical practices we contract with tend to have more acute or complex needs. They may have respiratory failure, sepsis, or chronic lung diseases like asthma and pulmonary fibrosis. Their level of care ranges from ambulatory to ICU.

My time spent on patient care varies with patient volumes and the needs of the healthcare organizations we are contracted with. Some weeks it is over 90% clinical and other weeks it is more of a mix of clinical and nonclinical responsibilities.

A typical day at work

As a physician entrepreneur, one thing is certain: uncertainty! There is never a dull moment. My daily work schedule is fairly dynamic and it gets adapted according to urgency, potential impact, and opportunities. Gone are the days of set schedules. Basically, after addressing the most pressing matters, I dedicate my energy to a broad mix of activities including patient care, business development, innovation, marketing, strategy, and learning.

Unconventional aspects

One thing that sets my work apart from that of most physicians is there is a lot of risk involved in terms of financial, professional, and personal areas. My focus is on finding innovative ways to positively impact people on a larger scale — especially people with sleep disorders. Although I dedicate most of my waking hours to building Telemedora, I get to learn exciting new things daily and then I try to incorporate that learning into my daily activities.

Sleep disorders such as sleep apnea impact one billion people across the globe and, of those, at least 70 million are in the United States. But access to sleep specialists is limited, with only one board-certified sleep medicine physician for every 45,000 people in the United States. Many healthcare facilities have a gap in specialty coverage. This gives me the opportunity to both address a patient's need and solve a pain point for clients.

Without the usual safety net of perks like paid time off, bonuses, and benefits that come with an employed position, I find it important to embrace uncertainty and the "why" behind what I'm doing.

Best parts of the job

The thing I enjoy the most is the ability to reimagine care so I can make a difference in a patient's life and have impact on a bigger scale. I also enjoy the ability to direct my energy toward a meaningful goal that I am very passionate about. When patients express appreciation for the care they receive or send positive feedback, it makes this uphill endeavor worth the sweat. Also, I get to be part of some very cool events. For instance, in summer of 2023, my startup made it to the finals of a global telehealth pitch competition. Qualifying for this as a female minority physician entrepreneur made this even more special.

Challenges faced

It is challenging to get buy-in to the idea that virtual care is care. There is also reluctance to embrace new technologies, even when they are approved by the FDA. Another challenge is simply resistance to change. Some people in healthcare talk about wanting change, yet the same people are afraid of change.

Qualifications and skills needed for this career

The necessary medical qualifications for virtual care depend on the type of care you are providing. My triple-board certification in pulmonary, critical care, and sleep medicine required seven years of training after medical school. You need to be tech-savvy and embrace technology. Having good webside manner plays a vital role in virtual care, as well.

To be an entrepreneur in the virtual medicine space, you need the courage to take calculated risks, resilience to rise above challenges, grit to keep going, and superb time management skills. You need to be a lifelong learner and embrace technology.

Obtaining an MBA gave me the knowledge of the business of medicine. MIT's Artificial Intelligence in Healthcare certification allowed me to gain better insights into the applications of artificial intelligence within the digital health space.

Advice for students and physicians

Be ready for the grind. There are no short-cuts when you embark on a practice or healthcare endeavor. Adaptability and flexibility are essential for entrepreneurs to allow for personal and professional growth. It is okay to fail. Failure comes with the territory of entrepreneurship. Get up, brush up, and get back in the game!

It is a privilege to be a clinician and it is even more of a privilege to be a physician entrepreneur. Do what is right. Doing the right thing makes all the difference. Be this differentiating factor.

Be able to live happily while living well below your means after finishing training so you save enough to fund your dream project. Most people underestimate the amount of money required to get any business up and running. Regardless of what work you are doing, keep investing in your personal and professional growth.

CAREERS WITH UNCONVENTIONAL JOB CLASSIFICATIONS AND WORK ARRANGEMENTS

Physicians work an average of 50 hours per week.[25] That is 11 more hours than the typical working American. Spending too many hours at work is one of the top contributors to burnout.[226] Various unconventional job classifications and work arrangements allow for less time spent at work while still progressing your career.

Some alternative work arrangements do require a full-time commitment, but come with other benefits that ultimately increase job satisfaction or work-life balance. These can be flexibility in scheduling, the ability to pick and choose your tasks or assignments, or having extended time off mid-career.

You may have heard of the employment types described in the upcoming chapters, but perhaps did not consider them to be viable options in the medical profession. More and more, medical professionals — even those engaged in clinical work — are seeking out or negotiating these flexible and adaptable arrangements.

Flexible and alternative work schedules

A gradual movement away from full-time employment structured around the standard workday has been ongoing for decades. Workers want flexibility regarding when and how much they work. You may not feel this movement applies to you as a doctor; however, healthcare has experienced some of the fastest growth in nonstandard work arrangements across all industries.[227] Many arrangements are available to physicians who actively seek them out. These come in the form of flexible workweeks, alternative work schedules, and breaks in work continuity.

FLEXIBLE WORKWEEKS

Inflexible schedules are a leading cause of job dissatisfaction among doctors,[228] so flexibility should be a factor in your job search. A flexible workweek, or "flextime," schedule grants the autonomy to tailor your work hours to meet your individual needs or preferences, while adhering to management's parameters. A major benefit is better work-life balance without reducing your total work hours or requiring a pay cut.

A popular type of flexible schedule, the compressed workweek, condenses the standard weekly workload into fewer than the typical five workdays. This can take various forms, such as four 10-hour days and an additional day off each week. If four working days per week is not possible, another option is working nine-hour blocks on most days, resulting in a day off every other week.

Similarly, a variable workweek distributes hours differently across different days. You can choose to work longer hours on some days and fewer on others. For instance, you might add an hour to your schedule Monday through Thursday to have a half-day clinic on Fridays.

Primarily due to the need for prescheduled patient appointments, flexible scheduling options do not always align seamlessly with clinical work. The most fitting jobs combine patient care with administrative responsibilities. Physicians working in outpatient clinics may use their core hours for patient appointments while allocating flexible hours to administrative tasks.

Even for full-time clinicians with demanding patient care responsibilities, some creativity can make flextime scheduling feasible. Collaboration with APPs to handle patient appointments during designated off-hours or working with a neighboring practice to manage urgent patient calls during specific times are possible approaches.

Despite the challenges, flexible scheduling is gaining popularity in medicine. A 2023 survey found that 59% of hospitalist groups had implemented increased scheduling flexibility over the prior year.[229]

JOBS WITH ALTERNATIVE WORK SCHEDULES

In contrast to flextime, some less conventional jobs have a rigid schedule, but with hours falling outside the standard workday.

Working as a nocturnist

More than three-quarters of hospitalist programs now incorporate dedicated night-shift physicians (known as nocturnists) into their staffing models.[230] Most nocturnist opportunities are in internal medicine and pediatrics, although some hospitals employ nocturnists for busy specialty services such as intensive care, cardiology, and surgery.

There are a few compelling reasons for working as a nocturnist. One is the potential for higher pay, with nocturnists earning 15% more than their daytime counterparts, on average.[231] In some cases, this higher salary actually requires shorter shifts or fewer shifts per month than is required for daytime hospitalists. The nocturnist schedule opens more daytime hours for personal priorities.

Night shifts involve fewer meetings, rounds, teaching responsibilities, and administrative tasks compared to daytime shifts, allowing the nocturnist to focus more on the practice of medicine itself. They also offer more autonomy, since the nocturnist is one of the few — if not the only — physicians on duty at night. Unlike the rotating shift work common in emergency medicine, nocturnists have the benefit of a consistent night schedule and do not need to constantly adjust their sleep patterns.

After-hours and weekend work

After-hours and weekend-only work can serve as either a primary or supplemental job. These positions, which span inpatient and outpatient settings, are found in urgent care centers, hospitals, and physician groups seeking coverage for their full-time providers. Shifts can range from a few hours to a full 24 hours.

After-hours opportunities are usually associated with moonlighting, often viewed as a means for residents and fellows to earn extra income; however, attending physicians are great candidates for these positions, especially ones requiring board certification. Internal medicine physicians earn the most through secondary work of this type, averaging $64,000 in extra income per year. Family medicine physicians and cardiologists are not far behind.[232]

As-needed and on-call jobs

In the past, doctors were perpetually on call and were expected to respond to their own patients' needs around the clock. Now, most healthcare organizations have structured on-call rotations. This has created jobs where doctors are contracted to fill in when the need arises, which might be during vacations or unforeseen staffing shortages.

As-needed positions go by a few names in healthcare, including as-needed, per diem, and backup. Some institutions maintain float pools of clinicians to sporadically cover shifts. Call-only positions can involve reporting to the hospital when needed, or they can be exclusively taking phone calls from home and giving verbal orders.

Practices using as-needed and on-call doctors range from primary care group practices to transplant surgery programs.

FLEXIBILITY IN WORK CONTINUITY

A final type of work flexibility allows for variations in continuity of employment, including both shorter and longer breaks from clinical practice. Sometimes we take breaks out of necessity, like for medical leave of absence. Breaks can also be deliberate, to help align our careers with professional goals, personal aspirations, or life circumstances.

Seasonal work

Seasonal work is commonplace in some industries. Retail stores hire help for the holidays and accounting firms hire extra staff during tax season, for example. We don't regularly think about seasonal jobs in medicine, but they do exist and can be excellent for balancing clinical practice with extended time off.

Seasonal positions are utilized when the demand for healthcare services varies throughout the year. Organizations may hire staff directly or temporary staffing agencies. Hospitals, emergency departments, and clinics in and around tourist destinations are possibilities. Certain national parks, including Yosemite and Yellowstone, operate seasonal medical clinics. Some hospitals and offices strategically hire extra clinical staff to manage surges in patient volume during specific times of the year, like flu season. Some large summer camps hire seasonal physicians to oversee nursing staff and occasionally treat campers directly.

One advantage of seasonal work over most locum tenens jobs is the potential for recurring assignments year after year.

Sabbaticals

In a traditional career trajectory, we work continuously until we retire. This approach is not the best for everyone. An alternative is taking mini-retirements or extended breaks throughout our working years.

The most common way for professionals to take career breaks is through sabbaticals. A sabbatical is a prolonged leave from work with an agreement that the employee will return to their same job afterward. Most sabbaticals are for somewhere between one and three months, although longer sabbaticals of up to a full year are not unheard of. Employees often retain benefits such as health insurance during the sabbatical; less commonly, they continue to receive a salary.

Sabbaticals are historically associated with universities and academic positions, but are increasingly offered in the private sector, with 11% of employers offering unpaid sabbaticals and 5% offering paid sabbaticals.[233]

Some employers without formal policies may allow for sabbaticals on a case-by-case basis.

Engaging in research, obtaining further training, completing an internship program, volunteering, and traveling are all possible pursuits during a sabbatical. You are most likely to gain approval for a sabbatical by presenting a well-defined plan outlining how it will contribute to your work abilities and professional development.

An alternative to taking a formal sabbatical is to simply quit your job, take an extended break, and then begin a new job. This requires careful financial planning and the stress of a job search but provides more flexibility in timing. Some physicians are hesitant to take unstructured time off from their career for fear of leaving an unjustified gap on their resume; however, this should not be a concern when the time off is deliberate.

FINDING AND NEGOTIATING ALTERNATIVE WORK SCHEDULES

Positions with flexible alternative work schedules may take some time to find, but begin your search by using multiple channels, including job boards, company websites, professional organizations, and your network. This is a situation in which larger bureaucracies may be preferable over small companies. Established corporations with many employees are more likely to have policies relating to flexible work arrangements and are more likely to direct efforts toward improving division of labor and hand-off coordination.

When evaluating any position as a secondary job, review the contract from your primary employer to avoid violating any noncompete agreements or other stipulations related to outside work.

To negotiate a schedule change with your current employer, start by reviewing any existing internal policies and procedures regarding scheduling. You may need to negotiate an informal agreement based on the buy-in and good-will of your supervisor. Success in these negotiations depends on how effectively you present your proposal for the adjusted schedule. Be prepared to address questions about how the schedule change will impact your work, other staff members, and patient care.

Some state and local governments have implemented legislation pertaining to flexible working arrangements. For instance, San Francisco's Family Friendly Workplace Ordinance allows workers to request flexible or predictable working arrangements to fulfill caregiving responsibilities, and Vermont has similar legislation permitting workers to request workplace flexibility for any reason. These laws can be an added tool in your planning and negotiations.

Locum tenens

Derived from the Latin term "to hold a place," locum tenens refers to temporarily taking over for another physician in their absence or in an unfilled position. This arrangement has become prevalent, with 94% of hospitals and healthcare administrators reporting they use locum tenens physicians.[234]

Only a small fraction of physicians engage in locum tenens work, but nearly all who do are pleased with their experience.[235] This career path offers the chance to take control of work-life balance while exploring new places, settings, and opportunities.

PRACTICING AS A LOCUM TENENS PHYSICIAN

Locum tenens physicians provide medical care to patients based on an agreed-upon scope of services and schedule. The specific duties vary depending on assignment, facility needs, and other factors. There is a great deal of variety in locums work, such that it can appeal to physicians with many different timelines, career goals, and personal situations.

Locums work can take place in hospitals, outpatient clinics, private group practices, and, less commonly, other settings like long-term care facilities. Assignment length can be as short as a few days and as long as a year or more. In assignments referred to as *locum to permanent*, organizations hire a locums physician with the goal of eventually hiring them for a long-term, employed position.

Locums work comes with flexibility and a bit of adventure. It also offers independence, allowing you to have more control over how, when, and where you practice medicine. Early-career physicians can use locum assignments to explore different practice settings or to test drive an organization or location before making a commitment. It can be a way to experience new places while still earning an income and paying off student loans. For mid- to late-career physicians, locums can offer a change of pace and place. Locum assignments can bridge a gap between full-time jobs without taking a financial hit. They can also serve as a transition to retirement while continuing to practice on a part-time basis.

There is a misconception that locum physicians deliver lower-quality care in comparison to permanent physicians; however, studies show that treatment by locum physicians and permanent physicians results in similar patient outcomes.[236,237]

GETTING INTO LOCUM TENENS

Locums work requires medical licensure in the state where you will be working. Board certification is needed in most cases. There is work available for physicians of all specialties, with the most in-demand specialties being family medicine, OB/GYN, cardiology, psychiatry, internal medicine, anesthesiology, and general surgery.[238] Experience requirements vary, but many positions require a minimum of two years of clinical experience and may require life support certifications.

Agencies and direct contracting

You will need to decide whether to work with a staffing agency or to contract directly with a healthcare organization. By far the more popular route is to go through an agency. Agencies match physicians to assignments, but also coordinate the placement and onboarding process, including licensing, credentialing, privileging, and travel and housing arrangements.

It is acceptable to ask agencies for details about their processes, what types of physicians they work with, and any other pertinent details before getting into discussions about a specific assignment.

Doing repeat work with one agency after developing a good relationship with them is common. That said, there is no rule you must limit yourself to one agency. Assignment availability often drives agency choice. Small agencies sometimes specialize in certain medical specialties or geographic locations but cannot compete with the sheer number of assignments advertised by larger agencies.

Most physicians who contract directly with a facility have a pre-existing relationship with them. The benefits to this approach include direct communication, potential for higher compensation due to no middle-man fees, and more ability to tailor your contract to meet your needs.

Finding and securing an assignment

Start your locums job search by looking on agency websites. Most agencies post open assignments publicly, so you can search for opportunities matching your specialty and location interests. Medical job boards are another place to look, as they often include both permanent and locum tenens positions. Networking with colleagues in your specialty who have done locums work is another way to hear about open assignments.

Express your interest in an assignment and ask for additional details. If it is a fit, the agency will present your information and credentials to their client. Some organizations will want to speak with you directly. If you do not already hold a license in the state where the assignment is, the agency will help you obtain one.

Contracts are the backbone of locum tenens assignments; they define the expectations and obligations of both parties. All contract elements are potentially up for negotiation. When negotiating through an agency, keep in mind agencies primarily serve the interests of their clients, who are the healthcare organizations who are paying their fees.

Risks of locums work

Most staffing agencies cover malpractice insurance; some require the physician to provide their own coverage. Check that the coverage matches the scope of work you will be doing.

If you accept a locums assignment in a state that you have not lived or worked in, learn the state's requirements related to licensing, prescribing, and practicing. You might be asked to perform tasks or sign off on documents unfamiliar to you. Even if you are told these tasks are routine for the doctor you are filling in for, don't hesitate to ask questions and proceed with caution.

The National Association of Locum Tenens Organizations, which sets industry standards and ethical guidelines for locum tenens staffing companies, is a helpful resource.

FINANCIAL CONSIDERATIONS

Locums work carries the potential for higher pay than long-term, employed positions. The average pay is $32 per hour more than earned by salaried physicians with a permanent job.[239] According to a 2020 survey, the average hourly rate for locum tenens physicians was $162 per hour, with rates exceeding $200 per hour for specialists in high demand.[235]

The rate offered to you is only a portion of what the facility is paying to the locum tenens agency. Hospitals pay a premium for locum tenens agency services, which means locums physicians cost employers between 25% to 30% more than permanent staff.[240] The first rate you are offered is rarely the best rate you can negotiate.

Locum assignments may offer special pay to further increase compensation. For example, they might provide higher rates for holidays or weekends, and shift differentials may apply for working evening or night shifts. Escalator clauses may stipulate pay rate increases over time or with performance. Get clarity on compensation for on-call hours and whether you are eligible for overtime pay if you spend time charting or completing administrative tasks beyond the regular workday.

Locum agencies facilitate licensing and credentialing, and they typically cover all associated costs. They also cover or reimburse for travel and lodging during an assignment. As with base compensation, these benefits are negotiable. Your travel arrangements and accommodations can have a big impact on your comfort and stress level during an assignment. Ask which expenses they cover, any coverage limits, and the process for obtaining reimbursement for out-of-pocket expenses.

Part-time work and job sharing

Although more than half of physicians want to work fewer hours,[241] only about 20% work fewer than 40 hours per week.[190] Too many of us believe that going part-time means sacrificing income, prestige, and career advancement opportunities. We assume a part-time job is not a viable option. We fear part-time work will make us appear less committed or less capable. These assumptions are misguided. Let's give part-time work a second look.

PART-TIME PRACTICE LOGISTICS

Working excessive hours has long-term consequences, including problems related to physical health, mental health, safety, and productivity. Decreasing work hours leads to tangible improvements. Physicians who work part-time report lower levels of burnout.[1] Part-time work also provides the freedom and flexibility to balance career and personal obligations. Many positions allow schedule adjustment as needed, which can be particularly beneficial for those with personal obligations.

Part-time work can range from a few hours per week to as many as 32 hours per week, depending on the employer and specific job requirements. Part-time clinical positions can involve fewer workdays per week, half-day clinics, shorter shifts, or other arrangements.

W-2 employment as a part-time physician offers stable, consistent hours and salary, while 1099 contract work provides more flexibility but lacks worker protections. Private practice physicians can also work part-time by cutting back on office hours, hiring additional providers, or other strategies to ensure patients continue to have access to care. One potential drawback is that a part-time doctor in a group practice may not be eligible for partnership.

If you are planning ahead in your career, consider that part-time options are most readily available for the non-procedural specialties. Physicians in academia may face challenges in securing grant funding or achieving tenure. In hospital settings, part-time physicians may have limited control over their schedules. None of these should be reasons to avoid pursuing any specific specialty or practice setting; they are simply things to keep in mind.

Transitioning from full-time to part-time

For those wishing to transition from full-time to part-time but remain with the same employer, a good place to begin is by reviewing your organization's policies — some policies address part-time employment, which will help you in raising this topic with your supervisor and human resources department. Of note for U.S. government employees, nearly every federal agency has a program for part-time employment. When making your case for part-time work, emphasize how the change can benefit both you and the organization. Be specific about the hours and schedule you want to work. You may want to propose a trial period for the new arrangement.

Sometimes the transition to part-time work calls for finding a new employer.

JOB SHARING

The concept of job sharing originated in the 1970s to help mothers stay in the workforce but has expanded to be an option for all types of workers. Still, it remains underutilized in the United States. Close to half of the organizations in the United Kingdom and Australia make job sharing available,[242,243] compared to 16% of U.S. employers.[244]

Job sharing restructures professional positions that cannot be easily reduced to standard part-time positions. It involves two workers dividing the duties and compensation of one full-time role; the compensation is prorated accordingly. Job sharing's success relies on a partnership between the two employees and their ability to accomplish the full set of responsibilities between them.

When carefully planned and thoughtfully executed, job sharing is a viable approach for employed physicians and practice owners. Published accounts of job sharing in medical practice are limited but do include successful examples in both family medicine and anesthesiology practices.[245,246]

Job sharing structures

The precise structure of a job share depends on the specifics of the position, the preferences of the partners, and the needs of the employer. In most job shares, one of the two partners is always working during normal business or clinic hours. Work time can be divided by splitting up each day (for example, mornings and afternoons) or by alternating days or weeks. There may be a small amount of overlap on some days to allow for partners to touch base and provide a handover of uncompleted tasks or patient caseloads.

Dividing work responsibility can be simple for some positions, such as those following a work queue or appointment schedule. It is more complicated for leadership positions involving long-term projects and addressing organizational needs. More important than the precise distribution of work is that the partners agree to it and the work gets done.

The flexibility of job sharing goes beyond the work schedule; it ensures reliability, with one partner covering for the other when needed. Sharers can also divvy their work such that each partner spends more time on tasks or types of cases that appeal to them. For example, a physician who likes to take their time with patients might agree to see the bulk of patients with more complex medical issues, for example.

How to start job sharing

Job sharing is primarily employee-driven; employers rarely advertise jobs as being open to a job share arrangement. Ask your current or prospective employer whether they would allow it. Similarly, it is unlikely the employer will take full responsibility for finding a partner for your job share. While this requires more effort on your part, it increases the chances you will end up working with someone who is a good match for you.

Partners can be someone you already know, such as an existing colleague or a physician spouse who practices in the same specialty. That said, only about half of job sharing workers know their partner beforehand.[247] Try networking within your organization, medical society, or professional associations. The smoothest job-share implementations occur when one or both partners are already employed by the organization. Managers are more likely to entertain a job-sharing proposal having already worked with at least one of the partners. Workplace processes and systems are not developed with job sharing in mind, so persistence may be required in getting it approved and implemented.

Job-sharing in residency

Job sharing in residency is an option for physicians who want to complete a post-graduate training program without the typical grueling schedule. The AMA's FREIDA residency and fellowship database tracks whether programs allow job sharing, which they refer to as "shared schedule positions."

ADDRESSING CHALLENGES OF PART-TIME PRACTICE

Part-time work can lead to schedule creep, in which you spend more time working than your schedule on paper lays out. The extra work is often not spent on direct patient care, but on charting, paperwork, and other tangential tasks. Many physicians who are technically part-time employees report working close to 40 hours per week.[248] On-call duty can be a contentious issue, with part-time physicians sometimes expected to take as much call as their full-time counterparts. They are also the first requested to cover extra shifts.

Anticipate and address these issues early and directly. Set clear boundaries with your employer and communicate your expectations for your schedule, work hours, and on-call requirements. Be diligent in tracking your work hours so you have accurate information if you need to have a conversation with your employer.

Without being proactive, you may miss out on promotions, leadership roles, or other career advancement opportunities as a part-time doctor. Make an effort to communicate and demonstrate your commitment and to voice your professional goals. Find supporters in management or leadership who will vouch for you.

Having a part-time job can mean less job security. Part-time workers are often the first to be laid off. If possible, be open to the possibility of transitioning to full-time, adjusting your schedule, or changing jobs in the case of an economic crisis or budget cuts.

COMPENSATION AND BENEFITS

Income. The elephant in the room. Many physicians do not want to take a salary cut, but a part-time job makes it possible to earn a solid income while having more time to enjoy that income. In fact, more than half of physicians report they would consider taking a salary reduction to have better work-life balance.[249]

On an hourly basis, part-time physicians actually earn more than full-time physicians. According to a 2020 survey, the median hourly rate for part-time doctors was $105, compared to $94 for those working full-time.[250]

Part-time work may also offer a partial solution to physicians affected by the gender pay gap in medicine. Female physicians earn less than male physicians on average, but the pay gap is smaller among those who work part-time.[251]

Financial considerations for job sharing

A worker in a job share receives half the salary of a full-time employee in exchange for roughly half the work. However, job sharing can increase opportunities for promotion or career advancement (accompanied by increases in compensation) when compared to conventional part-time work.

The employer needs to allocate more than the cost of a full-time role held by one worker to a job-sharing role. This covers overlapping work hours between partners for collaboration and handovers, as well as expenses related to training and equipment for two workers. The added costs are justifiable, but you may need to explain the benefits to your employer.

Benefits

Indirect compensation makes up nearly a third of a full-time employee's total compensation,[252] so don't ignore it when evaluating a potential part-time job. Most part-time positions lack comprehensive benefit plans, but some employers may be open to negotiation regarding benefits. Do research on the cost to purchase certain benefits such as disability insurance.

Most benefits for job share employees are prorated, although some employers provide the same annual contribution toward insurance that they offer for full-time employees. The personal situations of each job share partner can influence the benefits package, as well. For instance, if one partner receives health insurance through their spouse, the employer might allow the other partner to receive the full health insurance benefit.

The gig economy

It has become second nature to order products and services with the tap of a screen. You have probably hailed an Uber ride, ordered a meal through DoorDash, used Instacart to stock your pantry, or hired a handyman with TaskRabbit.

Behind each transaction is a real person for whom these platforms represent a flexible and autonomous income source. Platform-mediated services are the fastest growing facet of the gig economy, and there are opportunities for all types of workers, including physicians.

GIG ECONOMY BASICS

The gig economy revolves around short-term positions filled by workers who are independent of any parent company. Positions come in many types but primarily entail on-demand work found and traded in a digital marketplace with low barriers to entry.

There are 65 million gig workers in the United States.[253] This figure has been rising 27% more quickly than payroll employees over the past two decades.[254] The gig economy has reshaped the nation's employment and received a huge amount of media attention in the process.

Businesses turn to the gig economy to achieve flexibility, cost-efficiency, and agility in their operations. Utilizing gig workers allows them to optimize their workforce for specific tasks without the commitments and costs associated with hiring traditional employees. Business models driven by the gig economy offer scalability, better allowing companies to adjust to market fluctuations and changing customer demands.

For gig workers, the benefits are similar: working when wanted without a long-term commitment, but with the ability to adjust the amount of work as desired.

The platform-mediated gig economy

Platform-mediated gig work centers around on-demand tasks and services facilitated through an app or a website that creates an interface between gig workers and clients. Workers can accept or bid on gigs posted to a digital marketplace. Alternatively, some platforms allow workers to post a service offering, and customers can compare options.

Gig platforms share a few key characteristics, including that they are discrete and time-limited tasks or agreements. Payment is tied to a deliverables or task completion.

GIG PLATFORMS FOR CLINICAL WORK

We usually think of physician "gigs" as either locum tenens assignments or nonclinical contract work, such as freelance medical writing and expert witness work. These engagements have traditionally been the mainstays of supplemental income for physicians, although the scope of opportunities has broadened with the rise of the gig economy.

Healthcare gig platforms bridge a gap between patients and medical services. Many facilitate direct connections with physicians, with little to no healthcare system involvement. They allow doctors to provide care without a full-fledged practice and without dedicated marketing efforts. Another appealing feature is the zero-hour contracts offered by most platforms, meaning work is done without a stipulation for a specific time commitment. You are never on-call and you are not expected to show up for rounds or appointments at a specific time each day.

Available gig platforms expedite patient care, tackle healthcare staffing issues, and address other needs in the clinical space.

Virtual patient visits

The most popular clinical gig platforms match patients to clinicians for on-demand virtual encounters conducted by either video, phone, or text. Appointment wait time is negligible. As opposed to most telemedicine employers, providers work as ad hoc contractors, logging in when they want.

Compensation is often a set fee per encounter, ranging from around $20 to $35. Some platforms allow physicians to set their own fees. The platform company handles patient payments and insurance billing (if insurance is accepted).

Examples incorporating this model are Amwell, Doctor on Demand, Hims & Hers, MDLIVE, PlushCare, Recuro, and Teladoc. These and other on-demand care platforms have been experimenting with various models for provider scheduling and service delivery. Some may require you to set your availability in advance but allow you to adjust it from week to week and even day to day. Some give doctors full flexibility over when they work but require a minimum number of hours per week.

In-person patient visits

Not all healthcare gig platforms operate strictly within the digital realm. Recognizing the need for face-to-face evaluations and in-person care, they can serve as intermediaries connecting patients with clinicians for in-home visits on-demand. The concept is compelling, though this business model is more complex and geographically bound than platforms focusing solely on virtual care.

HEAL is among the largest platforms of this type, operating across eight states. Other examples include Pager, which offers services in and around New York City, and SOS Doctor House Call, which primarily operates in southern California.

Personalized health and medical information

A few platforms provide personalized information to users with health- and medical-related questions. These address an unmet need between general online health information and formal doctor's visits.

Virtual care platform HealthTap uses this model to give visibility to their network doctors, who can then charge a fee to users who book appointments for virtual care. Another platform, JustAnswer, connects users with experts across various fields to get their questions answered. Physicians can claim questions within their areas of expertise and receive compensation based on the question type and how long the user has been waiting.

Staffing platforms for clinical gigs

Digital apps also assist clinicians in finding gig work. Most platforms in this space, such as Nomad and Medely, have concentrated on nurses and allied health professionals, although a few have been successful in establishing connections between physicians and practices for telemedicine work. For instance, Wheel and SteadyMD connect physicians to virtual care gigs while also streamlining processes like credentialing, onboarding, and compliance. Their partners include digital health companies, labs, pharmacies, and other employers needing remote physician services.

Physician-patient matching

Some platforms' main service is to connect patients to physicians rather than to provide actual medical services. These can be valuable for physicians to expand their practice or fill open appointment slots.

One example is MediBid, which offers competitive bidding on medical services. Patients post their healthcare needs, such as medical procedures, surgeries, or consultations. In response, physicians pay a fee to bid on delivering the requested services. Patients evaluate the responses and accept a bid.

DoctorSpring and 2nd.MD are platform-mediated services facilitating connections between patients and specialists for second opinion consults. They match users with specialists based on case details shared by the patient.

CONSIDERATIONS FOR WORKING IN THE GIG ECONOMY

Work within the gig economy is supplementary income source for most physicians. Work volume and pay can be unpredictable. Platforms can adjust their business models and marketing strategies at any time and with little notice. Gig workers do not receive the same protections and benefits that employees have.

More than 40% of gig workers use multiple gig platforms simultaneously.[255] Clinical and nonclinical gig work can be combined to optimize your time and income. Freelancing platforms such as Upwork and Catalant focus on matching workers to clients seeking specialized skills and streamlining the contract and payment processes.

The gig economy is in constant flux. Digital tech startups emerge, adapt, and get acquired quickly. If you do not initially find an app or platform that suits you, revisit the options frequently.

When doing gig work involving telemedicine, it is helpful to have multiple state medical licenses. Obtaining and maintaining licenses is expensive, so always ask if the platform company will cover these costs. Reputable organizations have legal counsel to ensure compliance with state telemedicine regulations, but you should still familiarize yourself with these rules.

Susan M. Trocciola, MD, FACS

Locum Tenens Cardiothoracic Surgeon

Practice setting

I am a locum tenens cardiothoracic surgeon. I travel all over the country to work at different hospitals. I mainly practice in an inpatient setting, but also see patients in outpatient offices. Small- to medium-sized hospitals most frequently need locum tenens coverage for cardiothoracic surgery, although I have covered in a few large facilities. I work in academic, nonprofit, and for-profit hospitals. Assignments are often in remote locations, but I balance this with assignments near the beach or large cities.

I work for a few large locum firms that place me at different hospitals. Some assignments are short (for example, a few weekends). Others last one to two years, requiring one or two weeks per month at the same hospital.

Employment type and schedule

I am a 1099 contract worker. I have full control over when and where I work, and I choose to work part-time. During the summer I try to work one to two weeks per month. During the winter months, I work three to four weeks per month, mainly in warm locations to escape the cold of New York. I can take time off to spend with family or to go on vacation. Working on holidays is not required, although some locum physicians choose to work holidays for the extra pay.

After giving them my approval, the locum company presents my information to a client. They negotiate payment rates directly with the client. Once I am accepted for an assignment, the company arranges my schedule and travel.

The locum company gets paid by the hospital for the work I do and they, in turn, pay me. I negotiate my rate with the locum company. I have successfully given myself a raise every four to six months. I currently earn between $4,000 and $6,500 per day.

I take call almost every night while I am on a locum assignment; however, I get paid for answering phone calls or going into the hospital. My payment structure is that I get a base pay for up to two hours of work and an hourly rate for any time worked over two hours. So, if I get stuck for two hours waiting for a case to start, I am getting paid. If I have an emergency case that goes on all night, I am paid for every minute I am in the hospital. Although I work about one half as many days as my last full-time job, I make more as a locums surgeon. The ability to earn a lot of money over a short period of time adds to the enjoyment of locums tenens work.

Patient population and clinical work

While on assignment, 90% of my time is spent taking care of patients. Since I do cardiac and thoracic surgery, I mostly work with older patients. The one word I would use to describe my patients is grateful. Patients are happy they do not have to travel for their surgery, which is made possible by the hospital hiring a locums surgeon.

A typical day at work

I try to choose a mix assignment types, so my typical day varies. I pick assignments that are busy so I get an opportunity to operate frequently. I usually arrive at the hospital at about 7:00 a.m. and round on inpatients. I go to the operating suite at about 8:00 AM. In the afternoon, I round again on inpatients and see any new consults. On days I don't operate, I have office hours either in the morning or the afternoon. I finish by about 4:00 or 5:00 p.m. on most days.

I balance this with smaller assignments that are not as busy clinically and don't pay as much but are in a location I want to go — near a beach, in an interesting city, or close to friends and family. For these assignments, I may only work from 8:00 a.m. until 12:00 p.m. and then hold a pager for the rest of the day (while on the beach).

Unconventional aspects

Compared to most surgeons, the unconventional part of my job is I can work part-time and still function like a full-time surgeon (and earn the income of a full-time surgeon). Most years, I take a total of 12 to 14 weeks off throughout the year. This is far more than many cardiothoracic surgeons take.

The other unconventional part is being compensation for every hour I work. Many surgeons are paid a set fee for each type of surgery and a smaller fee for seeing consults or office patients.

Best parts of the job

I love going to hospitals that really need help and being able to provide good surgery to patients in need. I love that I can still operate on patients but do it on my terms. I love being able to work all over the country in places such as Miami, Florida, Tucson, Arizona, and Northern California. While the locums company pays for all my travel, I accumulate the loyalty program points to use for personal travel.

I am often offered full-time work at sites where I do locums. I have turned down many full-time opportunities, and that feels good. I don't think I will ever go back to a full-time employed position.

Challenges faced

The downside of locums is assignments sometimes get cancelled, usually by the hospital for financial reasons. I try to always have more than one assignment on the table. Even so, it can be frustrating to have a great assignment and then to have it suddenly cancelled.

Qualifications and skills needed for this career

To be successful as a locums, one must be motivated, independent, and flexible. You might not have all the exact equipment you need, so you need to adapt. At some sites, you will be busy and have to handle cases without any backup. At other sites, there may not be much work for you to do at all.

Most locum companies want physicians with no lawsuits and no reports to the National Practitioner Data Bank. You need to have references who can attest to the fact that you can practice independently.

Advice for students and physicians

An important part of my story is that I was diagnosed with stage III breast cancer about five years into my work as an attending surgeon. There was a concern that my disease had spread, and I will always remember the time I spent getting that workup. My only thought was, "Why did I work so much only to possibly die in my early 40s?" I was fortunate I did not have stage IV cancer, and my cancer was curable. However, this moment changed my life. My main piece of advice is to realize there is more to life than work.

I would not recommend being a locums directly after residency or fellowship. It is helpful to get mentored from more senior doctors. Locums is a great job for someone who does not want to work full-time or is burned out from full-time hospital employment. Locums does not provide health insurance or benefits; however, as a 1099 worker, you can take many more tax deductions and put money into independent, tax-deferred retirement accounts.

HOW TO THRIVE IN AN UNCONVENTIONAL CAREER

A s you contemplate your own unconventional career path, you'll likely find yourself with questions.

How will your unique situation influence your career trajectory?

Are you ready for a change? If so, where do you begin?

This final chapter transitions from job types to tailored strategies and information focused on ensuring satisfaction in your career.

CONSIDERATIONS BY CAREER STAGE AND SITUATION

The career options described in the previous chapters are not for a select few physicians. Many are possibilities for a variety of backgrounds and career stages. While your situation may feel unique, there are others who have faced similar challenges and proven strategies to design and adapt an unconventional career to fit your needs.

Medical students

If you are already contemplating an unconventional career while still in medical school, you likely are in one of two camps. You might have a clear vision of where you want to steer your career, and it happens to be a road less traveled. In this case, continue to educate yourself on career possibilities, since the unconventional ones will be lacking in your formal medical education. Focus on excelling in your classes and clinical rotations.

The other likely situation is that you are wrestling with doubts about your decision to pursue medicine. This book has introduced you to a vast array of career options. Hopefully, it revived your interest in medicine.

Regardless, don't quit. Finish medical school and do a residency. These will both open doors to many job opportunities.

Specialty choice is a momentous decision for medical students. The decision is often based on intuition, unfortunately. Try instead to take a systematic approach. Most medical specialties revolve around a specific organ system (e.g., nephrology, dermatology), a disease class (e.g., rheumatology, infectious disease), a procedure type (e.g., general surgery, plastic surgery), a type of medical technology (e.g., radiology, pathology), or a patient group (e.g., pediatrics, geriatrics). Some are a blend of two or more of these. Thinking about specialties in this manner can be a helpful starting point, especially when planning for an unconventional career path.

Keep in mind that the broader specialties, like internal medicine and emergency medicine, will prepare you for the widest range of unconventional careers.

Use elective rotations in your third and fourth years to explore unconventional fields. If your school lacks appealing options, look for off-site rotations or create a custom elective.

Find mentors who have had unconventional careers themselves. Engaging with them, even in casual discussions, can provide great insight.

Residents and fellows

You may have picked up this book because you are feeling overwhelmed or burned out amidst residency's long hours and rigorous requirements. Finish your program. Residency will make you board-eligible, and board certification will greatly expand your job prospects.

Residency and fellowship programs provide time for elective rotations. Use this time to gain experience in the unconventional clinical areas that interest you. Plan these rotations far in advance.

As a resident, you face the decision of whether to do a fellowship and what type to do. Many unconventional jobs do not require subspecialization; however, a fellowship can be beneficial if you envision having a niche clinical practice. Fellowships do not always receive accreditation or result in subspecialty board eligibility; this does not mean they are substandard or not worth your time. Many provide excellent training in lesser-known medicine subfields. There is no central database of unaccredited fellowships, so you will need to do some research to identify programs fitting with your interests.

Venture into unconventional work while you are still in training if you can. Moonlighting and side gigs provide experience, extra income, and a glimpse into the career path you are considering. It can be challenging to find employers who will hire residents and fellows, but the opportunities are out there if you search for them.

Early-career physicians

As a recent residency graduate or early-career physician, you probably feel both excited and uncertain about exploring unconventional career paths. This uncertainty may come from feeling inexperienced beyond familiar clinical settings. Many unconventional roles, though, do not require extensive experience; some have a steep learning curve, but it is manageable.

You may also feel a smidge of guilt for looking into unconventional roles early in your career. We are led to believe that physicians should "pay their dues" through years of grueling work. You may feel pressure to adhere to a predefined path for a while, but this is your life, your career, and your medical degree.

Finding work-life balance is a priority for early-career physicians. You are eager to advance in your career while also wanting to enjoy the peak years of your life. Unconventional careers can be the remedy. If a big, sudden change to your career path seems daunting, begin with a part-time or contract position to test the waters while maintaining income and stability.

Do your best to stay updated on trends in medicine and healthcare regulations, since they can lead to unconventional job opportunities. For instance, the ACGME occasionally recognizes new specialties and offers practice pathways for board certification without a fellowship. Recent examples include clinical informatics and addiction medicine. Other areas like obesity medicine and lifestyle medicine have active professional groups vying for specialty recognition. By gaining experience in a discipline like these, you can position yourself for future board certification without interrupting your career for fellowship training.

Mid- and late-career physicians

Inertia can hinder mid- and late-career physicians from making a career change. Even if dissatisfied with your current role or trajectory, a familiar day-to-day routine can feel comfortable. Don't fall victim to this.

Your extensive experience is a key asset, and it extends beyond your primary practice area. Your past roles may not directly align with an unconventional career, but your acquired skills, insights, and problem-solving abilities are transferable. Your broad knowledge base can set you apart as a job candidate and will enhance your effectiveness in a new, unconventional position.

When nearing retirement, you can utilize unconventional jobs to scale down practice through part-time or contract work or as a venue to explore something new before retiring. Physicians who have retired from their main practice can opt for part-time unconventional roles to stay active and engaged without the same stress and demands.

Returning to practice after a gap

You may have needed to take a break from practicing medicine for any number of reasons: raising kids, personal health, caring for an aging parent, or simply needing a change of pace. Returning to clinical practice comes with challenges. More than a third of physicians report difficulties reentering clinical practice after an inactive period.[256]

The leading concern for most doctors is feeling like their skills are rusty. Unconventional jobs with part-time or flexible schedules afford time for continuing education and a smoother transition back to work. Many of these roles operate at a slower pace, allowing you to update yourself on new medical guidelines and evidence. Some jobs might focus on a narrower therapeutic area, making it easier to become familiar with current standards.

If you prefer a more formal reintroduction to clinical practice, there are special programs designed for physicians returning to practice, such as Drexel University's Physician Refresher/Re-entry Program and the University of Texas Mini-Residency Program.

Another hurdle can be employers' requirements for recent clinical experience, particularly in larger hospitals and healthcare systems. Certain unconventional jobs can give you clinical experience and help you regain eligibility for other positions.

Many state medical boards have specific requirements for reinstating a lapsed medical license. Familiarize yourself with your state's rules early on so you can prepare. If they are overly burdensome, consider getting licensed in another state for telemedicine practice.

International medical graduates (IMGs)

The road to practicing medicine in the United States as an IMG is a long and arduous one. Some IMGs abandon this goal and end up working in jobs that underutilize their medical expertise. Don't let the process overwhelm you; it is attainable, as evidenced by 25% of U.S. practicing physicians being IMGs.[257]

The ACGME permits flexibility for exceptionally qualified applicants who do not meet standard eligibility criteria. You can support your application with clinical excellence, training programs, scholarship, and leadership. Completing a training program under these alternative circumstances will not lead to board eligibility but can still be a worthwhile experience and open doors, especially to unconventional jobs. Also investigate observerships and bridge programs designed for IMGs seeking U.S. certification.

Although your international experience may not directly count toward U.S. licensure, it can strengthen job applications. In some unconventional roles, your global perspective can offer a competitive advantage. For instance, cultural and language skills can be beneficial in positions serving immigrant communities.

Unfortunately, bias and discrimination sometimes affect IMGs in the job market. Seek out employers who value diversity and inclusion and who have a track record of hiring IMGs.

Leaders, mentors, and advisors

Whether you hold a formal appointment or provide informal guidance through mentorship or advising, you can deeply influence the career paths of medical students, trainees, and peers.

You may encounter individuals experiencing burnout or second-guessing their career choice. Some may be actively thinking about a career transition. Approach your conversations with an open mind. Foster their interest in an unconventional career instead of dissuading them. Encourage them to learn more about alternative career paths.

You might recognize that an advisee's skill set and interests align with an unconventional career. Although they may not have voiced it or recognized it, introduce the idea of an unconventional career and guide them toward resources to learn more.

Our medical education system focuses heavily on specialty choice. As a leader or mentor, try to broaden the conversation. Professional fulfillment in medicine relies on so much more than specialty; it depends on factors like the physical work environment, schedule, tasks, and workplace culture. Urge your mentees to delve into their career goals. Help them identify what their ideal job looks like.

As with specialty choice, salary and earning potential have less impact on overall career satisfaction than we assume. There is evidence that career decisions in the larger workforce are becoming less about money and more about lifestyle.[258] Help students and peers visualize what their lifestyle will look like for the various jobs they are considering.

Don't underestimate the power of mentoring. Whether solicited or unsolicited, and whether the mentee acts on your advice or not, your guidance is valuable.

FINDING AND LANDING UNCONVENTIONAL JOBS

The healthcare industry is home to many well-compensated unconventional jobs, although finding them can be tricky. The best opportunities rarely fall into your lap; you must be proactive. There are some subtleties to vetting jobs and negotiating the terms of employment that differ from traditional roles. Expect to put in upfront effort to maximize your long-term gains.

Job searching

Job postings offer a good starting point to find many job types. You can find unconventional jobs on physician-targeted job boards like PracticeLink and career centers run by medical associations. More so than traditional physician jobs, many unconventional openings appear on general job boards and aggregators such as Indeed and LinkedIn. The public sector, especially federal government jobs, follows different hiring procedures with most positions listed on USAJOBS.

Variation in job titles makes job searches challenging. For example, the role of *medical director* can vary by context. Organizations are now using newer terms like "provider" and "prescriber" more broadly to include physicians, NPs, PAs, and sometimes other licensed healthcare professionals. Use trial and error and adjust your search strategy as needed.

Do not dismiss recruiters in your search. Recruiters and search firms may have exclusive access to open positions. They can offer insights into industry trends and physician demand for the job types that interest you.

As always, leverage your professional network for leads, referrals, and information about potential jobs.

Evaluating job opportunities

Too often, doctors hesitate to make a career transition because they believe they are unqualified. Apply anyway. Job postings frequently overstate the requirements for candidates. Many employers value a broader range of experience, and your experience is more relevant than meets the eye. Many skills doctors possess such as communication, problem-solving, adaptability, and leadership are highly transferrable. Highlight examples in your applications and interviews.

When evaluating a potential job, don't make assumptions about the responsibilities, schedule, or payment structure; these may differ from what you have seen for conventional positions. Ask questions. If neither the in-house recruiter nor the hiring manager can provide clarity, this may be a red flag.

Another factor to consider is the potential for career advancement. Unconventional roles may not have a clear trajectory. Think about your exit strategy before you even enter. Are there paths to promotion within the company? Will you be able to leverage the skills and experience gained in this role for future positions at other organizations?

Try to connect with physicians who work for the company you are applying to. For many unconventional positions, your interviewers may not be physicians. Only your medical peers can give an authentic perspective of what it is like to practice medicine there.

Finally, be cautious. Amid countless reputable healthcare organizations who hire physicians for unconventional jobs, there are businesses that use unethical practices or prioritize profit over patient care.

Employment and contractor agreements

As excited as you may be when you get a job offer, do not sign the employment contract or contractor agreement without understanding and agreeing to what it says. Take a close look at the scope of work and responsibilities. Make sure you have ultimate authority to make decisions about your patients' medical treatment. Your employer can have policies, procedures, and protocols related to the clinical services they provide, but they cannot tell you how to practice medicine.

Noncompete clauses are common, but they can be remarkably restrictive for some unconventional jobs. These clauses can limit your ability to work for other organizations or in a specific geographic area after leaving the position. You may want to request removal of these in their entirety. You can also check on their enforceability, as some state laws do not uphold noncompete agreements for professionals.

Understand the terms and conditions that can lead to termination of your employment. Look for any notice periods, performance metrics, or specific situations which could lead to termination.

Clarify the ownership of intellectual property generated during your employment. At the very least, you should ensure you retain rights to any scholarly work or other intellectual property you develop on your own time outside the scope of your job.

Consider consulting with an attorney for particularly complex or high-stakes agreements.

Compensation and benefits

Physician compensation varies widely and depends on many factors, particularly in unconventional roles. Regardless of your background or the position you are applying to, one fundamental piece of advice holds true: Know your worth. Your expertise, your specialized skills, and the investment you have made in obtaining your credentials have significant value. Do not accept jobs that undermine the value you bring. Walk away from employers who undervalue you.

More money does not necessarily mean more happiness, but it does matter. One study revealed that physicians earning between $250,000 and $299,999 per year were 98% more likely to report being very content with their medical careers compared to their counterparts earning significantly less.[259] So it is worth negotiating for a compensation package that works for you.

You can negotiate more than your base salary or hourly pay. Relocation assistance, sign-on bonuses, partnership opportunities, and more paid time off are all options. You can request a stipend for added responsibilities, such as teaching students or supervising APPs. Review your contract for clauses mentioning annual increases, periodic salary renegotiations, or predefined growth milestones, as these are also items for negotiation.

Be sure you are clear on whether the company will pay for or reimburse expenses related to your responsibilities, including costs associated with medical license upkeep, CME, and equipment. Review the type of coverage and policy limits of the malpractice insurance the employer offers. If you are responsible for your own insurance, get a quote so you can factor in the expense as you think through your job offer.

Benefits can be a substantial component of overall compensation, especially for full-time employees. Health insurance, disability insurance, life insurance, retirement plan contributions, student loan repayment programs, and other benefits have great value. Benefits for part-time employees differ among employers, so clarify the details about what is offered.

STARTING AN UNCONVENTIONAL PRACTICE

Medical practice has shifted away from private practice. Fewer than half of physicians work in a physician-owned practice, and only 14% are in solo practice.[260] Despite this trend, independent private practice remains feasible. This is especially true if there is something to differentiate your practice from the competition, like a clinical niche or less common payment option.

Being an employee has advantages: a steady paycheck, established operational procedures, and fewer administrative responsibilities, to name a few. Owning a practice has benefits too, particularly autonomy. You decide your scope of services, the patients you treat, and the procedures you perform. You choose the hours. You retain the profits.

Of course, venturing into an unconventional solo practice requires careful planning and significant effort. You may choose to hire a lawyer and other professional consultants to help you open your practice. Regardless, take the time to familiarize yourself with relevant federal and state laws. Some states have regulations specifying the business entity types that licensed professionals can use to practice. Ensure your practice will comply with HIPAA, healthcare fraud and abuse laws such as Stark and the anti-kickback statute, state prescribing laws, and insurance regulations.

Your practice needs to be financially viable. The financial planning for practices accepting insurance can be relatively straightforward but requires time to establish coding and billing processes and go through credentialing processes with insurance companies. Practices relying on self-pay or alternative payment models may require more effort to determine a profitable pricing structure and effective marketing strategy.

If you intend to offer services that insurance companies do not typically cover, carefully mull over your reasons for doing this and be transparent with your patients about the risks and expected benefits. Along these lines, standard malpractice insurance policies may not be sufficient when providing less conventional services, so work with your provider to tailor your coverage, if needed.

A great benefit of starting a private practice today is the abundance of tech solutions to streamline operations. These include robust EHRs, telemedicine interfaces, billing software, scheduling applications, and other tools. When selected thoughtfully, your practice's technology stack will decrease the time you spend on administrative tasks and can even decrease the number of staff you need to hire. There are also many apps and software services geared toward small business owners of all types which can be assets for solo practice owners who want to reduce expenses. These can make it feasible to do your own accounting, website design, marketing, and more.

CAREER MANAGEMENT FOR UNCONVENTIONAL PHYSICIANS

Landing a great job — even your "dream job" — does not automatically lead to a satisfying career. You need to actively manage your career.

Career management is the process of intentionally and proactively planning and developing your career over the long-term. When done effectively, you will achieve your goals, have work-life balance, find personal fulfillment, and enjoy financial security. Managing your career should start by having clear and attainable professional goals. Regularly take a self-assessment of your skills, interests, and values, as these can shift over time.

The concept of a protean career is particularly relevant to physicians with unconventional jobs. Protean careers are characterized by change, flexibility, and adaptability. They include nontraditional career paths, multiple job changes, and entrepreneurial ventures. They are driven by the individual rather than by an organization.

Holding down a full-time job in medicine can leave little room for anything else. It is tempting to sideline opportunities for networking, continuous learning, and professional development that are not directly connected to your current job. But try your best to make the time for these, as they are critical in a protean career and will pave the way for future unconventional opportunities.

CONCLUSION

Physicians have become increasingly frustrated with the expectations and confines of the healthcare system, but they still want to make a meaningful difference in the lives of their patients and communities. As we search for ways to address our frustrations, unconventional medical careers are gaining recognition and acceptance within our profession.

What is considered unconventional now may, with time, become the new norm. It is up to us to demonstrate that unconventional roles can not only contribute significantly to the medical workforce, but also bring satisfaction and passion back to our work.

We can redefine our profession. This book offers two key points toward accomplishing that goal. First, there is no rule dictating that physicians must hold a certain type of job or adhere to a standard career path. Second, deviating from customary, full-time work in a hospital or clinic doesn't necessitate leaving medicine or transitioning to a nonclinical role that excludes patient care. Clinical opportunities span many types and formats.

So many decisions in life seem final at the time we make them. But one of the beauties of having a medical degree is the flexibility it offers. You can pivot in many directions without going back to school, doing another residency, taking a huge hit to your salary, or otherwise uprooting your life. If the idea of something atypical piques your interest, go for it — you can always redirect your career later.

Tech industry pioneer Alan Kay once remarked, "The best way to predict the future is to invent it." Likewise, the best way to ensure a fulfilling career is to aggressively shape it, seeking out and seizing opportunities that align with your passions and values.

References

1. The Physicians Foundation. *2020 Survey of America's Physicians: COVID-19 Impact Edition*. https://physiciansfoundation.org/wp-content/uploads/2020/09/2020-Physicians-Foundation-Survey-Part2.pdf

2. Stajduhar T. *On the Verge of a Physician Turnover Epidemic: Physician Retention Survey Results – February 2021*. Jackson Physician Search; 2021. https://www.jacksonphysiciansearch.com/wp-content/uploads/2021/02/Jackson-Physician-Search_2021-White-Paper_Physician-Retention-Survey-Results.pdf

3. Landon BE, Reschovsky JD, Pham HH, Blumenthal D. Leaving Medicine: The Consequences of Physician Dissatisfaction. *Med Care*. 2006;44(3):234–242. doi:10.1097/01.mlr.0000199848.17133.9b

4. U.S. Census Bureau. Census Bureau Reports Nearly 77 Million Students Enrolled in U.S. Schools. Census.gov. News Release. December 3, 2019. https://www.census.gov/newsroom/press-releases/2019/school-enrollment.html

5. Love HE, Schlitt J, Soleimanpour S, Panchal N, Behr C. Twenty Years of School-based Health Care Growth and Expansion. *Health Aff (Millwood)*. 2019;38(5):755–764.

6. Ran T, Chattopadhyay SK, Hahn RA, Community Preventive Services Task Force. Economic Evaluation of School-Based Health Centers: A Community Guide Systematic Review. *Am J Prev Med*. 2016;51(1):129–138. doi:10.1016/j.amepre.2016.01.017

7. Guo JJ, Wade TJ, Pan W, Keller KN. School-based Health Centers: Cost–Benefit Analysis and Impact on Health Care Disparities. *Am J Public Health*. 2010;100(9):1617–1623.

8. Cooley WC, Sagerman PJ. American Academy of Pediatrics, American Academy of Family Physicians, and American College of Physicians, Transitions Clinical Report Authoring Group. Supporting the Health Care Transition from Adolescence to Adulthood in the Medical Home. *Pediatrics*. 2011;128(1):182–200.

9. Statistical Briefing Book. Office of Juvenile Justice and Delinquency Prevention. January 1, 2023. https://ojjdp.ojp.gov/statistical-briefing-book/corrections/faqs/qa08522

10. Pinnacle Health Group. *2021 Annual Physician Compensation Survey*. Pinnacle Health Group; 2021. https://www.scribd.com/document/636713720/2021-Physician-Compensation-Report-updated-0821

11. Futterman L. SFIA'S Topline Report Shows Physical Activity Rates Increased for a Fifth Consecutive Year. Sports and Fitness Industry Association. February 22, 2023. https://sfia.org/resources/sfias-topline-report-shows-physical-activity-rates-increased-for-a-fifth-consecutive-year/

12. Deitsch R. 2022 Olympics: Beijing Games Draw Lowest Primetime Viewership Ever on NBC. *The Athletic.* https://theathletic.com/4182007/2022/02/21/2022-olympics-beijing-games-draw-lowest-primetime-viewership-ever-on-nbc/. Published February 21, 2022.

13. Florio M. NFL National Revenue Reaches $11.98 Billion in 2022 — NBC Sports. *NBC Sports.* https://www.nbcsports.com/nfl/profootballtalk/rumor-mill/news/nfl-national-revenue-reaches-11-98-billion-in-2022. July 19, 2023.

14. National Federation of State High School Associations. High School Sports Participation Continues Rebound Toward Pre-Pandemic Levels. September 21, 2023. https://www.nfhs.org/articles/high-school-sports-participation-continues-rebound-toward-pre-pandemic-levels

15. Goldman Sachs Ayco. *2021 Executive Benefits Survey.* Goldman Sachs; 2021. https://www.ayco.com/content/dam/ayco/pdfs/us/en/literature/2021-executive-benefits-survey.pdf

16. Komaroff AL. Executive Physicals: What's the ROI? *Harv Bus Rev.* 2009;87(9):28–30.

17. The Hollywood Reporter Staff. Doctor Ratings: Best Doctors in Los Angeles. *The Hollywood Reporter.* September 10, 2014. https://www.hollywoodreporter.com/news/general-news/doctor-ratings-best-doctors-los-731354/

18. Ito R. L.A.'s Concierge Medical Services Woo VIPS with Plush Amenities—but Not Everyone Thinks That's Healthy. *Los Angeles Magazine.* April 1, 2021. https://lamag.com/featured/concierge-medicine-los-angeles

19. Schwartz N. The Doctor Is In. Co-Pay? $40,000. *The New York Times.* June 3, 2017. https://www.nytimes.com/2017/06/03/business/economy/high-end-medical-care.html

20. Nittle N. Interesting Facts and Information About the U.S. Indigenous Population. ThoughtCo. September 13, 2021. https://www.thoughtco.com/interesting-facts-about-native-americans-2834518

21. Indian Health Service. *Indian Health Disparities.* Indian Health Service; 2019. https://www.ihs.gov/sites/newsroom/themes/responsive2017/display_objects/documents/factsheets/Disparities.pdf

22. Americans for the Arts. Artists in the U.S. Workforce 2006-2020. March 9, 2021. https://www.americansforthearts.org/by-program/reports-and-data/legislation-policy/naappd/artists-in-the-us-workforce-2006-2020

23. Ackermann B, Driscoll T, Kenny DT. Musculoskeletal Pain and Injury in Professional Orchestral Musicians in Australia. *Med Probl Perform Art.* 2012;27(4):181–187.

24. Dick RW, Berning JR, Dawson W, Ginsburg RD, Miller C, Shybut GT. Athletes and the Arts—The Role of Sports Medicine in the Performing Arts. *Curr Sports Med Rep.* 2013;12(6):397–403.

25. Kane L. Medscape Physician Compensation Report 2023: Your Income vs Your Peers'. Medscape Public Health. April 14, 2023. https://www.medscape.com/slideshow/2023-compensation-overview-6016341

26. Substance Abuse and Mental Health Services Administration. *2021 National Survey of Drug Use and Health*. SAMHSA News Releases; 2021. https://www.samhsa.gov/data/release/2021-national-survey-drug-use-and-health-nsduh-releases

27. National Institute on Drug Abuse. Drug Overdose Death Rates. June 30, 2023. https://nida.nih.gov/research-topics/trends-statistics/overdose-death-rates

28. American Board of Emergency Medicine. *American Board of Emergency Medicine Annual Report 2021-2022*. ABEM; 2022. Accessed November 3, 2023. https://www.abem.org/public/docs/default-source/default-document-library/abem-21-22-annual-report_final.pdf

29. Substance Abuse and Mental Health Services Administration. Opioid Treatment Program Directory. Accessed October 14, 2023. https://dpt2.samhsa.gov/treatment/directory.aspx

30. Substance Abuse and Mental Health Services Administration. Federal Guidelines for Opioid Treatment Programs. *HHS Publ No SMA PEP15-FEDGUIDEOTP*. January 2015. https://store.samhsa.gov/sites/default/files/pep15-fedguideotp-federal-guidelines-for-opioid-treatment-programs.pdf

31. Kao L, Pizon A. Medical Toxicology Fellowship Training Is Available to Applicants from Many Specialties. *J Med Toxicol*. 2018;14:177–178.

32. Van Dam A. Analysis | The Average Doctor in the U.S. Makes $350,000 a year. Why? *Washington Post*. August 4, 2023. https://www.washingtonpost.com/business/2023/08/04/doctor-pay-shortage

33. Doximity & Curative. *2023 Physician Compensation Report*. Accessed November 3, 2023. https://press.doximity.com/reports/doximity-physician-compensation-report-2023.pdf

34. Rikard SM, Strahan AE, Schmit KM, Guy Jr GP. Chronic Pain Among Adults—United States, 2019-2021. *Morb Mortal Wkly Rep*. 2023;72(15):379.

35. Schappert SM, Burt CW. Ambulatory Care Visits to Physician Offices, Hospital Outpatient Departments, and Emergency Departments: United States, 2001-02. *Vital Health Stat 13*. 2006;(159):1–66.

36. Gaskin DJ, Richard P. The Economic Costs of Pain in the United States. *J Pain*. 2012;13(8):715–724.

37. Simon LS. Relieving Pain in America: A Blueprint for Transforming Prevention, Care, Education, and Research. *J Pain Palliat Care Pharmacother*. 2012;26(2):197–198.

38. Bonica JJ. The Role of the Anesthetist in the Management of Intractable Pain. *Proc R Soc Med*. 1954;47(12):1029–1032.

39. AAPM Council on Ethics. Ethics Charter from American Academy of Pain Medicine. *Pain Med*. 2005;6(3):203–212.

40. Shipton EE, Bate F, Garrick R, Steketee C, Shipton EA, Visser EJ. Systematic Review of Pain Medicine Content, Teaching, and Assessment in Medical School Curricula Internationally. *Pain Ther*. 2018;7:139–161.

41. Provenzano D, Kamal KM, Giannetti V. Evaluation of Primary Care Physician Chronic Pain Management Practice Patterns. *Pain Physician*. 2018;21(6):E593–E602.

42. Tepper SJ, Dahlöf CG, Dowson A, et al. Prevalence and Diagnosis of Migraine in Patients Consulting Their Physician with a Complaint of Headache: Data from the Landmark Study. *Headache*. 2004;44(9):856–864.

43. Begasse de Dhaem O, Burch R, Rosen N, Shubin Stein K, Loder E, Shapiro RE. Workforce Gap Analysis in the Field of Headache Medicine in the United States. *Headache*. 2020;60(2):478–481.

44. Gawande A. *Being Mortal: Medicine and What Matters in the End*. New York: Metropolitan Books; 2014.

45. Deaths and Mortality. Centers for Disease Control and Prevention. National Center for Health Statistics. January 17, 2023. https://www.cdc.gov/nchs/fastats/deaths.htm

46. Definitive Healthcare. Top 20 Physician Group Specialties with the Most Growth Over the Last Five Years. Definitive Healthcare. June 1, 2023. https://www.definitivehc.com/resources/healthcare-insights/top-physician-group-specialties-most-growth

47. National Center for Health Statistics. Hospice Care. Centers for Disease Control and Prevention. August 31, 2022. https://www.cdc.gov/nchs/fastats/hospice-care.htm

48. Stevenson DG, Grabowski DC, Keating NL, Huskamp HA. Effect of Ownership on Hospice Service Use: 2005–2011. *J Am Geriatr Soc*. 2016;64(5):1024–1031.

49. Center to Advance Palliative Care. *Growth of Palliative Care in U.S. Hospitals: 2022 Snapshot*; 2022. https://www.capc.org/documents/download/1031/

50. State Statuses. Death with Dignity. 2023. https://deathwithdignity.org/states/

51. Compassion & Choices. *Medical Aid-in-Dying Utilization Report*; 2023. https://www.compassionandchoices.org/docs/default-source/default-document-library/medical_aid_in_dying_utilization_report_12-13-2022.pdf

52. Emanuel EJ, Onwuteaka-Philipsen BD, Urwin JW, Cohen J. Attitudes and Practices of Euthanasia and Physician-Assisted Suicide in the United States, Canada, and Europe. *JAMA*. 2016;316(1):79–90.

53. American Medical Group Association. *Medical Group Compensation and Productivity Survey*; 2022. https://my.amga.org/store/s/product-details?id=a1B2E0000079GooUAE

54. Alexander L. The Benefits of Obesity Medicine Certification. *Am J Lifestyle Med*. 2019;13(2):161–164.

55. Custom Market Insights. *U.S. Weight Loss Market Size, Trends, Share, Forecast 2030*; 2023. https://www.custommarketinsights.com/report/us-weight-loss-market/

56. Greaney ML, Cohen SA, Xu F, Ward-Ritacco CL, Riebe D. Healthcare Provider Counselling for Weight Management Behaviours Among Adults with Overweight

or Obesity: A Cross-Sectional Analysis of National Health and Nutrition Examination Survey, 2011–2018. *BMJ Open.* 2020;10(11):e039295. doi:10.1136/bmjopen-2020-039295

57. Bennett WL, Wang NY, Gudzune KA, et al. Satisfaction with Primary Care Provider Involvement is Associated with Greater Weight Loss: Results from the Practice-Based POWER Trial. *Patient Educ Couns.* 2015;98(9):1099–1105.

58. Hampl SE, Hassink SG, Skinner AC, et al. Executive Summary: Clinical Practice Guideline for the Evaluation and Treatment of Children and Adolescents with Obesity. *Pediatrics.* 2023;151(2):e2022060641.

59. LaRosa J. How to Set Up a Successful Medical Weight Loss Program. Market Research Blog. May 17, 2022. https://blog.marketresearch.com/how-to-set-up-a-successful-medical-weight-loss-program

60. Pfuntner A, Wier LM, Stocks C. *Most Frequent Procedures Performed in U.S. Hospitals, 2010.* HCUP Statistical Brief #149. February 2013. http://www.ncbi.nlm.nih.gov/books/NBK132428/

61. American Red Cross. U.S. Blood Supply Facts. Accessed October 14, 2023. https://www.redcrossblood.org/donate-blood/how-to-donate/how-blood-donations-help/blood-needs-blood-supply.html

62. Lin Y, Khandelwal A, Kapitany C, Chargé S. Transfusion Camp: Successes and Challenges in Scaling and Expanding a Transfusion Medicine Education Program. *Transfus Apher Sci.* 2023 Feb;62(1):103629.

63. U.S. Government. *Requirements for Blood and Blood Components Intended for Transfusion or for Further Manufacturing Use.* Vol 21 CFR Part 630. https://www.ecfr.gov/current/title-21/part-630

64. Finnegan J. Now More Than 9,000 Urgent Care Centers in the U.S., Industry Report Says. *Fierce Healthcare.* February 26, 2020. https://www.fiercehealthcare.com/practices/now-more-than-9-000-urgent-care-centers-u-s-industry-report-says

65. Page L. 10 Statistics on Urgent Care Centers. Becker's Hospital Review. February 16, 2011. https://www.beckershospitalreview.com/hospital-management-administration/10-statistics-on-urgent-care-centers.html

66. Ho V, Metcalfe L, Dark C, Vu L, et al. Comparing Utilization and Costs of Care in Freestanding Emergency Departments, Hospital Emergency Departments, and Urgent Care Centers. *Ann Emerg Med.* 2017;70(6):846-857.e3. doi:10.1016/j.annemergmed.2016.12.006

67. Merritt Hawkins. *Convenient Care: Growth and Staffing Trends in Urgent Care and Retail Medicine;* 2015. https://www.ihaconnect.org/About-IHA/Documents/Merritt%20Hawkins/mhawhitepaperconvenientcarePDF.pdf

68. Amirault B. Who Works in Urgent Care Clinics? Solvhealth.com. October 10, 2018. https://www.solvhealth.com/blog/who-works-in-urgent-care-clinics

69. Weinick RM, Bristol SJ, DesRoches CM. Urgent Care Centers in the U.S.: Findings from a National Survey. *BMC Health Serv Res.* 2009;9(1):79. doi:10.1186/1472-6963-9-79

70. Sawyer W, Wagner P. *Mass Incarceration: The Whole Pie 2023*. Prison Policy Initiative. March 14, 2023. https://www.prisonpolicy.org/reports/pie2023.html

71. Fair H, Walmsley R. *World Prison Population List (13th Edition)*. World Prison Brief; 2021. https://www.prisonstudies.org/sites/default/files/resources/downloads/world_prison_population_list_13th_edition.pdf

72. Maruschak LM, Buehler ED. Census of State and Federal Adult Correctional Facilities, 2019–Statistical Tables. Bureau of Justice Statistics. November 2021;301366.

73. Maruschak LM, Minton TD. Correctional Populations in the United States, 2017–2018. Bureau of Justice Statistics. NCJ 252157. August 2020:1–17.

74. Minton TD, Zeng Z. Jail Inmates in 2020–Statistical Tables. NCJ 303308. December 2021;303308.

75. Wang L, Sawyer W. *New Data: State Prisons Are Increasingly Deadly Places*. Prison Policy Initiative. June 8, 2021. https://www.prisonpolicy.org/blog/2021/06/08/prison_mortality/

76. California Correctional Health Care Services. Physician Careers. Accessed October 14, 2023. https://cchcs.ca.gov/careers/physician/

77. Starr P. *The Social Transformation of American Medicine*. New York: Basic Books; 2017. https://www.hachettebookgroup.com/titles/paul-starr/the-social-transformation-of-american-medicine/9780465093038/?lens=basic-books

78. Driscoll C. Is There a Doctor in the House. *Am Acad Home Care Physicians Newsl*. 1991;3(1):7–8.

79. Taler G. House Calls for the 21st Century. *J Am Geriatr Soc*. 1998;46(2):246–248.

80. Meyer GS, Gibbons RV. House Calls to the Elderly—A Vanishing Practice Among Physicians. *N Engl J Med*. 1997;337(25):1815–1820.

81. Stall N, Nowaczynski M, Sinha SK. Systematic Review of Outcomes from Home-Based Primary Care Programs for homebound Older Adults. *J Am Geriatr Soc*. 2014;62(12):2243–2251.

82. Boling PA, Retchin SM, Ellis J, Pancoast SA. Factors Associated with the Frequency of House Calls by Primary Care Physicians. *J Gen Intern Med*. 1991;6:335–340.

83. Kao H, Conant R, Soriano T, McCormick W. The Past, Present, and Future of House Calls. *Clin Geriatr Med*. 2009;25(1):19–34.

84. Harris-Kojetin L, Sengupta M, Lendon J, Rome V, Valverde R, Caffrey C. Long-term Care Providers and Services Users in the United States, 2015-2016. *Vital Health Stat*. 2019;3(43). https://stacks.cdc.gov/view/cdc/76253

85. Harrington C, Carrillo H, Garfield R, Published ES. *Nursing Facilities, Staffing, Residents and Facility Deficiencies, 2009 Through 2016*. Medicaid; 2018. https://www.kff.org/medicaid/report/nursing-facilities-staffing-residents-and-facility-deficiencies-2009-through-2016/

86. Ågotnes G, McGregor MJ, Lexchin J, Doupe MB, Müller B, Harrington C. An International Mapping of Medical Care in Nursing Homes. *Health Serv Insights*. 2019;12. doi:10.1177/1178632918825083

87. Welch W, Oliveira I, Blanco M, Sommers B. *Ownership of Skilled Nursing Facilities: An Analysis of Newly-Released Federal Data.* Office of the Assistant Secretary for Planning and Evaluation, U.S. Department of Health and Human Services. December 15, 2022. https://aspe.hhs.gov/reports/ownership-skilled-nursing-facilities

88. Kim S, Ryskina KL, Jung HY. Use of Clinicians Who Focus on Nursing Home Care Among U.S. Nursing Homes and Unplanned Rehospitalization. *JAMA Netw Open.* 2023;6(6):e2318265. doi:10.1001/jamanetworkopen.2023.18265

89. Katz PR, Karuza J, Intrator O, Mor V. Nursing Home Physician Specialists: A Response to the Workforce Crisis in long-Term Care. *Ann Intern Med.* 2009;150(6):411–413.

90. Levinson D. Adverse Events in Skilled Nursing Facilities: National Incidence Among Medicare Beneficiaries. Agency for Healthcare Research and Quality Patient Safety Network. March 19, 2014. https://psnet.ahrq.gov/issue/adverse-events-skilled-nursing-facilities-national-incidence-among-medicare-beneficiaries

91. Grand View Research, Inc. *U.S. Mobile Clinics Market Size & Share Analysis Report* 2030; Grand View Research; 2023. https://www.grandviewresearch.com/industry-analysis/us-mobile-clinics-market-report

92. Mobile Health Map. Mobile Clinic Impact Tracker. Mobile Health Map at Harvard Medical School. Accessed October 14, 2023. https://www.mobilehealthmap.org/tableau-public-data/

93. Malone NC, Williams MM, Smith Fawzi MC, et al. Mobile Health Clinics in the United States. *Int J Equity Health.* 2020;19(1):1–9.

94. Hill CF, Powers BW, Jain SH, Bennet J, Vavasis A, Oriol NE. Mobile Health Clinics in the Era of Reform. *Am J Manag Care.* 2014;20(3):261–264.

95. Song Z, Hill C, Bennet J, Vavasis A, Oriol NE. Mobile Clinic in Massachusetts Associated with Cost Savings from Lowering Blood Pressure and Emergency Department Use. *Health Aff (Millwood).* 2013;32(1):36–44.

96. Liao O, Morphew T, Amaro S, Galant SP. The Breathmobile™: A Novel Comprehensive School-Based Mobile Asthma Care Clinic for Urban Underprivileged Children. *J Sch Health.* 2006;76(6):313–319.

97. Landi H. Dollar General Pilots Mobile Clinics as It Targets a Bigger Presence in Healthcare. *Fierce Healthcare.* January 20, 2023. https://www.fiercehealthcare.com/providers/dollar-general-pilots-mobile-clinics-it-targets-bigger-presence-healthcare

98. The Advisory Board. How to Avoid the "Million-Dollar Patient"? Mobile Clinics, MD Says. Advisory Board Daily Briefing. October 18, 2017. https://www.advisory.com/daily-briefing/2017/10/18/mobile-clinics

99. NACCHO. Directory of Local Health Departments. Accessed October 14, 2023. https://www.naccho.org/membership/lhd-directory

100. Beck AJ, Boulton ML. Trends and Characteristics of the State and Local Public Health Workforce, 2010–2013. *Am J Public Health.* 2015;105(S2):S303–S310

101. Association of State and Territorial Health Officials. *Profile of State and Territorial Public Health.* Association of State and Territorial Health Officials. Arlington, VA: ASTHO; 2017. https://www.astho.org/topic/public-health-infrastructure/profile/

102. Economic Research Institute. Public Health Physician Salary. October 14, 2023. https://www.erieri.com/salary/job/public-health-physician/united-states

103. Sellers K, Leider JP, Bogaert K, Allen JD, Castrucci BC. Research Full Report: Making a Living in Governmental Public Health: Variation in Earnings by Employee Characteristics and Work Setting. *J Public Health Manag Pract.* 2019;25(2 Suppl):S87.

104. NP Fact Sheet. American Association of Nurse Practitioners. 2022. https://www.aanp.org/about/all-about-nps/np-fact-sheet

105. American Academy of Physician Associates. *About AAPA Fact Sheet.* 2023. https://www.aapa.org/download/77924/

106. Najmabadi S, Honda TJ, Hooker RS. Collaborative Practice Trends in U.S. Physician Office Visits: An Analysis of the National Ambulatory Medical Care Survey, 2007–2016. *BMJ Open.* 2020;10(6):e035414.

107. Everett CM, Schumacher JR, Wright A, Smith MA. Physician Assistants and Nurse Practitioners as a Usual Source of Care. *J Rural Health.* 2009;25(4):407–414.

108. State Practice Environment. American Association of Nurse Practitioners. October 2022. https://www.aanp.org/advocacy/state/state-practice-environment

109. Peterson LE, Phillips RL, Puffer JC, Bazemore A, Petterson S. Most Family Physicians Work Routinely with Nurse Practitioners, Physician Assistants, or Certified Nurse Midwives. *J Am Board Fam Med JABFM.* 2013;26(3):244–245. doi:10.3122/jabfm.2013.03.120312

110. Martin B, Alexander M. The Economic Burden and Practice Restrictions Associated with Collaborative Practice Agreements: A National Survey of Advanced Practice Registered Nurses. *J Nurs Regul.* 2019;9(4):22–30.

111. Phoenix BJ, Chapman SA. Effect of State Regulatory Environments on Advanced Psychiatric Nursing Practice. *Arch Psychiatr Nurs.* 2020;34(5):370–376.

112. American Medical Association. *Work-Related & Independent Medical Examinations*; 2022. https://code-medical-ethics.ama-assn.org/ethics-opinions/work-related-independent-medical-examinations

113. Baum K. Independent Medical Examinations: An Expanding Source of Physician Liability. *Ann Intern Med.* 2005;142(12):974–978. doi:10.7326/0003-4819-142-12_Part_1-200506210-00007

114. SEAK. How Much Does An IME (Independent Medical Examination) Cost? SEAK, Inc., Blog. December 12, 2019. https://seak.com/blog/uncategorized/how-much-does-an-ime-independent-medical-examination-cost/

115. Liddy C, Rowan MS, Afkham A, Maranger J, Keely E. Building Access to Specialist Care Through e-consultation. *Open Med.* 2013;7(1):e1.

116. Mantena S, Keshavjee S. Strengthening Healthcare Delivery with Remote Patient Monitoring in the Time of COVID-19. *BMJ Health Care Inform.* 2021;28(1): e100302. doi:10.1136/bmjhci-2020-100302

117. Insider Intelligence. The Technology, Devices, and Benefits of Remote Patient Monitoring in the Healthcare Industry. Insider Intelligence Insights. January 19, 2023. https://www.insiderintelligence.com/insights/remote-patient-monitoring -industry-explained/

118. Mackintosh N, Terblanche M, Maharaj R, et al. Telemedicine with Clinical Decision Support for Critical Care: A Systematic Review. *Syst Rev.* 2016;5(1):176. doi:10.1186/s13643-016-0357-7

119. Kappell S. Remote Patient Monitoring Economics. *Med Econ.* 2022;99(8):35–36. Accessed October 17, 2023. https://www.medicaleconomics.com/view/ summer-bootcamp-remote-patient-monitoring-economics

120. DiGiovanna T, Rosen T, Forsett R, Sivertson K, Kelen GD. Shipboard Medicine: A New Niche for Emergency Medicine. *Ann Emerg Med.* 1992;21(12):1476–1479. doi:10.1016/s0196-0644(05)80065-4

121. Buni C. Ernest Shackleton—The Greatest Adventures of All Time. *Time.* September 12, 2003. https://content.time.com/time/specials/packages/arti cle/0,28804,1981290_1981354_1981610,00.html

122. Lyon RM, Wiggins CM. Expedition Medicine—The Risk of Illness and Injury. *Wilderness Environ Med.* 2010;21(4):318–324. doi:10.1016/j.wem.2010.09.002

123. U.S. Department of Veterans Affairs. Clinical Deployment Teams (CDT). VHA Office of Emergency Management. January 25, 2023. https://www.va.gov/ VHAEMERGENCYMANAGEMENT/CDT/index.asp

124. Donner H. The Expedition Physician. In: *Expedition and Wilderness Medicine.* 1st ed. London: Cambridge University Press; 2008:2. doi:10.1017/CBO9780511722202

125. U.S. Department of State. About the U.S. Department of State. https://www.state. gov/about/

126. Budiman A. Key Findings About U.S. immigrants. Pew Research Center. August 20, 2020. https://www.pewresearch.org/short-reads/2020/08/20/key-findings -about-u-s-immigrants/

127. Centers for Disease Control and Prevention. Technical Instructions for Panel Physicians. September 28, 2023. https://www.cdc.gov/immigrantrefugeehealth/ panel-physicians.html

128. CIA. Browse CIA Jobs—Physician. CIA Careers. Accessed October 16, 2023. https://www.cia.gov/careers/jobs/physician-2/

129. Goel S, Angeli F, Dhirar N, Singla N, Ruwaard D. What Motivates Medical Students to Select Medical Studies: A Systematic Literature Review. *BMC Med Educ.* 2018;18(1):16. doi:10.1186/s12909-018-1123-4

130. UN High Commissioner for Refugees. *Global Trends: Forced Displacement in 2022.* UNHCR; 2022. Accessed October 16, 2023. https://www.unhcr.org/ global-trends-report-2022

131. United States Agency for International Development. *FY 2022 Agency Financial Report: Progress Beyond Programs.* UNAID; 2022. https://www.usaid.gov/reports/agency-financial-report/fy-2022

132. Medecins Sans Frontieres. *International Activity Report 2020.* 2020. Accessed October 16, 2023. https://www.msf.org/sites/default/files/2021-07/international-activity-report-2020.pdf

133. Medecins Sans Frontieres. Career Opportunities & Benefits. 2023. Accessed October 16, 2023. https://www.doctorswithoutborders.org/careers/work-field/pay-benefits

134. World Tourism Organization. Tourism on Track for Full Recovery as New Data Shows Strong Start to 2023. May 9, 2023. https://www.unwto.org/news/tourism-on-track-for-full-recovery-as-new-data-shows-strong-start-to-2023

135. Angelo KM, Kozarsky PE, Ryan ET, Chen LH, Sotir MJ. What Proportion of International Travellers Acquire a Travel-Related Illness? A Review of the Literature. *J Travel Med.* 2017;24(5). doi:10.1093/jtm/tax046

136. International Society of Travel Medicine. Online Clinic Directory. Accessed October 16, 2023. https://www.istm.org/AF_CstmClinicDirectory.asp

137. Hill DR, Ericsson CD, Pearson RD, et al. The Practice of Travel Medicine: Guidelines by the Infectious Diseases Society of America. *Clin Infect Dis Off Publ Infect Dis Soc Am.* 2006;43(12):1499-1539. doi:10.1086/508782

138. Kogelman L, Barnett ED, Chen LH, et al. Knowledge, Attitudes, and Practices of U.S. Practitioners Who Provide Pre-Travel Advice. *J Travel Med.* 2014;21(2):104–114. doi:10.1111/jtm.12097

139. Keystone JS, Dismukes R, Sawyer L, Kozarsky PE. Inadequacies in Health Recommendations Provided for International Travelers by North American Travel Health Advisors. *J Travel Med.* 1994;1(2):72–78. doi:10.1111/j.1708-8305.1994.tb00566.x

140. Shappell S, Detwiler C, Holcomb K, Hackworth C, Boquet A, Wiegmann D. Human Error and Commercial Aviation Accidents: An Analysis Using the Human Factors Analysis and Classification System. *Human Factors: The Journal of the Human Factors and Ergonomics Society.* 2007;49(20:227–242.

141. Thamer SB, Bello J, Stevanovic M, Obat D, Buckey JC. Nationwide Survey of Medical Student Interest in and Exposure to Aerospace Medicine. *Npj Microgravity.* 2023;9(1):44.

142. Gendreau MA, DeJohn C. Responding to Medical Events During Commercial Airline Flights. *N Engl J Med.* 2002;346(14):1067–1073.

143. Ortega H. A Special Specialty. *Aerosp Med Hum Perform.* 2020;91(3):121–122. doi:10.3357/AMHP.913PresPage

144. Defense Finance and Accounting Service. Medical Corps Board Certification Pay, Incentive Pay (IP) and Retention Bonus (RB) — FY2024. September 19, 2023. https://www.dfas.mil/militarymembers/payentitlements/Pay-Tables/HPO4/

145. U.S. Bureau of Labor Statistics. Employer-Reported Workplace Injuries and Illnesses, 2021–2021 A01 Results. Economic News Release. November 9, 2022. https://www.bls.gov/news.release/osh.nr0.htm

146. American College of Occupational and Environmental Medicine. *ACOEM Physician's Practice Income & Benefits Survey*. ACOEM; 2013.

147. American College of Occupational and Environmental Medicine. *ACOEM Physician's Practice Income and Benefits Survey*. ACOEM; 2018.

148. Organisation for Economic Co-operation and Development. Ocean Shipping and Shipbuilding. *The Ocean*. https://www.oecd.org/ocean/topics/ocean-shipping/

149. NOAA Headquarters. U.S. Fishing Generated More than $200 Billion in Sales in 2015; Two Stocks Rebuilt in 2016. *ScienceDaily*. May 9, 2017. https://www.sciencedaily.com/releases/2017/05/170509161134.htm

150. Defense Manpower Data Center. DoD Personnel, Workforce Reports & Publications. DMDC website. 2023. https://dwp.dmdc.osd.mil/dwp/app/dod-data-reports/workforce-reports

151. Bishop JM, Hildreth LA, Lindly JM, Luan WP, Minneci M, Prugh GM. Analysis of DoD Accession Alternatives for Military Physicians: Readiness Value and Cost. Alexandria, VA: The Institute for Defense Analysis; 2019. https://www.ida.org/-/media/feature/publications/a/an/analysis-of-dod-accession-alternatives-for-military-physicians-readiness-value-and-cost/p-10815.ashx

152. Stortz SK, Foglia LM, Thagard AS, Staat B, Lutgendorf MA. Comparing Compensation of U.S. Military Physicians and Civilian Physicians in Residency Training and Beyond. *Cureus*. 2021;13(1).

153. Thorne G. The Ketamine Clinic Craze: Legalities and Possibilities. Harris Sliwoski LLP Blog. March 4, 2020. https://harrisbricken.com/psychlawblog/the-ketamine-clinic-craze-legalities-and-possibilities/

154. Whiting PF, Wolff RF, Deshpande S, et al. Cannabinoids for Medical Use: A Systematic Review and Meta-Analysis. *JAMA*. 2015;313(24):2456-2473.

155. Sarris J, Sinclair J, Karamacoska D, Davidson M, Firth J. Medicinal Cannabis for Psychiatric Disorders: A Clinically-focused Systematic Review. *BMC Psychiatry*. 2020;20(1):1–14.

156. Sanacora G, Frye MA, McDonald W, et al. A Consensus Statement on the Use of Ketamine in the Treatment of Mood Disorders. *JAMA Psychiatry*. 2017;74(4):399–405. doi:10.1001/jamapsychiatry.2017.0080

157. Office of the Commissioner. *FDA at a Glance*. U.S. Food & Drug Administration; 2023. https://www.fda.gov/about-fda/economics-staff/fda-glance

158. Clark CM, Shaver AL, Aurelio LA, et al. Potentially Inappropriate Medications Are Associated with Increased Healthcare Utilization and Costs. *J Am Geriatr Soc*. 2020;68(11):2542–2550. doi:10.1111/jgs.16743

159. Liew TM, Lee CS, Shawn KLG, Chang ZY. Potentially Inappropriate Prescribing Among Older Persons: A Meta-Analysis of Observational Studies. *Ann Fam Med*. 2019;17(3):257–266. doi:10.1370/afm.2373

160. Aronson JK. What Do Clinical Pharmacologists Do? A Questionnaire Survey of Senior UK Clinical Pharmacologists. *Br J Clin Pharmacol.* 2012;73(2):161–169.

161. Ley TJ, Rosenberg LE. The Physician-Scientist Career Pipeline in 2005: Build It, and They Will Come. *JAMA.* 2005;294(11):1343–1351.

162. U.S. Food and Drug Administration. Device Classification Under Section 513(f)(2)(De Novo). Published online October 16, 2023. https://www.accessdata.fda.gov/scripts/cdrh/cfdocs/cfpmn/denovo.cfm?id=den040007

163. Hotze TD, Shah K, Anderson EE, Wynia MK. "Doctor, Would You Prescribe a Pill to Help Me … ?" A National Survey of Physicians on Using Medicine for Human Enhancement. *Am J Bioeth.* 2011;11(1):3–13. doi:10.1080/15265161.2011.534957

164. Juengst ET. Aging and the Aged: VI. Anti-Aging Interventions: Ethical and Social Issues. In Encyclopedia of Bioethics, 3rd ed., Vol. 1. SG Post (ed.). New York: Macmillan Reference USA; 2004: 112-116. Gale eBooks, link.gale.com/apps/doc/CX3402500037/GVRL?u=22516&sid=bookmark-GVRL&xid=bdaeb76c

165. United States Government Accountability Office. *Genetic Services: Information on Genetic Counselor and Medical Geneticist Workforces.* USGAO; 2020. https://www.gao.gov/assets/gao-20-593.pdf

166. Raspa M, Moultrie R, Toth D, Haque SN. Barriers and Facilitators to Genetic Service Delivery Models: Scoping Review. *Interact J Med Res.* 2021;10(1):e23523. doi:10.2196/23523

167. The Match. *Match Results Statistics: Medical Genetics.* National Resident Matching Program. October 20, 2022. https://www.nrmp.org/wp-content/uploads/2022/10/Medical-Genetics-MRS-Report.pdf

168. Jenkins BD, Fischer CG, Polito CA, et al. The 2019 U.S. Medical Genetics Workforce: A Focus on Clinical Genetics. *Genet Med.* 2021;23(8):1458–1464. doi:10.1038/s41436-021-01162-5

169. Cohen E, Ettouati W, Lippman S. *Proposal for a Self-Supporting Program of Graduate Studies Master of Science Degree in Precision Medicine.* University of California San Diego. October 4, 2021. https://senate.ucsd.edu/media/547492/2021-11-08-som-proposed-interdisciplinary-ms-in-precision-medicine.pdf

170. Fontanarosa PB. Alternative Medicine Meets Science. *JAMA.* 1998;280(18):1618. doi:10.1001/jama.280.18.1618

171. National Center for Complementary and Integrative Health. Congressional Justification FY 2023. Department of Health and Human Services. 2023. https://www.nccih.nih.gov/about/budget/congressional/fy2023

172. Anastasi J. *The Use of Complementary and Alternative Medicine by the American Public.* Washington, DC: Institute of Medicine; 2005.

173. National Center for Complementary and Integrative Health. Complementary, Alternative, or Integrative Health: What's In a Name? NCCIH; 2021. https://www.nccih.nih.gov/health/complementary-alternative-or-integrative-health-whats-in-a-name

174. Winslow LC, Shapiro H. Physicians Want Education About Complementary and Alternative Medicine to Enhance Communication with Their Patients. *Arch Intern Med.* 2002;162(10):1176–1181.

175. Integrative Medicine Physician Salary in USA – Average Salary. Talent.com. Accessed October 31, 2023. https://www.talent.com/salary

176. Joos S, Musselmann B, Szecsenyi J, Goetz K. Characteristics and Job Satisfaction of General Practitioners Using Complementary and Alternative Medicine in Germany — Is There a pattern? *BMC Complement Altern Med.* 2011;11:1–6.

177. Buttorff C, Ruder T, Bauman M. Multiple Chronic Conditions in the United States. RAND Corporation; 2017. https://www.rand.org/pubs/tools/TL221.html

178. Centers for Disease Control and Prevention. Health and Economic Costs of Chronic Diseases. National Center for Chronic Disease Prevention and Health Promotion (NCCDPHP). March 23, 2023. https://www.cdc.gov/chronicdisease/about/costs/index.htm

179. Willett WC. Balancing Life-Style and Genomics Research for Disease Prevention. *Science.* 2002;296(5568):695–698. doi:10.1126/science.1071055

180. Rosenfeld RM. Physician Attitudes on the Status, Value, and Future of Board Certification in Lifestyle Medicine. *Am J Lifestyle Med.* 2022; 18(1):118–130. doi:10.1177/15598276221131524

181. American Society of Plastic Surgeons. *Inaugural ASPS Insights and Trends Report: Cosmetic Surgery 2022.* 2022. https://www.plasticsurgery.org/documents/News/Trends/2022/trends-report-cosmetic-surgery-2022.pdf

182. American Society for Dermatologic Surgery. Survey on Dermatologic Procedures. 2016. https://www.asds.net/Portals/0/PDF/procedures-survey-results-infographic-2016.pdf

183. Moeller M. The 2022 Medical Spa State of the Industry Executive Summary in Context. American Med Spa Association. January 24, 2023. https://americanmedspa.org/blog/the-2022-medical-spa-state-of-the-industry-executive-summary-in-context

184. American Med Spa Association. *Guidelines for Non-Invasive Medical Aesthetic Practices (Medical Spas).* AMSA:2020.

185. Ahmed O. *States Must Expand Telehealth to Improve Access to Sexual and Reproductive Health Care.* Center for American Progress. May 21, 2020. https://www.americanprogress.org/article/states-must-expand-telehealth-improve-access-sexual-reproductive-health-care/

186. Planned Parenthood. Who We Are. Planned Parenthood website. https://www.plannedparenthood.org/about-us/who-we-are

187. Lague DC Casandra Cashman,Ian. Primary Care Providers Can Help Safeguard Abortion. *Sci Am.* June 24, 2022. https://www.scientificamerican.com/article/primary-care-providers-can-help-safeguard-abortion/

188. Pitasi MA, Beer L, Cha S, et al. Vital Signs: HIV Infection, Diagnosis, Treatment, and Prevention Among Gay, Bisexual, and Other Men Who Have Sex with Men

— United States, 2010-2019. *MMWR Morb Mortal Wkly Rep.* 2021;70(48):1669–1675. doi:10.15585/mmwr.mm7048e1

189. Matthews AK, Brandenburg DL, Johnson TP, Hughes TL. Correlates of Under-utilization of Gynecological Cancer Screening Among Lesbian and Heterosexual Women. *Prev Med.* 2004;38(1):105–113. doi:10.1016/j.ypmed.2003.09.034

190. The Physicians Foundation. *2018 Survey of America's Physicians.* 2018. https://physiciansfoundation.org/wp-content/uploads/physicians-survey-results-final-2018.pdf

191. Grosse E. 'Pajama Time': Unraveling The 'Whys' Behind Physician Burnout. *Forbes.* December 5, 2022. https://www.forbes.com/sites/forbestechcouncil/2022/12/05/pajama-time-unraveling-the-whys-behind-physician-burnout/

192. NHE Fact Sheet | CMS. https://www.cms.gov/data-research/statistics-trends-and-reports/national-health-expenditure-data/nhe-fact-sheet

193. Bishop TF, Press MJ, Keyhani S, Pincus HA. Acceptance of Insurance by Psychiatrists and the Implications for Access to Mental Health Care. *JAMA Psychiatry.* 2014;71(2):176–181. doi:10.1001/jamapsychiatry.2013.2862

194. Doherty R, Medical Practice and Quality Committee of the American College of Physicians. Assessing the Patient Care Implications of "Concierge" and Other Direct Patient Contracting Practices: A Policy Position Paper from the American College of Physicians. *Ann Intern Med.* 2015;163(12):949–952. doi:10.7326/M15-0366

195. KFF. 2022 Employer Health Benefits Survey. October 27, 2022. https://www.kff.org/mental-health/report/2022-employer-health-benefits-survey/

196. Hammond JB. Cash Only Doctors: Challenges and Prospects of Autonomy and Access. *UMKC Rev.* 2011;80:307.

197. Niu C. *2022 Franchising Economic Outlook.* International Franchise Association. https://www.franchise.org/sites/default/files/2022-02/2022%20Franchising%20Economic%20Outlook.pdf

198. Nijmeijer KJ, Fabbricotti IN, Huijsman R. Is Franchising in Health Care Valuable? A Systematic Review. *Health Policy Plan.* 2014;29(2):164–176.

199. Kalim F. The Subscription Economy Has Grown Over 435% in 9 Years (and the Uptick Is Expected to Continue). Media Makers Meet. March 4, 2021. https://mediamakersmeet.com/the-subscription-economy-has-grown-over-435-in-9-years-and-the-uptick-is-expected-to-continue/

200. 25 Simple Concierge Medicine Industry Statistics and Trends, Updated for 2023! Concierge Medicine Today. Accessed October 13, 2023. https://conciergemedicinetoday.org/25-concierge-medicine-industry-statistics-and-trends-updated-for-2019/

201. The Physicians Foundation. *2016 Survey of America's Physicians: Practice Patterns & Perspectives.* 2016. https://physiciansfoundation.org/wp-content/uploads/2018/01/Biennial_Physician_Survey_2016.pdf

202. Mapper. Direct Primary Care Frontier. https://mapper.dpcfrontier.com/

203. Direct Primary Care Coalition. What Is Direct Primary Care? https://www.dpcare.org

204. Forrest BR. Breaking Even on 4 Visits per Day. *Fam Pract Manag*. 2007;14(6):19–24.

205. Huff C. Direct Primary Care: Concierge Care for the Masses. *Health Aff (Millwood)*. 2015;34(12):2016–2019.

206. Konstantinovsky M. Many Doctors Are Switching to Concierge Medicine, Exacerbating Physician Shortages. *Scientific American*. October 9, 2021. https://www.scientificamerican.com/article/many-doctors-are-switching-to-concierge-medicine-exacerbating-physician-shortages/

207. A Look Back and Forward ... 2012-2015 and 2022 Poll of Concierge Physician Salaries. Concierge Medicine Today. December 31, 2022. Accessed October 13, 2023. https://conciergemedicinetoday.org/2022/12/31/a-look-back-and-forward-2012-2015-and-2022-poll-of-concierge-physician-salaries/

208. Ko JM, Rodriguez HP, Fairchild DG, Rodday AMC, Safran DG. Paying for Enhanced Service: Comparing Patients' Experiences in a Concierge and General Medicine Practice. *The Patient*. 2009;2(2):95-103. doi:10.2165/01312067-200902020-00005

209. Busch F, Grzeskowiak D, Huth E. *Direct Primary Care: Evaluating a New Model of Delivery and Financing*. Society of Actuaries; 2020. Accessed November 3, 2023. https://www.soa.org/49c889/globalassets/assets/files/resources/research-report/2020/direct-primary-care-eval-model.pdf

210. *2021 Review of Physician and Advanced Practitioner Recruiting Incentives*. Merritt Hawkins; 2021.

211. Paddock E, Prince RJ, Combs M, Stiles M. Does Micropractice Lead to Macro-satisfaction? *J Am Board Fam Med JABFM*. 2013;26(5):525–528. doi:10.3122/jabfm.2013.05.120278

212. Graff K. A Micropractice/Community Partnership Model for Lifestyle Medicine. *Am J Lifestyle Med*. 2017;12(2):124–127. https://doi.org/10.1177/1559827617726524

213. Akifox. How To Get Started in Solo Practice. SoloDoc. October 1, 2004. https://akifox.blogspot.com/2004/10/how-to-get-started-in-solo-practice.html

214. Parvus Medical Suites. What Is a Micropractice? January 4, 2023. https://parvusmedicalsuites.com/what-is-a-micro-practice/

215. Bernard R. Direct Care Financial Realities: What You Need To Know About Income and Overhead. MedicalEconomics. June 1, 2022. https://www.medicaleconomics.com/view/direct-care-financial-realities-what-you-need-to-know-about-income-and-overhead

216. Cohen A. Pittsburgh's Insurance-Free Doctor Charges $35 Per Visit. Bloomberg. December 13, 2019. https://www.bloomberg.com/news/articles/2019-12-13/pittsburgh-s-insurance-free-doctor-charges-35-per-visit

217. Guglielmo WJ. What's a Micropractice. *Med Econ*. 2006;83(23):51, 55–57. https://www.medicaleconomics.com/view/whats-micropractice

218. Horwitz AV. Outcomes in the Sociology of Mental Health and Illness: Where Have We Been and Where Are We Going? *J Health Soc Behav.* 2002;43(2):143–151.

219. Pylypchuk Y, Barker W. *Use of Telemedicine Among Office-Based Physicians, 2021.* Office of the National Coordinator for Health Information Technology; 2023. https://www.healthit.gov/sites/default/files/2023-03/DB65_TelemedicinePhysicians.pdf

220. Snoswell CL, Chelberg G, De Guzman KR, et al. The Clinical Effectiveness of Telehealth: A Systematic Review of Meta-analyses from 2010 to 2019. *J Telemed Telecare.* 2023;29(9):669–684.

221. Totten AM, Womack DM, Eden KB, et al. *Telehealth: Mapping the Evidence for Patient Outcomes From Systematic Reviews.* Agency for Healthcare Research and Quality (U.S.); 2016. http://www.ncbi.nlm.nih.gov/books/NBK379320/

222. Atmojo JT, Sudaryanto WT, Widiyanto A, Ernawati E, Arradini D. Telemedicine, Cost Effectiveness, and Patients Satisfaction: A Systematic Review. *J Health Policy Manag.* 2020;5(2):103–107.

223. Nochomovitz M, Sharma R. Is It Time for a New Medical Specialty?: The Medical Virtualist. *JAMA.* 2018;319(5):437–438.

224. Perrin A, Duggan M. *Americans' Internet Access: 2000-2015.* Pew Research Center; 2015. https://www.pewresearch.org/internet/2015/06/26/americans-internet-access-2000-2015/

225. Barber M. How Much Does Telemedicine Cost Without Insurance? Solv. March 28, 2022. https://www.solvhealth.com/blog/how-much-does-telemedicine-cost-without-insurance

226. Kane L. "Death by 1000 Cuts": Medscape National Physician Burnout & Suicide Report 2021. Medscape Public Health. January 22, 2021. https://www.medscape.com/slideshow/2021-lifestyle-burnout-6013456

227. Katz LF, Krueger AB. The Rise and Nature of Alternative Work Arrangements in the United States, 1995–2015. *ILR Rev.* 2019;72(2):382–416.

228. LocumTenens.com. The Future of Work: Redefining the Role of Physicians in the Gig Economy. January 17, 2023. https://www.locumtenens.com/media/d02lkftg/the-future-of-work-survey-report.pdf

229. Society of Hospital Medicine. SHM's State of Hospital Medicine Report. 2023. https://www.hospitalmedicine.org/practice-management/shms-state-of-hospital-medicine2/

230. Beresford L. The State of Hospital Medicine in 2018. *Hosp Natl Assoc Inpatient Physicians.* 2019;23(1):1-11. https://www.the-hospitalist.org/wp-content/uploads/legacy/journals/thehospjan19_lowres_digital.pdf

231. Trask A. News Flash! Nocturnists Are in High Demand. *The Hospitalist.* September 11, 2017. https://www.the-hospitalist.org/hospitalist/article/146776/news-flash-nocturnists-are-high-demand/

232. Armon B. Must-Knows about Moonlighting. July 21, 2021. https://magazine. practicelink.com/magazinearticles/must-knows-about-moonlighting-summer -2021/

233. Sammer J. Sabbaticals Could Be the Solution to Employee Burnout. SHRM. November 3, 2022. Accessed October 13, 2023. https://www.shrm.org/ resourcesandtools/hr-topics/benefits/pages/sabbaticals-could-be-the-solution- to-employee-burnout.aspx

234. Nabity J. The Pros and Cons of Physician Locum Tenens. Physicians Thrive. December 23, 2020. https://physiciansthrive.com/physician-compensation/ locum-tenens/

235. Staff Care, Inc. *2021 Survey of Locum Tenens Physicians and Advanced Practitio- ners.* 2021. https://www.amnhealthcare.com/siteassets/amn-insights/whitepapers/ staffcare2021providersurvedited.pdf

236. Blumenthal DM, Olenski AR, Tsugawa Y, Jena AB. Association Between Treatment by Locum Tenens Internal Medicine Physicians and 30-Day Mortality Among Hospitalized Medicare Beneficiaries. *JAMA.* 2017;318(21):2119–2129.

237. Chiu RG, Nunna RS, Siddiqui N, Khalid SI, Behbahani M, Mehta AI. Locum Tenens Neurosurgery in the United States: A Medicare Claims Analysis of Out- comes, Complications, and Cost of Care. *World Neurosurg.* 2020;142:e210-e214.

238. CompHealth. Top Specialties for Locum Tenens: 7 High-Demand Specialties in 2022. CompHealth Blog. March 30, 2022. https://resources.comphealth.com/ top-specialties-locum-tenens/

239. CompHealth. How Does Locum Tenens Pay and Salary Work for Physi- cians? CompHealth Blog. August 16, 2023. https://resources.comphealth.com/ how-locum-tenens-pay-works/

240. Locum Tenens Guy. Finding Best Locum Tenens Companies in 2023. The Locum Tenens Guy Blog. December 31, 2022. https://thelocumguy.com/best-locum -tenens-companies/

241. 2017 Great American Physician Survey Results. Physicians Practice. Septem- ber 11, 2017. https://www.physicianspractice.com/view/2017-great-american -physician-survey-results

242. Elsmore K. *Caring and Flexible Working.* Department for Work and Pensions: London; 2009.

243. Mudditt J. How Job Sharing Is Going Mainstream. Westpac Wire. Published June 22, 2021. https://www.westpac.com.au/news/money-matters/2021/06/ how-job-sharing-is-going-mainstream/

244. Matos K, Galinsky E, Bond J. *National Study of Employers.* Society for Human Resource Management, Families and Work Institute, When Work Works; 2016.

245. Worzniak MJ, Chadwell M. A Job-Share Model for the New Millennium. *Fam Pract Manag.* 2002;9(8):29–32.

246. Lopez J. What Is Job sharing? A Physician Tells All.... CareerCodeBlueHq. October 3, 2019. https://careercodebluehq.com/career-choice/what-is-job-sharing -a-physician-tells-all/

247. Daniels L. Job Sharing at Senior Level: Making It Work. Capability Jane. 2011. https://workingfamilies.org.uk/wp-content/uploads/2014/09/jobsharekeyfindings. pdf

248. Darves B. Part-Time Physician Practice on the Rise. NEJM CareerCenter Resources. October 29, 2011. https://resources.nejmcareercenter.org/article/ part-time-physician-practice-on-the-rise/

249. Baggett S, Martin K. Medscape Physician Lifestyle & Happiness Report 2022. Medscape Public Health. January 14, 2022. https://www.medscape.com/ slideshow/2022-lifestyle-happiness-6014665

250. MGMA DataDive Provider Compensation Data. 2020. https://www.mgma.com/ datadive/provider-compensation

251. Ly DP, Seabury SA, Jena AB. Differences in Incomes of Physicians in the United States by Race and Sex: Observational Study. *BMJ*. 2016;353:i2923.

252. U.S. Bureau of Labor Statistics. Employer Costs for Employee Compensation Summary. News Release. December 15, 2023. https://www.bls.gov/news.release/ ecec.nr0.htm

253. MBO Partners State of Independence in America Report 2023. MBO Partners. https://www.mbopartners.com/state-of-independence/

254. Wells N. The "Gig Economy" Is Growing — And Now We Know By How Much. October 13, 2016. https://www.cnbc.com/2016/10/13/gig-economy-is-growing- heres-how-much.html

255. Smith R, Leberstein S. *Rights on Demand: Ensuring Workplace Standards and Workplace Security in the on-Demand Economy*. National Employment Law Project. September 2015. https://www.nelp.org/wp-content/uploads/Rights-On- Demand-Report.pdf

256. Adams KE, Allen R, Cain JM. Physician Reentry: A Concept Whose Time Has Come. *Obstet Gynecol*. 2008;112(3):706–707.

257. Association of American Medical Colleges. *Physician Specialty Data Report*. 2022. https://www.aamc.org/data-reports/workforce/data/active-physicians-who -are-international-medical-graduates-imgs-specialty-2019

258. Chamberlain A. What Matters More to Your Workforce than Money. *Harv Bus Rev*. January 17, 2017. https://hbr.org/2017/01/what-matters-more-to-your -workforce-than-money

259. Leigh JP, Kravitz RL, Schembri M, Samuels SJ, Mobley S. Physician Career Satisfaction Across Specialties. *Arch Intern Med*. 2002;162(14):1577–1584.

260. Kane CK. Recent Changes in Physician Practice Arrangements: Private Practice Dropped to Less Than 50 Percent of Physicians in 2020. *Policy Research Perspectives*. American Medical Association. 2021:5.